The Voice of Memory

The Voice of Memory

Interviews 1961–1987

Primo Levi

*Edited by Marco Belpoliti and
Robert Gordon
Translated by Robert Gordon*

The New Press
New York

This collection © 2001 by Polity Press

First published in Italy as *Primo Levi: Conversazioni e interviste 1963–87*, edited by Marco Belpoliti © 1997 Guilio Einaudi, 1997, with the exception of the interviews beginning on pages 3, 13, 23, and 34 (for further details see Acknowledgments page).

First published in the United Kingdom by Polity Press in association with Blackwell Publishers Ltd, 2001
Published in the United States by The New Press, New York, 2001
Distributed by W.W. Norton & Company, Inc., New York

ISBN 1-56584-645-1 (hc.)
CIP data available.

The New Press was established in 1990 as a not-for-profit alternative to the large, commercial publishing houses currently dominating the book publishing industry. The New Press operates in the public interest rather than for private gain, and is committed to publishing, in innovative ways, works of educational, cultural, and community value that are often deemed insufficiently profitable.

The New Press, 450 West 41st Street, 6th floor, New York, NY 10036
www.thenewpress.com

Set in Plantin
Printed in the United States of America

10 9 8 7 6 5 4 3 2 1

Contents

Part IV: Literature and Writing   115

Part V: Auschwitz and Survival   177

Part VI: Judaism and Israel   259

Preface

Robert Gordon

Primo Levi is now firmly established as one of the essential writers of our century. His two principal works on the Holocaust[1] – *Se questo è un uomo* (*If This is a Man*, 1947), a spare but searing account of his eleven months 'in the depths' of Auschwitz, and *I sommersi e i salvati* (*The Drowned and the Saved*, 1986), a collection of essays revisiting the moral and historical dilemmas of that event and the memory of it forty years on – stand like twin pillars of humane meditation on the century's darkest moment. Indeed, it is hard to think of another figure of comparable stature who wrote and spoke of these unbearable events with such accessible economy, wit and persistence over such a long period of time.

Levi's extraordinary impact on the reading public within Italy, but perhaps even more so in the English-speaking world, has been variously and at times controversially explained. Whilst for many it is the pellucid clarity and unburdened directness of his prose that attracts, for others it is his rather ambivalent status as a 'non-Jewish Jew' (his own phrase) that allows him to bridge the gap between the 'Jewish' Holocaust and the wider world looking on. However, as recent attention to his *œuvre* in Italy, led by the work of Marco Belpoliti, has shown,[2] both these explanations are inadequate to account for the power and resonance of his writing. There is another Levi, more complex and disquieting, more hybrid and contradictory and hence more rich and rewarding, a Levi who belies the calm sage many have taken him to be. At the very least, the multiplicity of identities and voices within Levi must be taken as fundamental to our understanding of him. This volume of interviews shows us another of those identities, another of Levi's roles which filtered through into his writing and went towards making up the figure we so much admire and listen to.

Above I referred to Levi as someone who both wrote and spoke of the camps. The purpose of the present volume is encapsulated in that simple pairing of writing and speech. As Marco Belpoliti points out in his essay 'I am a Centaur' below, Levi's career or *métier* as a writer, itself a complement to his primary career as an industrial chemist, constantly ran parallel to and intersected a third *métier*, as a talker. Levi the interviewee is one part, the recorded part, of Levi's career as a talker.

As Levi notes in *The Drowned and the Saved*, survivors can be split into two schematic types, those who talk and those who stay silent.[3] Neither role is voluntary, he says; both are psychopathological impulses. At the moment of return from the camps, the impulse to talk even superseded the fear – felt by him and all his fellow inmates in the camps – that no one would listen to what they had to say. When two oral historians indicated to Levi in a 1982 interview that they had spoken to several survivors who had only now begun to talk about their camp experience, he was at one level incredulous:

LEVI: . . . But as to why Elena Recanati or Natalia Tedeschi haven't spoken until now, surely it's because they've only now been tracked down. Did they refuse to say anything before?

No, they say that after their return, they felt so deeply misunderstood, that they were not believed, that they lost the desire to say anything more.

LEVI: For myself I didn't feel that incomprehension. As you know, *If This is a Man* had a difficult career. It only became well known ten years after it was written. But nevertheless, I found understanding, solidarity, I never had any difficulty in telling the stories I had to tell. (see below p. 241)

Indeed, far from having difficulty in the months following his return to Turin in October 1945, Levi poured forth the stories he had to tell to whoever would listen – friends, family and strangers in trains, trams, offices and homes. This was all the more striking given his later discretion and restraint in choosing whom to tell (see, for example, his comments on not talking to his children at all about his deportation, p. 232 below). In due course, the stories would be written down and coalesce into *If This is a Man*. Writing and talking went hand in hand from the outset with Levi.

At this first stage of his work, when familiar lines of shared reflection on the genocide had not yet been laid down, the moral impulse behind his stories was muted, even though it is as a subtle moralist that Levi is increasingly coming to be valued. Levi was one of many returnees to speak and write, in public and in private, in the months following their repatriation, but he, like others, was primarily laying his own ghosts to rest and also setting the record rather than issuing a call to moral enquiry. Hence the powerful but lapidary imperative in the poem 'Shema' that prefaces *If This is a Man*: 'Meditate that this has been'. The poem echoes in a number of ways the Hebrew prayer after which it is named, not least in its ritual orality, its exhortation to repeat its words (as Levi paraphrases it) 'in your homes and as you go on your way, / as you go to sleep and as you rise...'. Levi's own talking of the camps in these months shares something of this orality, with its awe but also its solemn stasis, as each 'recitation' renews the trauma as well as heals it.

The voice of 'Shema' and *If This is a Man* nevertheless also contains clues to the moral or ethical turn that Levi's writing and talking was increasingly to take. The preface of the book, for example, famously describes his task as 'a calm study of certain aspects of the human mind'. This becomes more evident still when Levis finds a public stage in the mid-1950s. In one of the interviews in this volume, he suggests that his return to writing – that is, his reworking of *If This is a Man* for a second edition in 1958 and the subsequent writing of *The Truce* (1963) – was actually triggered by a new-found vocation for public speaking and public dialogue:

In 1955 – to mark the tenth anniversary of the liberation of the camps – they organized a photographic exhibition on the deportations, in Turin and elsewhere. Until then I had felt a fearful panic about speaking in public. During the war and the Racial Laws, I was part of a very small group of Jewish youths in Turin who had set themselves the task of showing how the Bible and Fascism were incompatible. [...] Since any form of associationism was forbidden, unless licensed by the police, there was a local policeman at all the meetings: poor thing, he sat in a corner, not understanding a word, smoking his pipe, reading the newspaper or sleeping.

When I had to get up and speak I was terrified. I ineptly read my piece on antisemitism... I was 19 and I swore to myself that I would never speak in public again, that I was not up to it. And I stuck to my promise until 1955 when I went to that exhibition to explain the meaning of those photographs. And I found an audience of young people who were so enthusiastic, warm and nice that I was overwhelmed: I saw that my book, even though it had sold so poorly, had

spread around, had left a mark, had touched people. This too drove
me towards writing *The Truce*. (pp. 164–5 below)

Once again, talking and writing intersect. At this point, Levi's talking
becomes moral rather than psychopathological, public and 'civic'
rather than private; it is dialogue rather than monologue, response
rather than ritual reiteration. And in his description of the enthusiastic 'young people' he spoke to, we can see what was to be the
dominant constituency for this new phase of his career, especially
after the early 1960s when his books became set texts in Italian
schools: students. Levi spoke at schools, conferences and public
meetings on literally hundreds of occasions, repeating his own stories
but also answering questions and engaging with his audience. These
encounters ostensibly had little to do with record, with history or with
the written word, and indeed only very few of them have survived in
recorded or transcribed form. But over the course of the years Levi
became a professional, even a consummate talker, crystallizing – in
part through a form of variant repetition quite different from the
liturgical repetition evoked by 'Shema' – that balance between
restrained formality and orality that Marco Belpoliti pinpoints
below in his analysis of Levi's language. Levi speaks as if writing
and writes as if speaking, with an emotional and syntactic lucidity
that draws his reader or listener into engaged, reflective contact.

The first two phases in Levi's career as a talker – first, talk as
trauma, then talk as pedagogy and exchange – in a sense represent
the prehistory of the Levi anthologized in this book. Sporadically in
the 1960s and 1970s, but with a dramatic crescendo in the 1980s,
Levi's talking increasingly took the form of the media interview, in
journals and newspapers, on radio and television. This new form of
encounter is assessed by Levi with his usual ironic acuity in moments
of his own writing. Perhaps the most important of these reflections is
in his 'self- interview', which first appeared in *La Stampa* in 1976 and
was then included in a longer version in new editions of *If This is a
Man* as an 'Afterword' (see below pp.184–207), where he sifts
through twenty years of questioning about the camps – mostly by
schoolchildren – to ask himself eight key questions, on the Final
Solution, Germany and Germans, racism and anti-Semitism. But it
is worth also noting three other less well-known corners of his work
where he pokes fun at the interview form through characteristically
playful transposition and parody of it. First, there is his radio short
'Intervista aziendale' ('Company Interview') of 1968, elaborated by
the experimental director Carlo Quartucci from an idea by Levi, in
which a documentary-style interview with workers in a factory

uncovers a Lamarckian industrial dystopia where workers inherit their factory skills genetically from their parents. Then there is the series of mock newspaper interviews with animals, of which he completed five in the last months of his life for the journal *L'Airone*. And finally, there is a story called 'L'intervista' ('The Interview') in *Racconti e saggi* (*The Mirror Maker*), in which an extraterrestrial chronicler compiling information about the Earth interviews the protagonist Elio on his way out of the factory night-shift.[4] All three of these examples show Levi using the interview form as a stylized way of interrogating the world, of stripping away its surfaces; but in each case also, the interview tends to reduce and simplify and the interviewee feels disoriented and uneasy at having to represent and explain his factory, his species, his world in such terms. The temptation to see here an analogue of Levi as he was constantly called upon to represent and encapsulate in simple terms the darkly rebarbative and complex world of the camps and also the 'species' of the survivor is strong indeed. Beneath the gentle satire and the formal games, as so often in Levi's work, we find a reflection on his own experience and an interrogation of the limits and possibilities of the form in question, here the interview which played such a prominent role in the final decades of his life.

The selection in this volume is intended to illustrate the range and variety of his interviews and also the patterns of reiteration and reworking of the familiar in Levi's responses. A many-sided Levi – with interests in, among other things, politics, literature, chemistry, science, religion, music, even mountaineering – emerges alongside the overwhelming gravity of his central experience and subject-matter, the *Lager*. It is as though his interviews describe a spiral movement, out from the centre of gravity – Levis himself described Auschwitz in a 1987 article as a 'black hole' – but then inexorably back again. Ultimately it is perhaps this movement through testimony and beyond and then back again that explains the sheer rounded humanity we feel when reading Levi; and also when spending some time in his company as he talks to others.

Life

A brief outline of Levi's life and work will serve as a useful guide to reading his interviews.

Born in 1919 into the small and largely assimilated Jewish community in Turin, Levi attended the Liceo Massimo d'Azeglio, a school once famous as a seedbed of liberal anti-Fascist views. His father Cesare was an electrical engineer, close to the dominant positivist circles of the city's intelligentsia, and Primo followed him in his voracious, eclectic reading and in his rejection of the humanist education on offer in the liceo. He opted to read chemistry at Turin university. Despite the obstacles set in his path by the 1938 Race Laws, he managed to graduate in 1941. Following a period in Milan and after the fall of Fascism and Italy's Armistice with the Allies in 1943, Levi joined the Resistance against the rump Fascists and the Nazi occupiers of northern Italy, but he was betrayed and captured almost immediately. Preferring to declare himself a Jew rather than risk execution as a partisan, he was imprisoned at the prison camp at Fossoli from where, in February 1944, he was deported to Auschwitz-Monowitz. He remained there until liberation by the Red Army in January 1945. He reached Turin again in October 1945 after a long, halting journey home described in *La tregua* (*The Truce*, 1963).

On his return, he wrote stories about his time in Auschwitz and, with doctor and fellow deportee Leonardo De Benedetti, a medical report on camp conditions for a general medical journal (*Minerva medica*). The stories were published in book form as *Se questo è un uomo* in 1947, by De Silva, having been rejected by Natalia Ginzburg and Cesare Pavese at Einaudi. The book was praised by a small number of reviewers (including the young Italo Calvino), but had little impact. Levi started a career as an industrial chemist and manager which would last for thirty years. He stopped writing with regularity, although it is now clear, despite his own declarations to the contrary, that he continued to think up and sketch out stories and poems throughout his apparent years of silence between the late 1940s and late 1950s.

In 1958, with interest in the Holocaust growing, Einaudi republished *Se questo è un uomo* in a slightly revised edition, to much greater acclaim. This success persuaded Levi to write more, and in 1963 he published *La tregua*, which won a prize and began to launch Levi into the role of writer *per se* for the first time. In 1966 and 1971 respectively, he published two collections of science-fantasy stories, *Storie naturali* (initially under a pseudonym, Damiano Malabaila) and *Vizio di forma*. Both contained stories written as divertissements over a period of years, some dating back to those same months in 1946 when he was talking and writing his first deportation stories. Their witty but often dark inventions have grown in stature over the years as both subterranean links with the Holocaust work and as their own literary qualities have become more evident. In particular, though, they are a focal point for Levi's important role as a bridge between 'the two cultures' of science and literature in Italy. As he tells Giuseppe Grassano (see below p. 126), a long-standing, if neglected tradition in Italian culture, from Galileo onwards, has seen no gulf between the two, and he positions himself, as a writer and a public figure, firmly within that tradition.

In confirmation of this happy synthesis, in 1975 he published *Il sistema periodico* (*The Periodic Table*, 1984), an autobiography loosely structured according to chemical elements. Each chapter centres on a real, fictional or metaphorical encounter with an element at a certain time of Levi's life. The book was hailed in America especially – Saul Bellow called it 'a necessary book' – and Levi's immense international reputation stems from this reception. His next work, *La chiave a stella* (1978; *The Wrench*, 1987), was, by contrast, very local in its style and theme: it consists of the work stories of a industrial rigger, Libertino Faussone, who, in his odd mixture of Piedmontese dialect and technical jargon, tells of his epic and intimate struggles with bridges, dams and the like. And yet, as several interviews show, Levi saw *The Wrench* as closely related to *The Periodic Table* in their shared celebration of the possibilities of a certain intelligent, problem-solving form of work, and generally put a great deal of his most heartfelt values into the figure of Faussone and his stories.

The Wrench, set in a Togliattigrad Levi had visited for work, stands among other things as a farewell meditation on his career as a chemist, and indeed, as he was writing it he was also going into retirement to become a full-time writer. His only fully fledged work of fiction, *Se non ora, quando?* (*If Not Now, When?*), the story of a Jewish partisan band in the Second World War, followed in 1982, winning two prestigious prizes, but also some criticism for its 'over-researched' reconstruction of the Ashkenazi Jewish culture of Eastern Europe. The 1980s saw a rapid crescendo in interviews and international acclaim, and Levi also began publishing several volumes of collected and new essays, stories, poems and articles. The year 1981 saw *Lilìt e altri racconti*, containing essays, camps stories and science-fiction stories and *La ricerca delle radici* ('The Search for Roots'), a fascinating commented anthology of his favourite or formative books. In 1983 came his translation of Kafka's *The Trial*, an occasion for an extraordinary and traumatic clash of temperaments. His collected poems appeared in 1984 under the Coleridgean title *Ad ora incerta* ('At an Uncertain Hour') and the following year came his most characteristically eclectic, 'encyclopaedic' (as Calvino called it) and curious volume of essays, *L'altrui mestiere* (*Other People's Trades*). More of his articles for *La Stampa* were collected for the 1986 volume *Racconti e saggi* (*The Mirror Makers*).

A year before his death, Levi drew together his reflections on Auschwitz in his most striking book, *I sommersi e i salvati* (*The Drowned and the Saved*, 1986). The essays – on memory, communication, the shame of the survivor, the Nazis' 'useless' violence, and the 'grey zone' of moral ambiguity between victim and oppressor – revisit many of the moral and historical questions thrown up by the Holocaust and are models in humane, ethical meditation. At the same time, they also contain moments of genuine anguish, anger and ambivalence. Indeed, this acceleration in publishing and public profile in the 1980s was by no means without its pressures and anxieties for Levi. He was vexed by periods of writer's block, frustrated by the distortions in his reception abroad (especially in America after 1984, where he felt he was being lionized but also absorbed into a model of the European Jewish writer which he knew he did not fit, only then to be criticized precisely for not fitting it) and deeply concerned by pernicious negationist and 'revisionist' accounts of the Holocaust appearing in France and Germany. He was also increasingly disillusioned with speaking to the young: he felt they no longer understood him nor had any notion of why what he had to say was important, let alone of the detailed complexity of what he was trying to describe. Nevertheless, he remained active, talking, writing and planning future writing throughout his final years. He died in April 1987, believed by most to have killed himself, although several voices continue to argue that there is no substantial evidence that he committed suicide.[5]

Notes

1   Like many others, Levi disliked the term 'Holocaust' and for good reason, but as he says in a 1979 interview with Giorgio Segrè, 'the word cannot be avoided now' (p. 269 below).

2   As well as editing the Italian edition of this book, *Conversazioni e interviste. 1963–87* (Turin: Einaudi, 1997), Belpoliti has edited an important new edition of Levi's complete works (Primo Levi, *Opere*, vols i–ii, Turin: Einaudi, 1997) and a collection of critical essays (*Primo Levi*, Milan: Marcos y Marcos / Riga 13, 1997), and he is the author of a recent introduction to Levi's work (*Primo Levi*, Milan: Bruno Mondadori, 1999).

3   Levi makes this distinction at the start of the essay on 'Stereotypes', the seventh of *The Drowned and the Saved* (*Opere*, vol. ii, p. 1109).

4   For the pieces discussed here, see P. Levi and C. Quartucci, *Intervista aziendale* (Turin:RAI radiodramma, [1968]); the animal interviews in *Opere*, vol. ii, pp. 902–4 [the only one in *Racconti e saggi*], 1325–7, 1332–43 (all in English in *The Mirror Maker*, London: Methuen, 1990, pp. 28–

46, 57–61); and 'L'intervista' in *Racconti e saggi*, in *Opere*, vol. ii, pp. 863–5 (*The Mirror Maker*, pp. 11–13).

5 See Diego Gambetta, 'Primo Levi's Last Moments', *Boston Review*, Summer 1999, pp. 25–9.

'I am a Centaur'

Marco Belpoliti

For all that he was a shy and reserved person, in the course of his career Primo Levi agreed to take part in large number of interviews, conversations and dialogues, many of which appeared in print, with a wide variety of different interlocutors, from journalists and critics to students and fellow writers. So intense was this activity that he came to think of his role as a talker and witness as a third profession, to set alongside his more official and recognized careers as chemist and as writer. Indeed, almost twenty years after the republication of *If This is a Man* in 1958, he felt compelled to add a new chapter to the book, an Afterword aimed particularly at his young readers, in which he replied to the questions most frequently put to him.[1] The Afterword is a genuine example of what we might call the self-interview. What is more, orality had from the outset played an important role in his vocation as a writer, if we are to believe his account – often repeated in his interviews – of the first drafts of the stories that went to make up *If This is a Man*, first drafts based on stories told orally to relatives and friends, to strangers and chance travel companions, on trains, trams, public places, wherever he found himself.

The orality of Primo Levi the narrator is confirmed by the famous preface to *If This is a Man*, where he describes the need to tell the story to 'others' as an elementary necessity, a physical need; or in the 1946 poem about the dreams of his year in Auschwitz, which later became the epigraph to *The Truce*: 'tornare; mangiare; raccontare' (going home, eating, telling our story).[2] In this, Levi comes close to those characters in the short stories of Nikolai Leskov, whom Walter Benjamin described as 'having counsel', as offering their listeners practical advice, norms for living, proverbs; whose 'counsel, woven into the fabric of real life, is wisdom'.[3] Furthermore, in Levi's work, but also in his active life, the art of the storyteller is closely related to the art of listening: as he writes in *The Wrench*, 'just as there is an art of storytelling, strictly codified through a thousand trials and errors, so there is also an art of listening, equally ancient and noble, but as far as I know, it has never been given any norm'.[4] In an interview Levi gave to Italian television in the early 1970s, entitled 'The Profession of Storytelling' and dedicated to *If This is a Man*, there is a curious episode which epitomizes his attitude as a talker-cum-listener: at a certain point, the interviewer, instead of seeking answers from Levi, begins to answer his own questions himself. Levi calmly listens to him, in silence, his expression a mixture of curiosity and perplexity. The questioner is talking about the behaviour of Germans during Hitler's rule, a question to which Levi himself has no sure answer and one to which he returns in many of the interviews concerning his experience as a deportee to the German concentration camps.

The speaker's profession is, for Levi, necessary, dictated by a dual obligation: on the one hand, there are the demands from many of his listeners for explanations of aspects of the *Lager* he does not write of in his books (or that he touches on only briefly). These are demands for further excavation – as if beneath Levi's stories there could be a base truth, an explanation of explanations, a foundation on which his interlocutors could plant their feet solidly and all would be clear. On the other hand, Levi feels the need to clarify for himself, to explain to himself more precisely, to draw out what is implicit in his writing.

Listening to Levi reply to his interviewers' questions on the tapes or videos that have survived, one cannot help but be struck by how smooth and polished his speech is, how it is ready-made for the printed page. His spoken language is closer to written language, dictated by his quick reflexes, the reflexes of the chemist. He seems quite free from what Roland Barthes called the 'hysteria' of the spoken word, the continual attempt to hook the listener with a flow of 'buts' and 'sos', to bind him into his status as partner for the duration of the dialogue. On the contrary, Levi's language is always precise; the typical interjections of a one-to-one encounter – 'do you follow? are you listening? do you understand?' – are quite absent. In other words, in Levi's spoken language there is no drama, not even muted drama. Transcribing his words from tape, one realizes that they always come quickly to him: the task of adding punctuation is easy since, unless he is interrupted by his questioner, pauses in his speech are clear, natural. Even parentheses, digressions – all the diversions that point in spoken language to the secondary importance of this or that idea – are rare and always perfectly clear.

For Levi, the interview is an extension of the art of storytelling, a way of adding something further, something that he has saved from oblivion, a fragment that his so-called 'mechanical memory' can suddenly restore.[5] Often in conversation he sounds like the archaeologist of his own past: for example, in the first interview in Part II of this book, 'The Little Theatre of Memory' (another self-interview, this time made using extracts of music and songs), he sounds the depths of his own memory and tries to draw together the fragments into an organic design. The writer is always narrating, even when he entrusts his memories to the microphone, to an apparently ephemeral moment such as the interview. Indeed, the best way of getting to know the man and the writer, the chemist and the ex-deportee, is to read the words he offers to others. Levi takes advantage of his occasional listeners to recall neglected episodes from the camps, neglected by others but also by his younger self (when Levi tells stories he is never alone, he is always in the company of that other younger self who lived through the experience of Auschwitz and whose heir, descendant and beneficiary the older Levi is, as he says on several occasions). And the opposite is also true: Levi can tell the same story yet again, after so many other times of telling it, with the same words used with such precision in his writing. The art of storytelling, for him, is also the art of repeating oneself, of renewing the same old story for new listeners, with a modicum of necessary variation. In his stories, and thus also in these interviews, repetition is not an unthinking gesture: it is a carefully deliberated choice. It is the choice of the swiftest possible means so that the passage from mouth to ear always results in clear and effective communication.

'A book', Levi said more than once, 'has to be a telephone that works', and the metaphor of the phone points to a crucial aspect of communication in Levi – distance. There is a distance between narrator and listener; the narrator, of course, counsels his interlocutor, but there is always a certain distance between them (it is the *Lager* that produces the disparity, as well as the need for explanation prompted by the interlocutors, a need he himself feels acutely). In the early 1980s, as Levi began to reflect once more on his salvation, he tells one interviewer that the impulse to write a book about his time in Auschwitz came not only from the need to bear witness and to cure himself from the curse of Auschwitz – the word as salvation, the story as therapy – but also from the desire to feel different from those around him: 'think of Ulysses spending the night recounting his odyssey to Alcinous. Probably there is another motivation at work here, perhaps that almost banal need to testify to the facts, to make another understand that I am different from you, that I have seen things you have never seen, thus I am at a level above you.'[6]

In many interviews, Levi repeats that his first profession, chemistry, saved him from death and gave him his second profession, writing. It was his strange destiny to have received from one of the greatest tragedies of our century the gift of the word: so that we can almost see him – although he disliked prophets – in the image of Isaiah whose lips were touched by the Archangel with the burning firebrand, to confer on him the purity of speech. Levi the Jew – 'ebreo di ritorno' (returning Jew), as he describes himself whenever he is asked about his Judaism – acquired the ability to narrate directly from the hell of Auschwitz, and, once he had returned to life, the ability to purify his mouth of that contagion using the gift of the story, an inheritance which, like all divine or magic gifts, soon proved to be a double-edged sword. In *The Wrench* he uses Greek myth to tell the story of that gift, seeing himself in the clothes of Tiresias who meets the snake on the road and is turned into a woman: 'ever since then, being a chemist for all the outside world but feeling the blood of a writer in my veins, I felt as though I had two souls within my body, and two is one too many'.

The dialogues in this book show with great clarity the complex identity of this 'man of counsel', this 'enchanted traveller': chemist and writer, witness and writer, Jew and Italian. In one of the earliest interviews, with Edoardo Fadini in 1966, dedicated to the science-fiction stories published later that year as *Storie naturali* ('Natural Histories') under the pseudonym Damiano Malabaila (his literary alter ego), Levi declares: 'I am amphibian, a centaur [...] I am split in two. One half of me is of the factory, the technician and the chemist. The other half is quite separate from the first [...] and inhabits the world of writing, giving interviews, working on my past and present experiences. They are two halves of my brain. I live with this paranoiac split.'[7]

The Centaur, to whom Levi dedicated one of his most beautiful short stories, 'Quaestio de Centauris',[8] does not only represent the presence of opposites, but also the union of man and beast, of impulse and ratiocination, an unstable union destined to break down. The man-horse is an emblem of the radical internal opposition that every survivor lived through and which echoes like a biblical warning in the very title of Levi's first book. In many interviews, Levi constantly found ways to come back to the deep split that ran through him, rather than wishing to hide it or to forget it. He offers it to his listeners in part as a sort of self-revelation, but always also with a modest reluctance to give in wholly to the excessive curiosity of others. As he puts it, with a note of pride, in one radio interview, 'I guard my own privacy jealously'.[9] In these conversations, Levi tells us a lot about himself, about his family, his tastes, his life in general, so that it might even seem that his trumpeted discretion is only apparent. In reality, he allows us glimpses into his life because it was from the capital event of his life that his adventure as a storyteller and talker began, because the unhealing wound, in life and in memory, is what produces the need for the word, for clear communication.

In many encounters, Levi is asked if he would have been a writer had it not been for Auschwitz. Levi replies that without knowing 'what to say', without 'the content', there is no story. On another occasion, he goes so far as to say that without the *Lager* he would have been a failed writer. His second profession, which he more than once labels a non-profession (a lecture he gave in Turin after the publication of *The Periodic Table* (1975) was entitled 'The Writer Who is Not a Writer' ('Scrittore non scrittore')), not only gives great happiness, as is evident when he discusses writing, but is also the means for him to renew that old pain, the wrench. There is an almost standard reply that he uses after a certain date – around 1978 – when he is asked 'What are you writing now?' 'Nothing,' he says, 'I think I've exhausted all avenues'; or 'I've run out of supplies, I don't have much more to say'. In one of his last conversations, with Roberto Di Caro, in which he talks about the economy of narrative, there is a sense of weariness, of exhaustion in his words;[10] but this is nothing new. Acting just like a chemist or technician who carefully weighs up his own means and assesses what is available to him before starting in on an operation, Levi weighed up his own narrative resources on several occasions. When *The Truce* was published in 1963, he was asked about future projects and he mentions an idea for a book of factory stories, the adventures of a chemist, but he says he has not yet found the key motif, the way to make the subject interesting for the reader, although he himself is so enthused by it (Levi clearly had in mind at the time a story built around an epic motif, around memory, which, as Benjamin noted again, 'is the epic faculty *par excellence*', 'The Storyteller', p. 96). These hints are the embryonic form of a narrative project that resulted in not one but two books: *The Periodic Table* and *The Wrench*. 'And what about the *Lager* experience?', a journalist asks him after he receives the Campiello Book Prize for *The Truce* in 1963. 'Absolutely, not another word. Nothing. I've said everything I had to say. It's all over.'[11] But nothing finishes in Levi, everything returns continuously, through some intrinsic force. And so his affirmation that his subject-matter has run its course, besides being a superstitious gesture driven by the fear of losing his own prodigious storytelling abilities, is also an unequivocal sign of its continual recapitulation, of the impossibility of cutting himself off even for a moment from the inheritance of Auschwitz (there is not a single interview that does not refer, even if only in the introduction, to that place).

The other question Levi comes back to again and again – at times rejecting and at times accepting it – is the question of his being a writer. Levi is certainly a fully fledged writer, above all else an exceptional writer, since none of his books fits neatly into a specific genre, and this causes his questioners difficulties: what is *If This is a Man*? A testimony or a story? A memorial or a novel? And *The Periodic Table*? A *Bildungsroman* built up out of several short stories? And again, what sort of a book is *The Drowned and the Saved* from a literary point of view? He explains to Giuseppe Grassano that his identity as a writer is manifold, coming back once again, in 1979 now, to the theme of the Centaur: 'I am a "liceo" student with a humanistic education, but also a chemist and finally an ex-deportee. So I have at least three different sources for my writing.'

The foremost difficulty for the interviewer, then, at least until the early 1980s, is that of fixing the boundary between witness and writer, chemist and storyteller, between the narrator of the odyssey of Auschwitz and the writer of science-fiction stories. Then, suddenly, with the publication of *If Not Now, When?* in 1982, the problem seems to disappear, as if that work of fiction, that story of love and war, has smoothed over all the distinctions. But for Levi the problem is still there; indeed, in a sense it is sharper than ever. On the one hand, as the witness, Levi feels called upon to be truthful, and this problem – the truthfulness of his own affirmations – will return obsessively in these years, providing the impulse to write that masterpiece of self-reflection, *The Drowned and the Saved*, born not only as a reaction to the 'negationism' of figures such as Faurisson and Darquier de Pellepoix,[12] but also from inner motives, from an enquiry into his own work as a writer. On the other hand, his books are all, whether testimonial or essayistic (see, for example, *Other People's Trades* (1985), one of the last great examples of the tradition of the *elzeviro* (short essay) or *prosa d'arte* (art prose), in which Italian writers of the twentieth century have excelled), strongly literary works. Indeed, this literary quality is what sets Levi apart from the hundreds of stories and testimonies published in Italy and in Europe after the defeat of Nazism.

So, Levi's books are to differing degrees shot through with that 'fiction' proper to literature (he reflects on this in almost all of the interviews, explaining what real events lie behind this or that story, including stories he has been told by others). To be a writer, he reflects, is in a sense to betray the task of the witness, since it is natural for the written page to render the true story more convincing and more compelling. In this Levi shows, even compared to other narrators of the genocide of the Jews, an acute awareness of the problematic rapport between narration and reality, of the fact that every act of testimony is valid essentially in and of itself. In a filmed interview of 1974, the interviewer tries to compare Levi's account with that of one of his camp companions, the famous Pikolo of the chapter 'The Canto of Ulysses' in *If This is a Man*. All to no avail, because Pikolo does not remember a single thing of that crucial episode, he only recalls that he and Levi did speak at length, nothing of what they spoke about. Levi himself, in other conversations, emphasizes that there is always some discrepancy between what he narrates and what happened in reality, however much he continues to insist on the essential veracity of his work. He notes that few of the people who appear in his books have accepted the portrait he gives of them there. When he moves on to the field of pure invention, with the characters of *If Not Now, When?*, he confesses to journalists that he ran up against another unforeseen problem. The characters began to act like people, refusing to die, taking him by the hand and control-ling him (one of them will even come and visit his creator, in a couple of stories from the 1960s, 'Creative Work' and 'In the Park'[13]).

In a conversation on the sources of *The Wrench* in 1978, Levi speaks of himself, with his usual self-irony, as a 'counterfeiter'. In all probability, he is aware – although no one puts it to him in these terms – that the literature of our age is a strange place where nothing, not even that which is most horrifying and scandalous, appears before the reader as it is, a place where the true story loses its spark of truth and changes into something else, a leisure activity or a form of information. Walter Benjamin, once more, tells us that this is because literature in the modern age has substantially cut itself off from experience, it is no longer 'experience passed on from mouth to mouth' ('The Storyteller', p. 84), it no longer originates in an act of memory, it has lost perhaps once and for all its epic charge.

The presence of many professions in Levi (chemist, writer, witness, speaker) is not a chance happening: any profession is a natural gen-erator of stories, since stories are born in the workplace, in various workplaces (those 'other people's trades' pursued with such tenacity in the prose collection of that name). The profession of the writer is itself a form of artisanal craft, he declares shortly after the publication of *If Not Now, When?*, his first *novel* as he calls it. Like Faussone, the mechanical rigger of *The Wrench*, he talks of himself as a rigger of stories. Indeed, all his stories are ones we can ask to be continued (Benjamin again). In one interview Levi even says he has an idea for a sequel to *If Not Now, When?*; in others he explains how it had originally been born out of another story, together with a fragment recovered from the story of his own return to life.

Although Levi was from the outset a great talker, always ready to respond to his listeners, no published interviews have been found before 1961, when he is asked to respond to a questionnaire on the 'Jewish question' put together by an historical journal. Even between 1963 and 1978, the number of interviews is relatively low. Then, suddenly, from 1979 onwards, Levi – already a very well-known writer, the author of a set text studied in almost every school in Italy and also a frequent visitor to schools – becomes a public figure. Newspapers begin to ask his views on his life, his work as a chemist, his past, on the camps and his work as a writer. Most of Levi's 250 or so interviews are concentrated in a period of seven or eight years between 1979 and 1986, when he is no longer practising his first profession and has dedicated himself more intensely to his second, that of the writer. In this phase of his life, Levi only very rarely goes to schools to meet students, since the latter, he notes with regret more than once, now see the Second World War as an event lost in the distant past. For the first time, there are notes of pessimism about his third profession and this seems only to intensify with his various encounters with the press. He takes part in television programmes and he accepts into his home interviewers from all four corners of the world. For the international public, Levi has by the early 1980s become one of the best-known Jewish writers in the world, and this despite the fact that the translations of his books into English had passed almost unnoticed in previous decades (including in America and Israel). Levi himself is surprised and bewildered by this, as he explains in a 1986 interview with Risa Sodi, where he gives an account of his trip to America and the welcome he received, and notes 'by dint of being called a Jewish writer, I became one! I've already mentioned that I began to wonder if there any "goyim" lived in America. I didn't come across a single one of them! It almost becomes comical. My editor is Jewish and all his collaborators are Jewish. He introduced me exclusively to illustrious American Jews. I spoke to Jewish audiences.'[14]

As emerges clearly from the interviews and dialogues collected in this volume – but also from the many not included – even the Jewish side of his identity presents problems. Never letting go of his hybrid nature, he tells one interviewer he feels four-fifths Italian and one-fifth Jewish. But he immediately adds that he has grown very affectionate towards that one fifth and that he considers it fundamental to his identity. On several occasions, such as in the interview with the writer Edith Bruck, herself a Jewish concentration-camp survivor, he declares that he became Jewish after Auschwitz, that beforehand he had been simply a middle-class Italian boy.[15] Or again, to Giuseppe Grieco, 'I am Jewish by accident of birth. I am neither ashamed nor boastful about it. Being Jewish, for me, is a matter of "identity": an "identity", I must also say, that I have no intention of discarding.'[16]

In 1982, the invasion of southern Lebanon by Israeli troops provoked a strong reaction in public opinion both in Israel and amongst the Jewish Diaspora outside Israel to which Levi belonged. It was a critical moment for Levi, who had just returned from his second trip to Auschwitz since the end of the war. He was one of the promoters of an appeal for the withdrawal of the troops and for a peace process to guarantee a homeland to those who did not have one. The Italian press interviews Levi and here too, he revealed the subtlety of his thinking which, much like his thinking on the Lager and the theme of the 'grey zone', cannot be reduced to simple categories founded on predetermined mental or ideological schemas. This is an aspect of Levi's Judaism that is less well-known but just as important as others, another tile in the unusual mosaic that goes to make up his identity.

Reading this volume makes the special qualities of Primo Levi clearer than ever for us. If the collected interviews of many twentieth-century writers constitute a rich mine of information on their working habits, opinions, interpretations, likes and dislikes, Levi yet again represents an exception. His story, whether written or oral, is always a story of experience, in which words count as gestures, as ceremonial acts to guide us through the calamitous state of the twentieth century. It is up to the reader to pick up in his words and their transcription the sanction of truth that resonates, often in the dual guise of an unexpected optimism combined with a lucid pessimism. 'I am a centaur', he tells us. For Primo Levi, talker and writer, let Benjamin's closing words on the storyteller stand: 'His gift is the ability to relate his life; his distinction to be able to tell his entire life. The storyteller: he is the man who could let the wick of his life be consumed completely by the gentle flame of his story' ('The Storyteller', p. 107).

Notes

1 See below, pp. 184-207

2 Primo Levi, *If This is a Man/The Truce*, translated by S. Woolf (Harmondsworth: Penguin, 1979), pp. 15, 183.

3 See Walter Benjamin, 'The Storyteller. Reflections on the Work of Nikolai Leskov' in *Illuminations*, translated by H. Zorn (London: Pimlico, 1999), pp. 83–107 [p. 86].

4 Primo Levi, *The Wrench* (London: Michael Joseph, 1987), p. 35.

5 Levi uses the phrase 'mechanical memory' several times in *The Drowned and the Saved*, translated by R. Rosenthal (London: Michael Joseph, 1988).

6 Interview not included in this volume.

7 See below, p. 85

8 *Opere*, vol. i, pp. 505–16; not included in the English selection of Levi's stories, *The Sixth Day* (London: Michael Joseph,1990).

9 Interview with Dina Luce, RAI radiodue, 4 October 1982, not included here.

10 See below, p. 169–70.

11 See below, p. 81.

12 Robert Faurisson, a professor at the University of Lyons, was at the centre of negationism following his denial of the existence of the gas chambers in 1978. Also in 1978, Darquier de Pellepoix, former Vichy commissioner responsible for the deportation of Jews from France, claimed that the gas chambers were intended merely to kill fleas.

13 *Opere*, vol. i, pp. 651–60, 671–80; not in *The Sixth Day*.

14 Risa Sodi, 'An Interview with Primo Levi', *Partisan Review*, LIV, 3, 1987, pp. 355–66 [360].

15 See below, p. 262.

16 See below. p. 274.

Editors' Note

The interviews included here have been chosen from the two hundred or so published interviews and the fifty or so broadcast interviews given by Levi between 1961 and 1987. Before 1961, when Levi responded to the questionnaire on 'The Jewish Question' included in Part V here, there seem to be no interviews at all, despite the publication of *If This is a Man* in 1947 and its republication in 1958. After 1961, there is a group of interviews following the publication and success of *The Truce* in 1963, but then only a handful between 1964 and 1977. There is another flurry in 1978 with the publication of *The Wrench*, but it is only really between 1981 and 1986 (with a peak in 1982, with *If Not Now, When?*) that Levi becomes a frequent and multi-media interviewee and a public figure of sorts. The measure of frequency of these public encounters may not be the only nor indeed the best measure of a writer's status – Levi was known as a writer throughout the 1960s especially in schools, where he was giving dozens of unpublished talks – but it is one significant element in his public profile.

The most complete available list of all his interviews is to be found in Primo Levi, *Opere*, edited by Marco Belpoliti (Turin: Einaudi, 1997), vol. i, pp. cxvii–cxxvi, although there are almost certainly gaps still remaining of further published interviews (especially outside Italy) and of unpublished or untranscribed conversations. Some previously unknown transcriptions are included in the volume by Gabrielle Poli and Giorgio Calcagno, *Echi di una voce perduta* (Milan: Mursia, 1992).

The interviews included here come in three different textual forms: those answered in writing by Levi himself, those transcribed or 'written up' by the interviewer-journalist and those transcribed from recordings either previously or for this volume. They have been divided into sections for ease of orientation, although inevitably there is a large degree of overlap, at times even repetition between different interviews and different sections. We have not trimmed these repetitions as they are an integral part of Levi's long experience in giving interviews, as he himself acknowledges more than once. Titles of the interviews as published or broadcast have for the most part been retained, except in the case of the third section where book titles are used instead.

The first part, 'English Encounters', contains four of the most important of Levi's encounters with English-speaking writers and journalists, perhaps the most influential of which was his 1986 meeting with Philip Roth. Part II, entitled 'Life', shows aspects of Levi's experiences and interests, likes and dislikes, that are often overshadowed by his status as a Holocaust survivor. It opens with a sort of Italian version of *Desert Island Discs* where Levi uses music to remember his parents and childhood, aspects of the camps, his return home and marriage, but also his later work in radio. It then goes on to highlight aspects as diverse as his work as a chemist, his passion for mountaineering, his affection for the city of Turin, his involvement in campaigns for the morality of science. Part III, 'Books', selects examples from the rounds of interviews that accompanied the publication of eight of his books (with the significant exception of *If This is a Man*, although inevitably that first book pervades almost all the other interviews), to give a sense of the chronology of his career and his evolving thoughts on his own writing. The fourth part, 'Literature and Writing', includes interviews where Levi reflects in more general terms about his books and those of others, including, for example, his fascinating, ambivalent encounter (as translator) with Kafka. In Part V, 'Auschwitz and Survival', Levi tackles the event at the heart of his life and work and at the heart of all his interviews. Of particular interest here are the transcription of a TV documentary-interview following him back to the camp at Auschwitz and the long interview entitled 'The Duty of Memory', carried out as part of an oral history project. Finally Part VI is called 'Judaism and Israel' and it contains five interviews in which Levi addresses his identity as a Jew, through discussion of religious belief, tradition and education and the role of the 'Diaspora' Jew in relation to Israel.

In translating the interviews an attempt has been made to reflect the somewhat unusual spoken language used by Levi in his public conversations, as described by Marco Belpoliti in his introduction; that is, a spoken language which is fluent and accessible but which often smacks of the poise and formality of the written word. It should be noted that it has become common practice in Italian to use the German term *Lager* (camp) as a generic term for the Holocaust, and both because Levi disliked the term Holocaust (although he accepted it was unavoidable) and because it reflects his own usage, *Lager* has more often than not been retained in the translation. The editors have added brief informative notes to names and references which may not be clear to English readers or to young readers in general. These notes are generally only given once for each name or reference (see the Index when no note is given). Where possible, English titles of Levi's books have been used, except in cases where the books are untranslated or where the English editions differ significantly from the original.

Marco Belpoliti edited and carried out the research for the Italian edition. Robert Gordon translated the text, adapted the notes for the English edition and co-edited the book in collaboration with Marco Belpoliti. The sections and the selection for the English edition have been altered to reflect the different readership: in particular, Part I is new, and significant additions have been made to Part IV and V.

The editors would like to thank the following for their help: Alberto Cavaglion and Paola Valabrega, Giovanni Tesio, Sophie Nezri, Maddalena Gnisci, Ian Thomson, Daniela Amsallem, Carole Angier, Dea Rosselli, Silvia Lalía, Maria Sebregondi, Franco Nasi, Alessandro Carrera, Giuseppe Furghieri, Martin McLaughlin, Patrick Pauletto, Claudio Toscani, Giovanni Grassano, Bruno Vasari, Guido Lopez, Ada Luzzati and Silvio Ortona, Luca Scarlini, Anna Maria Levi, Pietro Crivellari, Roberto Vacca, Domenico Fiormonte, Yuri Sangalli, Corinna Salvadori Lonergan, Lorenzo Enriques, Eduardo Caianello, Nadia Fusini, Beniamino Placido.

Special thanks to Lucia, Lisa and Renzo Levi; Ernesto Ferrero, Paolo Fossati, Maria Perosino and Roberto Gilodi (at Einaudi); Lynn Dunlop at Polity Press and Jane Robertson; Federico Reviglio (*La Stampa* archive); *Il Giorno* archive; Michele Gulinucci, Ermanno Anfossi and Marco Zaccarelli (RAI); Dede Cavallari (Mediaset); Maria Grazia Rabiolo (Radio Svizzera Italiana); Michele Sarfatti and Liliana Picciotto Fargion (Centro di Documentazione Ebraica, Milan). And in particular to Elio and Luigi Grazioli, Claudia Verpelli and Barbara Placido.

Acknowledgements

The editors and publishers wish to thank the following for permission to use copyright material:

Gillon Aitken Associates Ltd on behalf of the author for 'Germaine Greer talks to Primo Levi', *Literary Review*, Nov. (1985) pp. 65–8. Copyright © Germaine Greer 1985;

Random House UK for Primo Levi, 'Afterword' from *If This is a Man* by Primo Levi, translated by Ruth Feldman, Vintage (1996) pp. 381–98;

Anthony Rudolf for 'Primo Levi in London', *London Magazine*, Oct. (1986) pp. 30–37;

Ian Thomson for 'Primo Levi in conversation with Ian Thomson', *PN Review*, 14:2 (1987) pp. 15–19;

The Wylie Agency on behalf of the author for Philip Roth, 'A Man Saved by his Skills', *New York Times Book Review*, 12.10.86, pp. 1, 38–9;

Every effort has been made to trace the copyright holders but if any have been inadvertently overlooked the publishers will be pleased to make the necessary arrangement at the first opportunity.

Part I
English Encounters

Germaine Greer Talks to Primo Levi (1985)

The interview was conducted in Italian; words occasionally given in inverted commas are words that Levi himself said in English.

In the first chapter of La chiave a stella [*The Wrench*] *Faussone says to the writer to whom he's going to tell his story: 'Now if you want to tell this, you'll work on it, you'll rectify it, you'll burnish it, take away the dross, give it a bit of pazazz and turn it into something.'*

Even though Faussone is an unreliable witness, I think he's saying something fundamentally true about what writers do, and I want to ask you about that manufacturing process as it applied to If This is a Man. *Any writer has to master reality and get it under his control if he's going to trap it between the covers of a book. How did you manage to tame the subject of* If This is a Man, *and make out of that horror an elegant, clear and sensitive book. I find the achievement staggering.*

I don't know how to answer. For one thing, it's forty years since I wrote it. And in those forty years I've constructed a sort of legend around that book, that I wrote it without a plan, that I wrote it on impulse, that I wrote it without reflecting at all.

The other people I've talked to about it accepted the legend. In fact, writing is never spontaneous. Now that I think about it, I can see that this book is full of literature, literature absorbed through the skin, even while I was rejecting it (because I was a bad student of

From the *Literary Review*, November 1985, pp. 15–19. A biographical introduction to the interview has been omitted.

Italian literature). I preferred chemistry. I was bored by lessons in poetic theory, the structure of the novel and all that. When the time came, and I needed to write this book, and I did have a pathological need to write it, I found inside myself a whole 'programme'. And it was that literature I'd studied more or less unwillingly, the Dante I'd had to do in high school, the Italian classics and so forth.

The virtuosity of If This is a Man *seems to me to reside in the rhythm of the unfolding of such a vast and appalling story and in the control of the tone of the narrator, who never seems to be unburdening himself. You don't actually find out very much about him: he was little, he could run, and he was a man people tended not to notice – which was just as well in the circumstances. Nevertheless, through the tone you feel the presence of a refined sensibility, a distinct personality, disabused, honest, undeceived and undeceivable.*

I think that it's precisely in this aspect, in being 'disabused' that you find the effects of my laboratory work. You couldn't afford to let yourself be taken in. It's always a good idea to go beyond appearances.

The first days were terrible – for everyone. There is a 'shock', a trauma connected with entrance into a concentration camp which can last five, ten, twenty days. Nearly all the people who died, died during this first phase. Our way of life had changed totally in the space of a few days, especially in the case of us western Jews. Polish and Russian Jews had done some hard training for the Auschwitz experience in the ghettos beforehand, and the shock for them was less severe. For us, the Italian, French and Dutch Jews, it was as if we had been plucked straight from our houses to a concentration camp.

But I could feel, along with fear and hunger and exhaustion, an extremely intense need to understand the world around me. To begin with, the language. I know a little German, but I felt I had to know a lot more. I went so far as to take private lessons, paid for with part of my bread ration. I didn't know that I was learning a really vulgar kind of German. I found that out on a business trip to a chemical factory in Leverküsen. The people I was dealing with, very polite German types, said 'How strange. Italians don't usually know any German, and those who do know a different kind of German. Where did you learn it?' So I told them. 'I learnt it in Auschwitz.' They were upset, for lots of reasons. We were being friendly together and at least some of them, perhaps all of them, had been Nazis.

It is always said that Levi is wonderful because he feels no hatred or resentment against the Nazis –

That doesn't seem all that true to me.

In fact, reading If This is a Man, *I am very aware of the superiority of the detached, sophisticated narrator – who detests any kind of interference in other people's lives – to these barbarous tormentors, and not just Nazis. You hardly ever mention the word 'Nazi', but you do say loud and clear that there's no point in trying to understand Germans.*

True enough. In fact, I tried very hard to understand Germans even afterwards. I signed on as a member of the Goethe Institute here in Turin for five years, and I've had lots of German friends.

If I can stick with this problem of the writer's re-invention of reality for a bit longer . . .

Well, I think there are writers who do it deliberately and intelligently, writers who do it intelligently and not deliberately, and ingenuous writers who do it without either planning it or wanting it. I believe that when I wrote *If This is a Man* I belonged to the third category. There's certainly distortion in it – if only because the camp I went to, Monowitz, was not typical of the complex of camps that was Auschwitz. It was seven kilometres from Auschwitz and it was not the same. While I thought I was writing the authentic story of the concentration camp experience, I was telling the story of my camp, of just one.

At that time, the selection of prisoners for extermination was more moderate; they took 10 or 15 per cent of the camp and not 40 or even 90 per cent as they did at Treblinka. They needed labour, you see. That's been documented: the conflict between the SS who wanted to kill everybody at once and German industry which, for reasons of money, not humanitarian considerations, said, 'A worker who dies within a week is no use to us. We want workers who last at least three months, six months.' All that came out at the Nuremberg trial. I found out years later from Borkin's book,[1] that my camp actually belonged to IG-Farben; it was a private camp. It didn't belong to the SS. And I was saved by my trade. In the selection of October 1944, I was passed over, because there was written on my card *Facharbeiter*, chemist. I was an unusual case, a specialized worker. And I'd like to add something else: all the stories of people who survived concentration camps have no general application. Every survivor is an exception, a miracle, someone with a special destiny. My special destiny was my training.

Your autobiographical writings, and in particular La tregua [*The Truce*], *are a modern version of* Robinson Crusoe, *but I suspect you're more sceptical, more pessimistic than Defoe.*

Sceptical certainly. Doubtful.

It is also true that you can't describe people without including an element of judgement in the description, isn't it? Would Sandro recognize himself from the account you give of him in The Periodic Table? [*Sandro Delmastro is the hero of a section of* The Periodic Table. *He was the first of the Piedmontese Resistance group to be killed in 1944.*]

No, he wouldn't recognize himself. He'd have protested. As his nephews in fact did protest. They attacked me violently, for stupid reasons: because I wrote that his father was a *capomastro* and in fact he was an industrial surveyor. It's always dangerous, transforming a person into a character. No matter how good the author's intentions, no matter how much he tries not to distort anything, or tries to improve the character of the person, to make it more noble or more beautiful, the person is always disappointed. Because everyone has an image of himself which is different from the image that other people have of them. It's as if I looked at myself in the mirror and saw a different face from the usual one. A human being is a 'unique', complicated object. When that object is reduced to a page, even by the best writers, it's reduced to a skeleton. It took Flaubert five hundred pages to describe Emma Bovary. I think if Sandro had lived, and I'd made him read the portrait of himself, he would have burst out laughing. He would have thought it comical that he'd turned into a written page. He was a young man who so loathed all forms of rhetoric that he'd have been afraid to find himself described as a hero, a saint, a warrior. He'd have laughed and said something in dialect, 'Balls!' probably.

Now that I'm retired I go to a swimming pool and nearly every Tuesday I meet Sandro's brother there. We greet each other, talk about the weather but he has always refused to talk to me about Sandro.

It is dreadful, isn't it? A writer's like a parasite whose excrement lasts longer than the thing it fed on.

That's true. But the writer's not only a parasite, he's also a creator. In the best cases, the book lasts longer than the man who wrote it and transmits a reality which isn't the true one.

And no matter what he confesses to, the narrator is always invulnerable.

Because he is in control. The author is omnipotent and can create the reality he wants.

The episode in La tregua[2] *that I found the most appalling and morally ambiguous was when those of you hiding out in the scarlatina ward heard other patients in the next room groaning for water and ignored their pleading.*

My subjective impression was very different. And still is today. I wrote to Charles, the Frenchman who was with me there, and we confessed to each other that those ten days were our 'finest hour'. Of course, we've censored and suppressed the fact that we didn't give water to everyone. However, we did try to save ten people's lives, and we succeeded, at least in part. We couldn't save four hundred, but perhaps we could save ten. And we did our best under the circumstances, even though we were both very sick. We remembered those ten days as our best time because we invented everything, the way to make the soup, the stove we made it on, the way to get water, even the medicines that we needed. We made our own world. There were hundreds around us who were not part of the world, but I think our calculation was the right one. It was better to try realistically to save ten than to succeed in saving no one.

I'm going to ask you the questions that Mordo Nahum [a character from La tregua] *and his friends used to discuss. What to you does the word 'know' mean?*

I don't know. I haven't asked myself that question since I was eighteen. I was surprised that Mordo Nahum and his friends asked it. Philosophy of science exists to labour over such questions, but I've remained a chemist in this. I know with my hands and my nose, with my senses, like any naive realist. It's not a matter of arriving at the deepest roots of knowing, but just of going down from one level to another, understanding a little more than before. When I understand what's going on inside a retort, I'm happier. I've extended my knowledge a little bit more. I haven't understood truth or reality. I've just reconstructed a segment, a little segment of the world. That's already a big victory inside a factory laboratory.

The next question of Mordo Nahum: what do you mean by 'spirit'?

The first people to practise distillation really thought they they were extracting the soul of things. I have to say I don't know. I really don't believe in an eternal soul.

The third of Mordo's conundrums: what do you mean by 'justice'?

To each his own. I think a primary approximation is to punish the guilty and reward the just. But it's very difficult to establish who is guilty and who is just. The trials they conduct in Italy, or for that matter anywhere else in the world, are not adequate. We can never be sure of establishing ultimate responsibility, of deciding whether a criminal is criminal by his own choice or because of his upbringing or his environment or the people who indoctrinated him, his teachers, his parents and so on. And so throughout the civilized world legal codes have been set up.

What is your religion?

I have none. Because my parents are Jewish, I constructed a Jewish culture for myself, but very late, after the war. After I got back, I found myself in possession of a supplementary culture and I tried to develop it. But not for religion. It's as if my religious sense had been amputated. I just haven't got one. I have what Freud called the oceanic sense. If you think about the universe at all, you become religious, but I don't have a problem with it.

Are you afraid of death?

I'm afraid of suffering, but not of death. I'm very afraid both of my own suffering and the suffering of others.

As you are one of the few Italian Jews to return from forced exile in the Lager, *did you not feel some kind of duty to steep yourself in the culture of a minority which was so nearly obliterated from history?*

I didn't think of it in that way. That's a role that has been imposed on me. I found it very surprising, to be introduced everywhere as an 'Italian Jew'. They compared me to Bashevis Singer,[3] misleadingly because my Jewish culture is all *post hoc*, all added on afterwards. I've studied Yiddish but it's not my language at all, and in Italy nobody speaks it. In America they put a label on me. I gave twenty-five interviews, and each one was on the theme, 'What it means to be a Jew in Italy.' Not much, I'm afraid.

I am interested in the fact that so many writers who have been successful in Italy lately have a second culture. Tomizza,[4] for example, is from Istria and his books are all in Italian, but he knows all about the culture of the valleys of the Cuneese, where they speak an Occitanian language. I'm Italian, but I'm also Jewish. It's like a having a spare wheel, or an extra gear. For practical reasons I set about studying Hebraic culture, whether Yiddish or biblical, as well as the way of life of Jews in various parts of the world, but with a detached interest, zoological again. However, the chapter on the culture of my Piedmontese Jewish forebears in *The Periodic Table* is written with love. I'm profoundly attached to Piedmont. I'm perfectly aware of the defects in the Piedmontese character, because they're my own defects.

Do you think a homeland is an essential thing? Is it essential for Jews to have a fatherland?

Mine is here, in Piedmont. I'd never think of going to Israel. But the first people who went to Israel didn't have this kind of homeland. They were either very religious people, or they were Poles, Russians, Romanians who were never allowed to think of the countries they lived in as their homes. The governments of their countries said to them, 'You're not a Russian, or a Pole or a Romanian. You're a "yid".' The pogroms continued after the war. Some of the Jews who miraculously survived the Holocaust died in postwar pogroms.

A great force was impelling people towards a homeland when in fact they no longer had one. This isn't my situation. I am a Jew of the Diaspora, a second-hand Jew in any case. The situation in Israel now is dramatic, tragic actually, partly for errors that have been made.

When I described the carriage full of young Zionists heading for Israel in *La tregua*, I was indicating a self-evident truth. There simply wasn't room in Europe any longer for these people. Europe was the land of massacres, the land of Auschwitz. There was a tremendous wave of emotion that I nearly got caught up in myself. I didn't know if my family had survived, or if this house was still standing, but my only thought after the liberation of Auschwitz was to come back to Italy. Lots of my ex-comrades asked me why I was returning to Italy. They thought Europe was a dangerous place. 'Come with us to Israel, to rehabilitate the land. By doing that we can rehabilitate ourselves. We'll go and build in order to rebuild ourselves.' It was a powerful argument. But it was a simplification. If you thought about the actual situation, the objective conditions . . . the country wasn't empty for one thing.

I had trouble with this in America. I had to give a talk to a group in Brooklyn and for the first time in my life I found myself in front of a totally Jewish audience. All old and all Jewish. I gave my talk, which I'd written in England. I'm not sure how much they grasped, given my terrible accent. As soon as I finished, they started asking questions about Israel and where I stood on the Arab–Israeli conflict. When I started to explain that I thought Israel was a mistake in historical terms, there was uproar and the moderator had to call the meeting to a halt.

Do you think there is a modern Jewish literature?

I think there are five hundred.

One reason I ask is that there is a Kafka story which reminds me very much of your sensibility and style –

You know I translated *The Trial* – it was part of a project of translation of writers by other writers. I didn't find it difficult, but it was very painful. I fell ill doing it. I finished the translation in a deep depression that lasted six months. It's a pathogenic book. Like an onion, one layer after another. Each of us could be tried and condemned and executed, without ever knowing why. It was as if it predicted the time when it was a crime simply to be a Jew.

A theme which struck me profoundly in If This is a Man *was that of the 'submerged' versus the 'saved'. Is there any value in the life of one of the 'submerged'?*[5]

Certainly – before he is submerged. But not when he is reduced to a 'husk'. But I wasn't talking about people who let themselves go under rather than behave in a brutal way in order to survive. There was nothing dignified in the 'submerged' of Auschwitz. They would not have given some of their portion to another. All the fabric of human relationships was destroyed.

In Ethiopia, for example, there are many Hurbineks. [Hurbinek is a crippled three-year-old who somehow escaped extermination along with the rest of his family to die a few days after liberation in March 1945, whose brief story is told in La tregua.] *In Western Europe we are like the ten of you who saved yourselves in the hospital room. Outside many more are 'submerged' than can be saved.*

  Humanity is like an iceberg; nine-tenths of it is 'submerged'. In the camps the 'submerged' had been pushed under by the Germans, but by the same token we are the Germans of the world.

Of course. The rest of the world is paying the costs of the colonial era.

So you see, I take If This is a Man *not as the story of an Italian Jew who wound up in Auschwitz in the closing years of the Second World War, but as a sort of allegory of the global situation. It raises all the important moral question of our time.*

Hm.

Notes

1   Joseph Borkin, *The Crime and Punishment of IG-Farben* (New York: Pocket Books, 1978).
2   The episode is first described in the final pages of *If This is a Man*.
3   Isaac Bashevis Singer (1904–91), the Nobel prizewinning Yiddish writer, was born in Poland and lived in America after 1935.

4   Fulvio Tomizza (1935–) is a prolific writer from Istria, the border region between Italy and the former Yugoslavia.

5   The ninth chapter of *If This is a Man* is called 'The Drowned and the Saved [or submerged]', as is Levi's 1986 book, published after this interview took place.

A Man Saved by his Skills (1986)

Philip Roth

On the September Friday that I arrived in Turin – to renew a conversation with Primo Levi that we had begun one afternoon in London the spring before – I asked to be shown around the paint factory where he'd been employed as a research chemist and, afterwards, until retirement, as factory manager. Altogether the company employs fifty people, mainly chemists who work in the laboratories and skilled laborers on the floor of the plant. The production machinery, the row of storage tanks, the laboratory building, the finished product in man-sized containers ready to be shipped, the reprocessing facility that purifies the wastes – all of it is encompassed in four or five acres a seven-mile drive from Turin. The machines that are drying resin and blending varnish and pumping off pollutants are never really distressingly loud, the yard's acrid odor – the smell, Levi told me, that clung to his clothing for two years after his retirement – is by no means disgusting, and the skip loaded with the black sludgy residue of the anti-polluting process isn't particularly unsightly. It is hardly the world's ugliest industrial environment, but a very long way, nonetheless, from those sentences suffused with mind that are the hallmark of Levi's autobiographical narratives. On the other hand, however far from the prose, it is clearly a place close to his heart; taking in what I could of the noise, the stench, the mosaic of pipes and vats and tanks and dials, I remembered Faussone, the skilled rigger in *The Monkey's Wrench*,[1] saying to Levi – who calls Faussone 'my alter ego' – 'I have to tell you, being around a work site is something I enjoy.'

From the *New York Times Book Review*, 12 October 1986, pp. 1, 40–1.

On our way to the section of the laboratory where raw materials are scrutinized before moving on to production, I asked Levi if he could identify the particular chemical aroma faintly permeating the corridor: I thought it smelled a little like a hospital corridor. Just fractionally he raised his head and exposed his nostrils to the air. With a smile he told me, 'I understand and can analyse it like a dog.'

He seemed to me inwardly animated more in the manner of some little quicksilver woodland creature empowered by the forest's most astute intelligence. Levi is small and slight, though not quite so delicately built as his unassuming demeanour makes him at first appear, and still seemingly as nimble as he must have been at ten. In his body, as in his face, you see – as you don't in most men – the face and the body of the boy that he was. His alertness is nearly palpable, keenness trembling within him like his pilot light.

It is probably not as surprising as one might think to find that writers divide like the rest of mankind into two categories: those who listen to you and those who don't. Levi listens, and with his entire face, a precisely modeled face tipped with a white chin beard that, at sixty-seven, is at once youthfully Pan-like but professorial as well, the face of irrepressible curiosity and of the esteemed *dottore*. I can believe Faussone when he says to Primo Levi early in *The Monkey's Wrench*, 'You're quite a guy, making me tell these stories that, except for you, I've never told anybody.' It's no wonder that people are always telling him things and that everything is recorded faithfully before it is even written down: when listening he is as focused and as still as a chipmunk spying something unknown from atop a stone wall.

In a large apartment house built a few years before he was born – and where he was born, for formerly this was the home of his parents – Levi lives with his wife, Lucia; except for his year in Auschwitz and the adventurous months immediately after his liberation, he has lived in this same apartment all his life.

The apartment is still shared, as it has been since the Levis met and married after the war, with Primo Levi's mother. She is ninety-one. Levi's ninety-five-year-old mother-in-law lives not far away; in the apartment immediately next door lives his twenty-eight-year-old son, a physicist; and a few streets off is his thirty-eight-year-old daughter, a botanist. I don't personally know of another contemporary writer who has voluntarily remained, over so many decades, intimately entangled and in such direct, unbroken contact with his immediate family, his birthplace, his region, the world of his forebears, and, particularly, with the local working environment which, in Turin, the home of Fiat, is largely industrial. Of all the intellectually gifted artists of this century – and Levi's uniqueness is that he is even more the artist-chemist than the chemist-writer – he may well be the most thoroughly adapted to the totality of the life around him. Perhaps in the case of Primo Levi, a life of communal interconnectedness, along with his masterpiece *Survival in Auschwitz*,[2] constitutes his profoundly civilized and spirited response to those who did all they could to sever his every sustaining connection and tear him and his kind out of history.

In *The Periodic Table*, beginning with the simplest of sentences – a paragraph describing one of chemistry's most satisfying processes – Levi writes, 'Distilling is beautiful.' What follows is a distillation too, a reduction to essential points of the lively, wide-ranging conversation we conducted, in English, over the course of a long weekend, mostly behind the door of the quiet study off the entrance foyer to the Levis' apartment. Levi's study is a large, simply furnished room. There is an old flowered sofa and a comfortable easy chair; on the desk is a shrouded word processor; perfectly shelved behind the desk are Levi's variously coloured notebooks; on shelves all around the room are books in Italian, German and English. The most evocative object is one of the smallest, an unobtrusively hung sketch of a half-destroyed wire fence at Auschwitz. Displayed more prominently on the walls are playful constructions skilfully twisted into shape by Levi himself out of insulated copper wire that is coated with the varnish developed for that purpose in his own laboratory. There is a big wire butterfly, a wire owl, a tiny wire bug, and high on the wall behind the desk are two of the largest constructions – one, the wire figure of a bird-warrior armed with a knitting needle, and the other, as Levi explained when I couldn't make out what the figure was meant to represent, 'a man playing his nose'. 'A Jew,' I suggested. 'Yes, yes,' he said, laughing, 'a Jew, of course.'

ROTH: *In* The Periodic Table, *your book about 'the strong and bitter flavor' of your experience as a chemist, you speak of a colleague, Giulia, who explains your 'mania about work' by the fact that in your early twenties you are shy of women and don't have a girlfriend. But she was mistaken, I think. Your real mania about work derives from something deeper. Work would seem to be your obsessive subject, even in your book about your incarceration at Auschwitz.*

Arbeit Macht Frei – Work Makes Freedom – are the words inscribed by the Nazis over the Auschwitz gate. But work in Auschwitz is a horrifying parody of work, useless and senseless – labour as punishment leading to

*agonizing death. It's possible to view your entire literary labor as
dedicated to restoring to work its humane meaning, reclaiming the word
'Arbeit' from the derisory cynicism with which your Auschwitz employers
had disfigured it. Faussone says to you, 'Every job I undertake is like a
first love.' He enjoys talking about his work almost as much as he
enjoys working. Faussone is Man the Worker made truly free through his
labors.*

LEVI: I do not believe that Giulia was wrong in attributing my
frenzy for work to my shyness at that time with girls. This shyness,
or inhibition, was genuine, painful and heavy, much more important
for me than devotion to work. Work in the Milan factory I described
in *The Periodic Table*. was mock-work which I did not trust. The
catastrophe of the Italian armistice of 8 Sept. 1943 was already in
the air, and it would have been foolish to ignore it by digging oneself
into a scientifically meaningless activity.

I have never seriously tried to analyze this shyness of mine, but no
doubt Mussolini's racial laws played an important role.[3] Other Jewish
friends suffered from it, some 'Aryan' schoolmates jeered at us,
saying that circumcision was nothing but castration, and we, at
least at an unconscious level, tended to believe it, with the help of
our puritanical families. I think that *at that time* work was actually for
me a sexual compensation rather than a real passion.

However, I am fully aware that *after* the camp my work, or rather
my two kinds of work (chemistry and writing) did play, and are still
playing, an essential role in my life. I am persuaded that normal
human beings are biologically built for an activity that is aimed
toward a goal, and that idleness, or aimless work (like Auschwitz's
Arbeit) gives rise to suffering and to atrophy. In my case, and in the
case of my alter ego Faussone, work is identical with 'problem-
solving'.

At Auschwitz I quite often observed a curious phenomenon. The
need for *lavoro ben fatto* – 'work properly done' – is so strong as to
induce people to perform even slavish chores 'properly'. The Italian
bricklayer who saved my life by bringing me food on the sly for six
months hated Germans, their food, their language, their war; but
when they set him to erect walls, he built them straight and solid, not
out of obedience but out of professional dignity.

*Survival in Auschwitz concludes with a chapter entitled 'The Story of Ten
Days', in which you describe, in diary form, how you endured from 18
January to 27 January 1945, among a small remnant of sick and dying*

patients in the camp's makeshift infirmary after the Nazis had fled west-ward with some 20,000 'healthy' prisoners. What's recounted there reads to me like the story of Robinson Crusoe in hell, with you, Primo Levi, as Crusoe, wrenching what you needed to live from the chaotic residue of a ruthlessly evil island. What struck me there, as throughout the book, was how much thinking contributed to your survivial, the thinking of a prac-tical, humane, scientific mind. Yours doesn't seem to me a survival that was determined by either brute biological strength or incredible luck, but was rooted, rather in your professional character: the man of precision, the controller of experiments who seeks the principle of order, confronted with the evil inversion of everything he valued. Granted you were a numbered part in an infernal machine, but a numbered part with a systematic mind that has always to understand. *At Auschwitz you tell yourself, 'I think too much' to resist, 'I am too civilized.' But to me the civilized man who thinks too much is inseparable from the survivor. The scientist and the survivor are one.*

Exactly – you hit the bull's-eye. In those memorable ten days, I truly did feel like Robinson Crusoe, but with one important difference, Crusoe set to work for his individual survival, whereas I and my two French companions were consciously and happily willing to work at last for a just and human goal, to save the lives of our sick comrades.

As for survival, this is a question that I put to myself many times and that many have put to me. I insist there was no general rule, except entering the camp in good health and knowing German. Barring this, luck dominated. I have seen the survival of shrewd people and silly people, the brave and the cowardly, 'thinkers' and madmen. In my case, luck played an essential role on at least two occasions: in leading me to meet the Italian bricklayer, and in getting sick only once, but at the right moment.

And yet what you say, that for me thinking and observing were survival factors, is true, although in my opinion sheer luck prevailed. I remember having lived my Auschwitz year in a condition of excep-tional spiritedness: I don't know if this depended on my professional background, or an unsuspected stamina, or on a sound instinct. I never stopped recording the world and people around me, so much that I still have an unbelievably detailed image of them. I had an intense wish to understand, I was constantly pervaded by a curiosity that somebody afterwards did, in fact, deem nothing less than cynical, the curiosity of the naturalist who finds himself transplanted into an environment that is monstrous, but new, mon-strously new.

Survival in Auschwitz *was originally published in English as* If This Is a Man, *a faithful rendering of your Italian title,* Se questo è un uomo *(and the title that your first American publishers should have had the good sense to preserve). The description and analysis of your atrocious memories of the Germans' 'gigantic biological and social experiment' is governed, very precisely, by a quantitative concern for the ways in which a man can be transformed or broken down and, like a substance decomposing in a chemical reaction, lose his characteristic properties.* If This Is a Man *reads like the memoirs of a theoretician of moral biochemistry who has himself been forcibly enlisted as the specimen organism to undergo laboratory experimentation of the most sinister kind. The creature caught in the laboratory of the mad scientist is himself the very epitome of the rational scientist.*

In The Monkey's Wrench *– which might accurately have been titled 'This Is a Man' – you tell Faussone, your blue-collar Scheherazade, that 'being a chemist in the world's eyes, and feeling . . . a writer's blood in my veins', you consequently have 'two souls in my body, and that's too many'. I'd say there's one soul, capacious and seamless; I'd say that not only are the survivor and the scientist inseparable but the writer and the scientist as well.*

Rather than a question, this is a diagnosis that I accept with thanks. I lived my camp life as rationally as I could, and I wrote *If This Is a Man* struggling to explain to others, and to myself, the events I had been involved in, but with no definite literary intention. My model (or, if you prefer, my style) was that of the weekly report commonly used in factories: it must be precise, concise, and written in a language comprehensible to everybody in the industrial hierarchy. And certainly not written in scientific jargon. By the way, I am not a scientist, nor have I ever been. I did want to become one, but war and the camp prevented me. I had to limit myself to being a technician.

I agree with you on there being only 'one soul . . . and seamless', and once more I feel grateful to you. My statement that 'two souls . . . is too many' is half a joke, but half hints at serious things. I worked in a factory for almost thirty years, and I must admit that there is no incompatibility between being a chemist and being a writer: in fact, there is a mutual reinforcement. But factory life, and particularly factory managing, involves many other matters, far from chemistry: hiring and firing workers; quarreling with the boss, customers and suppliers; coping with accidents; being called to the telephone, even at night or when at a party; dealing with bureaucracy; and many more soul-destroying tasks. This whole trade is brutally incompatible with writing. Consequently I felt hugely relieved when I reached retirement age and could resign, and so renounce my soul number one.

Your sequel to If This Is a Man (The Reawakening: *also unfortunately retitled by one of your early American publishers) was called in Italian* La tregua, *the truce. It's about your journey from Auschwitz back to Italy. There is a real legendary dimension to that tortuous journey, especially to the story of your long gestation period in the Soviet Union, waiting to be repatriated. What's surprising about* La tregua, *which might understandably have been marked by a mood of mourning and inconsolable despair, is its exuberance. Your reconciliation with life takes place in a world that sometimes seemed to you like the primeval Chaos. Yet you are so tremendously engaged by everyone, so highly entertained as well as instructed, that I wondered if, despite the hunger and the cold and the fears, even despite the memories, you've ever really had a better time than during those months that you call 'a parenthesis of unlimited availability, a providential but unrepeatable gift of fate'.*

You appear to be someone whose most vital needs require, above all, rootedness – in his profession, his ancestry, his region, his language – and yet when you found yourself as alone and uprooted as a man can be, you considered that condition a gift.

A friend of mine, an excellent doctor, told me many years ago, 'Your remembrances of before and after are in black and white; those of Auschwitz and of your travel home are in Technicolor.' He was right. Family, home, factory are good things in themselves, but they deprived me of something that I still miss: adventure. Destiny decided that I should find adventure in the awful mess of a Europe swept by war.

You are in the business, so you know how these things happen. *The Truce* was written fourteen years after *If This Is a Man*. It is a more 'self-conscious' book, more methodical, more literary, the language much more profoundly elaborated. It tells the truth, but a filtered truth. Beforehand, I had recounted each adventure many times, to people at widely different cultural levels (to friends mainly and to high school boys and girls), and I had retouched it *en route* so as to arouse their most favorable reactions. When *If This Is a Man* began to achieve some success, and I began to see a future for my writing, I set out to put these adventures on paper. I aimed at having fun in writing and at amusing my prospective readers. Consequently, I gave emphasis to strange, exotic, cheerful episodes – mainly to the

Russians seen close up – and I relegated to the first and last pages the mood, as you put it, 'of mourning and inconsolable despair'.

As for 'rootedness', it is true that I have deep roots, and that I had the luck of not losing them. My family was almost completely spared by the Nazi slaughter, and today I continue to live in the very flat where I was born. The desk here where I write occupies, according to family legend, exactly the spot where I first saw light. When I found myself 'as uprooted as a man could be' certainly I suffered, but this was far more than compensated afterwards by the fascination of adventure, by human encounters, by the sweetness of 'convalescence' from the plague of Auschwitz. In its historical reality, my Russian 'truce' turned to a 'gift' only many years later, when I purified it by rethinking it and by writing about it.

If Not Now, When? *is like nothing else of yours that I've read in English. Though pointedly drawn from actual historical events, the book is cast as a straightforward, picaresque adventure tale about a small band of Jewish partisans of Russian and Polish extraction harassing the Germans behind their eastern front lines. Your other books are perhaps less 'imaginary' as to subject matter but strike me as more imaginative in technique. The motive behind* If Not Now, When? *seems more narrowly tendentious – and consequently less liberating to the writer – than the impulses that generate the autobiographical works.*

I wonder if you agree with this – if in writing about the bravery of the Jews who fought back, you felt yourself doing something you ought *to do, responsible to moral and political claims that don't necessarily intervene elsewhere, even when the subject is your own markedly Jewish fate.*

If Not Now, When? followed an unforeseen path. The motivations that drove me to write it are manifold. Here they are, in order of importance:

I had made a sort of bet with myself: after so much plain or disguised autobiography, are you, or are you not, a full-fledged writer, capable of constructing a novel, shaping characters, describing landscapes you have never seen? Try it!

I intended to amuse myself by writing a 'Western' plot set in a landscape uncommon in Italy. I intended to amuse my readers by telling them a substantially optimistic story, a story of hope, even occasionally cheerful, although projected onto a background of massacre.

I wished to assault a commonplace still prevailing in Italy: a Jew is a mild person, a scholar (religious or profane), unwarlike, humiliated, who tolerated centuries of persecution without ever fighting back. It seemed to me a duty to pay homage to those Jews who, in desperate conditions, had found the courage and the skills to resist.

I cherished the ambition to be the first (perhaps only) Italian writer to describe the Yiddish world. I intended to 'exploit' my popularity in my country in order to impose upon my readers a book centred on the Ashkenazi civilization, history, language, and frame of mind, all of which are virtually unknown in Italy, except by some sophisticated readers of Joseph Roth [the Austrian novelist who died in 1939], Bellow, Singer, Malamud, Potok and of course yourself.

Personally, I am satisfied with this book, mainly because I had good fun planning and writing it. For the first and only time in my life as a writer, I had the impression (almost a hallucination) that my characters were alive, around me, behind my back, suggesting spontaneously their feats and their dialogues. The year I spent writing was a happy one, and so, whatever the result, for me this was a liberating book.

Let's talk finally about the paint factory. In our time, many writers have worked as teachers, some as journalists, and most writers over fifty have been employed, for a while at least, as somebody or other's soldier. There is an impressive list of writers who have simultaneously practised medicine and written books, and of others who have been clergymen. T. S. Eliot was a publisher, and as everyone knows, Wallace Stevens and Franz Kafka worked for large insurance organizations. To my knowledge only two writers of importance have ever been managers of a paint factory, you in Turin, Italy, and Sherwood Anderson in Elyria, Ohio. Anderson had to flee the paint factory (and his family) to become a writer; you seem to have become the writer you are by staying and pursuing your career there. I wonder if you think of yourself as actually more fortunate – even better equipped to write – than those of us who are without a paint factory and all that's implied by that kind of connection.

As I have already said, I entered the paint industry by chance, but I never had very much to do with the general run of paints, varnishes, and lacquers. Our company, immediately after it began, specialized in the production of wire enamels, insulating coatings for copper electrical conductors. At the peak of my career, I numbered among the thirty or forty specialists in the world in this branch. The animals hanging here on the wall are made out of scrap enameled wire.

Honestly, I knew nothing of Sherwood Anderson till you spoke of him. No, it would never have occurred to me to quit family and factory for full-time writing, as he did. I'd have feared the jump into the dark, and I would have lost any right to a retirement allowance.

However, to your list of writer/paint manufacturers I must add a third name, Italo Svevo, a converted Jew of Trieste, the author of *The Confessions of Zeno*, who lived from 1861 to 1928. For a long time, Svevo was the commercial manager of a paint company in Trieste that belonged to his father-in-law, and that dissolved a few years ago. Until 1918 Trieste belonged to Austria, and this company was famous because it supplied the Austrian Navy with an excellent anti-fouling paint, preventing shellfish incrustation, for the keels of warships. After 1918, Trieste became Italian, and the paint was delivered to the Italian and British Navies. To be able to deal with the Admiralty, Svevo took lessons in English from James Joyce, at the time a teacher in Trieste. They became friends and Joyce assisted Svevo in finding a publisher for his works.

The trade name of the anti-fouling paint was Moravia. That it is the same as the *nom de plume* of the noted Italian novelist is not fortuitous[4] both the Triestine businessman and the Roman writer derived it from the family name of a mutual relative on the mother's side. Forgive me for this hardly pertinent gossip. No, no, as I've hinted already, I have no regrets. I don't believe I wasted my time in the factory. My factory *militanza* – my compulsory and honourable service there – kept me in touch with the world of real things.

Notes

1 *The Monkey's Wrench* is the American title of *La chiave a stella* (*The Wrench* in the English edition).
2 *Survival in Auschwitz* is the American title of *Se questo è un uomo* (*If This is a Man* in the English edition).
3 Mussolini's anti-Semitic Race Laws, modelled on the Nazi Nuremberg Laws, were passed in 1938.
4 Alberto Moravia (pseud. Alberto Pincherle, 1907–90) was one of the most prolific and celebrated Italian novelists of the twentieth century.

Primo Levi in London (1986)

Anthony Rudolf

The number of books telling and retelling the Nazi attempt at genocide of the Jews is enormous. There are a handful of essential books, books of which it may legitimately be said: if you wish to approach an understanding of the 'Shoah' read *these*, all the rest are footnotes. One of the essential books is Primo Levi's chronicle *If This is a Man* and its sequel *The Truce*. Three other books by Levi, recently published in English translation by Michael Joseph, are cited in the following interview: *The Periodic Table*, *If Not Now, When?*, and *Moments of Reprieve*.

Primo Levi visited England with his wife for the first time in April 1986. I interviewed him twice, the first time in public during a Festival of Italian Jewry organized by Yakar, and the second time in his hotel. What follows is my edited version of those interviews.

A. R.

Italian Jewry is more assimilated than most if not all other Diaspora communities. Why is this?

The Rome Jewish community is the oldest Diaspora community in the world. There were Jews in Rome even before the destruction of the temple by Titus. The poet Horace, who lived in the first century B C, speaks of Jews there; and today, Roman Jews say they are more Roman than the Romans. So, you see, if Italian Jews are assimilated,

From the *London Magazine*, vol. 26, issue 7, October 1986, pp. 28–37.

it is because we have lived for so long as very small minorities within a majority Christian population. Bloody persecutions in Italy were very rare. It is true the Popes expelled Jews from Rome many times, but only to the small towns surrounding the city, after which they would return, to be expelled again at a later date. Mind you, the flourishing Jewish communities in southern Italy – Sicily, Bari, Ortona, Naples and elsewhere – disappeared completely when the rules which banished Jews from Spain in 1492 were extended to the parts of Italy occupied by Spain. Many of them migrated to northern Italy.

What happened to you and to other Italian Jews under Mussolini?

As a boy and as a young man, being Jewish was not all that important for me. My family was not religious. Jews in Italy speak and spoke only Italian. There was little difference between me and my friends. A schoolmate would ask, why don't you have a Christmas tree or take part in our festivals, and I would explain that outwardly I am like you but inwardly I am slightly different – I belong not exactly to a people but to a tradition slightly different from yours. This condition ended abruptly with the racial laws promulgated by Mussolini in 1938, which were identical to Hitler's Nuremberg ones. But Italians often disregard laws. This can be a virtue if the laws are bad, a sin if the laws are good. It was forbidden to have a Christian maid but everybody had one – when the doorbell rang you told her to go upstairs. It was forbidden to possess a radio, but everybody had one. But in important ways the situation was difficult and serious: Jews in jobs or positions dependent upon the government or fascist party were expelled.

And the Occupation?

We managed to find a way of living with the new laws between 1938 and 1943. On 8 September 1943, however, two-thirds of Italy fell into the hands of Hitler. An uncle and a cousin of mine were among those murdered. Week by week the situation of the Jews grew closer to that of Jews in Poland or Germany. Jews were obliged by law to be sent to concentration camps around the country. I fled to the mountains as a partisan, with a group of non-Jewish friends. To fight back was the right thing to do, but we were ill-prepared and untrained so we were quickly captured. The soldiers who captured me were Italian Fascists. I was recognized and owned up to being a Jew, out of a silly pride. Yes, it was silly, as events demonstrated later, but I wanted to make the point that not only Christians but Jews too were fighting Fascism. I was deported to Auschwitz.

There was no rule of law in the camps. What happened to the moral law within each individual?

In the camp we had a split morality. We never forgot the eternal morality of the Ten Commandments, but in daily life it could not be like that. We were surrounded by enemies and in those circumstances the Ten Commandments did not always apply. It was not possible to kill a German, but if it had been we would have done it. To steal was not considered a crime or a sin – but not from each other, of course, that really was a sin. On the other hand, stealing from the Germans – blankets, oil, anything – that was no sin. On the contrary, it was a matter of pride to steal without being caught or punished.

So the year spent outside the law was a self-contained experience, not affecting your attitudes in later life.

That is correct. The law had not disappeared. It was sleeping. In my first book I described the ten days which elapsed between the departure of the Germans and the arrival of the Russians. Eleven of us had by good fortune been left to ourselves in the hospital. The three with some strength left organized heating and food to the best of our ability – for ourselves and for the others, who were not our friends. It was an immediate return to common morality. I know many survivors. Most of them have returned to normal morality. Only a few seek revenge. In the camp to be a *Mensch* was a factor in survival. But not every survivor was a *Mensch*.

You wrote in If This is a Man *that the Greeks were the most coherent national nucleus in the camp.*

The Greeks were remarkable survivors, having been in Auschwitz for two years. They were dockers from Salonika. Very civilized, faithful to each other, clever, and inclined to seek out Italians because of Mediterranean solidarity. Do you remember my Greek in *The Truce*? I have made many attempts to trace him. As an industrial chemist after the war I had to buy coconut oil. Coconut oil is a world monopoly of Greek Jews. In every port in the world you find one or two Jewish Greeks, dealing only in coconut oil. There are no coconut palms in Greece so I don't know how they do it. We used coconut oil to manufacture varnishes. I used to receive representatives and travellers. They were all Jews stemming from Salonika, now living in Italy. I would ask them if they could help me retrace the itinerary of Leon Levi (whom I called Mordo Nahum in my book), and all of them told me there were perhaps one thousand Levis in Salonika, and of them thirty were called Leon Levi. I wrote twice to the Jewish community there, and never received a reply. Leon Levi could be heartless, but he gave me a pair of trousers. I would like to find him.

The Yiddish epigraph to your book The Periodic Table *reads: 'Ibergekumene tsores iz gut tsu dertseylin' – 'troubles overcome are good to tell'. The writer is one who shapes, controls, often horrendous material. Does this make him, despite everything, a happy man?*

He can be happy. But telling a story is not the privilege of the writer. Everybody can do it, orally, verbally. Everybody should do it. Of course if you tell a story in writing you have some hope of reaching one thousand or ten thousand people. Verbally, perhaps only ten or twenty, but in this case you see their faces, and this is an advantage the writer does not have.

You had the obligation, the necessity to tell?

Yes, and the happiness too. Also, for me it was a therapy to write *If This is a Man*. When I returned home I was not at peace at all. I felt profoundly disturbed. Some instinct drove me to tell the story. I told it verbally to everybody, even to unknown persons. And then somebody advised me, why not, if you are telling me this story, write it. So I tried, and by writing it I felt a sense of healing. And I was healed. That was my first book. My second book, *The Truce*, was written fifteen years later. This was not a matter of healing or of convalescence. It was the plain joy of recounting a story, and I think the reader can tell.

Reading and rereading the classics of Holocaust literature, including your own books, I am reminded of the Hagadah,[1] of the obligation to tell and retell the story. But I am also struck by the figure of Coleridge's Ancient Mariner, that man possessed by a burning inner necessity to tell his tale.

Yes, indeed. When I read Coleridge's poem after the war I was upset because I recognized myself in him. Until I wrote *If This is a Man* I acted exactly like that ancient sailor, grabbing people in the street. I remember a few days after my return home I had to travel between Turin and Milan to rebuild my career as a chemist. I well remember talking freewheel in a train with people I did not know. Among them was a priest. He was astonished, upset, and he asked me, why do you address people you don't know and I told him I had no choice, how could I refrain, how could I cease this urge within me to tell the tale.

The calm and reasonable tone of voice in your books has been much remarked upon. Is this tone a literary strategy or something personal to you?

It is not a strategy at all, it is me, it is my way of life. Generally speaking, I am not prone to anger or to revenge. My tone of voice is neither a virtue nor a vice, it is something in between. I am not particularly proud of being so calm; I have been criticized for it. But I disapprove strongly of the hysterical books on the Holocaust – the tone of voice is a crime, the descriptions often pornographic.

What do you think about Elie Wiesel?[2] My own feeling is that his first book, Night, *is a masterpiece but that afterwards the pressure falls off, with a consequent loss to the writing. His importance is that he is a professional witness, a perpetual celebrant of his own Hagadah. But you choose another path. You remained professionally a chemist. Some of your books (not all of which have been translated) deal with other subjects.*

Yes, Elie Wiesel chose a different path from mine, but in my opinion his personal history justifies him. After all, I was lucky: I didn't lose my family, I was the only member to be deported. When I returned to Italy I found my home, I found my family, I found a job. Elie Wiesel and I were in the same camp, of course, but probably we did not meet. He was a boy of sixteen, I was already a graduate of twenty-four. He spoke only Yiddish and Hungarian, I spoke Italian and a little French and German. We only got to know each other through our books. I agree with you that his masterpiece is *Night*. He belonged to a religious family and he lost, along with his family, his faith – or at least endangered it. It does not surprise me that he has this endless quarrel with God in whom he keeps believing but whom he keeps on not understanding. I do not find any artifice in his keeping faith with the same theme, because it is an inexhaustible theme.

You are also a poet, though not a prolific one. Your work falls into three phases. From 1943 to 1946 you wrote sixteen poems. Then twelve poems only in the next thirty years. But since 1978 you have written more poems than in the previous sixty years of your life.[3]

The first wave can be explained with reference to Adorno's famous statement that after Auschwitz to write poetry is barbaric. I would change it to: after Auschwitz it is barbaric to write poetry except about Auschwitz. The second wave since 1978 is perhaps connected with a new flow of vitality within me. I was in good health. I was satisfied with the newly published *If Not Now, When?* and, for me, writing poetry is like writing in another language. If you succeed in writing a good poem, then you are encouraged to write another one, especially if you receive a positive response from your wife, your relatives, your friends and the critics. It is, in chemical terms, an autocatalytic phenomenon – increasing on itself.

The personal response may be more important, or more normal, with a poem than with a novel.

Yes. Many of my poems were published in the Turin newspaper, *La Stampa*. With a short story or essay, there is little impact, little feedback. But with poems I receive letters of praise and many letters saying 'your poem is OK, but if I were to write it I propose the following variations . . . '

Your novel, If Not Now, When? *deals with the adventures of a band of Jewish partisans resisting in Eastern Europe. An East European Jew you are not. You seem to have wanted to appropriate the world of active resistance.*

To organize a resistance you must have trained people, this is the first condition. Secondly, you must have money. With money you can buy weapons, and with weapons you can organize an effective resistance. These factors were not completely absent in the camps. There were instances of resistance, but they did not aim at the impossible, namely liberation. People wanted to escape to join the partisans.

The title of the novel is taken, of course, from Hillel's famous remarks in Pirke Avoth.[4] *One phrase, among many, that struck me is spoken by your character Mendel: 'Blood is not paid for with blood, blood is paid for with justice.'*

In war, blood is paid for with blood, no two ways about it. But the occasion for Mendel's remark is not a real act of war. A partisan girl is shot in a German town by a German civilian for no reason just as the war ends, and in this instance the group of Jewish partisans commit a heavy retaliation, killing ten Germans for the one girl. Although he is not convinced, Mendel takes part.

The novel ends with a sentence about a newspaper report of the bombing of Hiroshima. Therefore I take it that, while Auschwitz and Hiroshima are not to be equated, it is legitimate to associate them in some way.

In future centuries, if there are any, the twentieth century will be known as the century of Auschwitz and Hiroshima. This is why I ended my book with a two-fold message, deliberately ambiguous, telling the birth of a child – which is the continuation of mankind – and the bombing of Hiroshima, the threat to that continuation. Some critics praised this ambiguity, others objected to it, saying Levi should have announced either a better or a worse future. Maybe the ambiguity was a bad idea. But the intention of my book was optimistic, and the general tone is positive. Perhaps I now repent the deliberate ambiguity.

You should not repent. Serious readers, serious human beings, can live with ambiguity. It is a threat only to rigid minds and brittle psyches. You are an Italian, a Jew, a survivor, a family man, a writer, a (retired) chemist. Let me turn to chemistry. Was there ever a conflict between literature and chemistry?

I was always fascinated by the shadow behind the real object in the laboratory, behind my structures of pipings and coolers. I always saw something, but it did not interfere with my practical work. I never went astray, drawn by my literary commitments. I was a serious chemist. There was no conflict. For thirty years I was a matter-of-fact chemist from nine to five, and a writer in the evening. Many times in the factory, both as a working chemist and a manager, I was asked by visiting reps if I was related to Primo Levi the writer and I said yes I am. Then I would say we were here to discuss business, we have to discuss business.

Was one of the attractions of chemistry its – I risk the phrase – inherent anti-Fascism?

Yes, indeed. In my opinion it *is* inherently anti-Fascist. But unfortunately we had famous chemists who were Fascists. Mind you, Fascism in Italy was not like in Germany, an elite matter of soil and blood. It was accepted cynically. Perhaps 5 per cent of Germans were members of the party. In Italy it was 90 per cent. (Of course we had a hard core too.) My professor of chemistry, to keep teaching, was obliged to wear a black shirt, but he didn't wear a real one, it was only a triangle in front, when he turned to the left or right you could see the triangle.

Your book The Periodic Table *describes human beings in terms of the chemical table of elements which we all learned at school. Do you think the table can be used as a source of metaphor by writers who are not also chemists?*

Yes, but you have to know how to read it, from left to right, with the active elements to the left, and the inert ones to the right. Human beings, too, range from the very active to the very inert. Imagine a human being described in terms of uranium! In my view it is illegal for a practising chemist to read the table this way, but I am now retired.

In the chapter 'Vanadium' where you describe your postwar correspondence with the laboratory chief you worked under in the camp, Dr Müller, you write: 'He perceived in my book (i.e. If This is a Man) *an overcoming of Judaism, a fulfilment of the Christian precept to love one's enemies.' You make no comment. I imagine no comment was needed.*

I am not a Christian. I am something of a Jew. I am a mild man but I don't feel inclined to love my enemies. I don't know if Müller was

Catholic or Lutheran but he read my book in his complicated way and he found in it something that wasn't there. I do not choose to kill my enemies but I am unable to love them. If an enemy is an enemy he is by definition somebody you can't love.

In your book Moments of Reprieve, *which has recently been published in America and will appear here later this year, you have a chapter on Rumkowski, the head of the Lodz ghetto. Now, the role of the Jewish councils is an absorbing and fascinating one.*

It was an ambiguous one. In some cases, with courage and cunning, some members of councils did contribute to rescuing people. But the question is impossible to resolve: you believe that by delivering up one hundred people you will save the lives of a thousand. Is that justified or not? I suppose the resistance in Warsaw were right. They said we must immediately stop any form of collaboration with the Germans, which they did. They didn't succeed in saving any lives, but they were all condemned anyway. They were the first to understand this. The council in Warsaw had not been persuaded that the final aim of the Germans was to destroy all the Jews.

Earlier we discussed Mendel's remark 'blood is not paid for with blood, blood is paid for with justice'. Does this apply to the situation of states, Israel for example? Perhaps it turns on a judgement about whether the state is at war or not. I recall, too, Büchner's prescient phrase in Danton's Death: *'Where self-defence ends, murder begins.'*[5]

Israel's enemies insist they are at war with her. Now, I don't believe in the morality or the political usefulness of retaliation, but it is beyond my scope and horizon to make a judgement. I try from time to time with Israeli friends, and they say, how can you allow yourself to judge something you know only through the newspapers.

But you, like myself, must have Israeli friends in the Peace Now movement who strongly disagree with certain policies.

Yes, of course. Unlike some countries, Israel has more than one head. But we must recognize that it is dangerous to hold back. My friend, Natalia Ginzburg,[6] wrote an essay at the time of the Yom Kippur war. In it she said that she preferred the old way of being a Jew, weaponless, humiliated and so on, as opposed to the new way: proud, strong, ready to fight etc. I wrote to her that I disagreed, that it is dangerous to be hesitant, history has proved it. She is a nice person, a fine writer, but she is not a thinker.

In If Not Now, When? *Mendel says 'Everybody is somebody else's Jew, because the Poles are the Jews of the Germans and the Russians.' Can this be applied elsewhere?*

Look, in a novel you are allowed to put words in the mouth of a character which you don't necessarily agree with yourself. Whose Jews are the Americans or the Chinese? But it *was* true of the Poles. As for your idea that the Palestinians are the Jews of the Jews (and that Palestinian nationalism was 'inspired' by Zionism) this is indeed part of the truth but, as we know, it is a complicated matter.

Dante is important to you, as to all serious Italian writers. One critic wrote that If This is a Man *could be said to describe your Inferno and* The Truce *your Purgatorio,* The Periodic Table *was your Paradiso.*

I don't believe in paradise on earth and even less in heaven. I don't think *The Periodic Table* describes a paradise unless you call normal life a paradise, which could be the case . . . If you are happy with daily life, living the life of a *Mensch* freely, then yes you can describe *The Periodic Table* as my Paradiso.

And hundreds of millions of people would indeed call that state of affairs paradise. This of course leads to a political question. You said earlier you don't believe in paradise on earth but I wonder if you believe in the idea of slow progress towards a paradise, the messianic age in Judaic terms.

Yes, although I am not a believer I strive for progress. It is impossible to live without hoping to do something, without expecting, however irrationally, that tomorrow will be better than today. I was never tempted by Christianity. The Jewish, as opposed to the Christian, vision of Messiah is more compatible with the everyday realities of our imperfect world.

Would some form of democratic socialism be the secular version of Jewish messianism?

I don't see any contradiction between democratic socialism and Judaism. I am basically a socialist, though not a member of the PSI. I believe in mutuality, community and a slow progress towards the messianic age.

Notes

1 The Hagadah is the prayer book of the Jewish festival of Passover, which includes the retelling of the story of Moses and the Jews' escape from slavery in Egypt.
2 Elie Wiesel (1928–   ) was born in Transylvania and deported to Auschwitz and other camps. He moved to France and then America after the war where he has became probably the best-known of all Holocaust survivors. He has written widely on the Holocaust, starting with *La Nuit* (1958), and was awarded the Nobel Peace Prize in 1986.
3 See *Ad ora incerta* (1984), in English as *Collected Poems* (Faber, 1988).
4 The Pirke Avoth are a collection of rabbinic sayings of the second century AD.
5 Georg Büchner (1813–37) was a German dramatist who died young of typhoid. *Dantons Tod* was written in 1835 and portrays the struggle between Danton and Robespierre.
6 Natalia Ginzburg (1916–91), the daughter of a Jewish father called Levi and member of an active anti-Fascist family in Turin, was a celebrated novelist and intellectual. She was a friend of Levi despite being largely responsible for Einaudi's decision to turn down *If This is a Man* in 1946/7.

Primo Levi in Conversation (1987)

Ian Thomson

Primo Levi endured almost the worst that the twentieth century has had to offer. In February 1944 he was deported, with 650 other Jews, to Auschwitz: 'a name without significance for us at the time, but it at least implied some place on earth'. Levi became *Häftling* – prisoner – 174517, and was shortly transferred to Buna, a rubber factory connected to the extermination camp. There he worked as a chemist until 27 January 1945, when the Red Army tanks finally arrived. Only three of the partisans survived. The need to 'tell the story, to bear witness' was afterwards so urgent that, some forty years on, Levi likened himself to Coleridge's Ancient Mariner: 'And till my ghastly tale is told / This heart within me burns'.

Levi told his tale in what are now deservedly considered masterpieces: *If This is a Man* (1947) and *The Truce* (1963) – 'the written forms of oral stories which I have told countless times after my escape from Auschwitz'. But it was almost a decade before *If This is a Man* won recognition in Italy. Levi first sent the typescript to Natalia Ginzburg at Einaudi; she rejected it. But Levi looked back on the incident as fortunate: 'If I'd had an immediate success with *If This is a Man*, I would have probably given up my career as a chemist, and without chemistry, I would not have written *The Periodic Table*.'

The Periodic Table (1975), a collection of part-autobiographical tales structured around elements of Mendelev's Table, finally confirmed Levi as, in Italo Calvino's words, 'one of the most important and gifted writers of our time'. Levi devoted himself fulltime to

From the *PN Review*, vol. 14, no. 2, 1987, pp. 15–19.

writing after 1977, when he retired from his position as manager-technician of a Turin chemical factory. But his connections with the chemical and scientific world remained as strong as ever: some of the most enthusiastic reviews of *The Periodic Table* appeared in *Chemical and Engineering News*, *Scientific American* and *New Scientist*. And without chemistry, Levi would not have survived Auschwitz: working at the Buna factory meant the SS considered him an 'economically useful Jew'.

Levi draws some fairly eccentric analogies from alchemy and chemistry in *The Periodic Table*. At one point he forges a comparison between the latter and Italian Fascism.

'Too eccentric, you think?', enquired Levi. 'But chemistry deals with Matter, with the clean and the easily quantifiable. Fascism dealt with the Spirit, with the dirty and the "unquantifiable". Under Mussolini, the very air we breathed was polluted with lies and propaganda; the teaching I received at school was contaminated by Fascist ideology. And the stress which the Fascists placed on the Spirit, on the "life-force" was bogus: without materials, without Matter, you cannot win a war, something which it took Mussolini a long time to realize: "Noi non abbiamo le arme, ma abbiamo il coraggio",[1] he said. Whereas the truth of the matter was that we had neither weapons nor courage.'

After Primo Levi graduated from Turin University in 1941 with a degree in chemistry, he worked as a chemist in a variety of jobs: extracting nickel from a large mine for a Turin metal company; as a laboratory assistant for a Milanese chemical plant. Levi looked back on these days with a certain nostalgia: relatively cheerful times compared to the horrors ahead. I wondered how much he had known then about Nazi atrocities against Jews.

'Nothing', said Levi. 'Well, almost nothing. The Italian newspapers, which at that time merely reproduced Nazi propaganda, gave very vague and partial accounts of how Jews in Poland had been *übertragen* – transferred – to certain "zones". From 1942 onwards, vague and sinister reports began to filter through from the Italian soliders returning from the Russian front. And they nearly all said the same thing: how they had seen the SS force Jews to dig their own graves, or how they had been thrown into rivers, or how Jewish men and women had been made to work on railroads in filthy rags, and how they had been made to lie down on the tracks in front of trains . . .

'There were vague rumours about atrocities committed by Russians against Jews. But they were nowhere near as ruthless as the Germans . . . When the Germans said "exterminate all" they meant it:

all deported, *all* exterminated. The Nazi death-camps were operated with the ferocious military rigour which was a Prussian inheritance, the savage discipline dramatized by Büchner in *Woyzeck*.[3]

'It's what is known in Germany as *Gründlichkeit*: fundamentalism, going to the very roots of something. Not a very Italian characteristic, to be sure. It's all to do with what I call a *mancanza di misura*: the inability to know when to stop, to strike a happy medium – something, I believe, which distinguishes you British from the Germans. But *Gründlichkeit* is a very ambiguous quality. Let me illustrate: several years ago a Bavarian girl wrote to me saying how disgraceful it was that Nazi atrocities were carefully glossed over at school. She seemed an intelligent girl, so I wrote back asking certain questions about postwar Germany. The girl sent me a postcard immediately, promising to reply in full as soon possible. Twenty days later I received a twenty-three-page letter from her, the product of indefatigable research: a thesis, in other words. "I haven't had enough time", she wrote at the end of it, "to write all I wanted." Now this is thoroughly *gründlich*: a national characteristic without which there would have been no Auschwitz, just badly run camps along the Russian lines.'

Levi was captured by the Fascist militia at Val d'Aosta on 13 December 1943. He was then transferred to Fossoli, near Modena, 'where a vast detention camp, originally meant for English and American prisoners-of-war, collected all the numerous categories of people not approved of by the new-born Fascist Republic'. On his way to Fossoli, Levi managed to tear into pieces and swallow his false identification papers, and to bury in the snow a notebook containing the addresses of partisans affiliated to the resistance movement to which he belonged: 'Justice and Liberty'.[3] When the SS arrived at the detention camp, Levi and the 650 other anti-Fascists were herded into deportation trains: 'goods wagons closed from the outside, with men, women and children pressed together without pity, like cheap merchandise, for a journey towards nothingness, a journey down there towards the bottom'. Levi hastily scribbled a postcard to his mother, addressed to her flat in Turin, and threw it out of the train; miraculously it reached its destination.

Turin was where Levi was born, in 1919, and it was where he returned after Auschwitz: 'swollen, bearded and in rags', as he wrote in *The Truce*. He was slight of build, very fair, with greyish-white hair. Horn-rimmed spectacles lent him a slightly professorial air. He had a neatly trimmed grey beard. The study in his Turin flat was almost bare of decoration: just an Anglepoise lamp, swivel chair and word processor. The only concession to ornament, apart from a sketch of a

half-destroyed wire fence at Auschwitz, was three bizarre creatures
(an owl, penguin and butterfly) modelled out of what looked like wire
coat hangers, perched high above a bookcase filled with scientific
journals. Our conversation was conducted in Italian, as Primo Levi
was rather too modest to admit that he spoke excellent English, as he
certainly did.

Levi was in short sleeves, the tattoo reading '174517' visible on his
left forearm: 'a typical German talent for classification', he said.
Tattooing is forbidden by Mosaic law: Leviticus 19.28. All the
more reason, then, for the Nazis to brand the Jews. And yet Levi
admitted to feeling a certain 'nostalgia' (his word) for Auschwitz, and
even looked back on his twenty months there as an 'adventure' (also
his word).

'An adventure', he said, 'in the sense that my experience of the
Lager was a sort of rite of passage, and the writing about it an... interior liberation. It was only after my humanity had been utterly
obliterated, only after I had written *If This is a Man*, that I felt a
true "man", a man in the sense of the title of that book... But more a
university than an adventure: I would almost say that I "graduated"
from the *Lager*... Auschwitz taught me how to get the measure of
somebody in a split second...

'It *is* a little paradoxical to say that I feel a certain nostalgia for
Auschwitz, of course. But the *Lager* coincided with my youth, and it
is for my youth, and for the few people with whom I made friends at
Auschwitz, that I feel nostalgia. Not that I have any desire to go back
to the camp as a *Häftling*. Obviously not. But the memory plays
strange tricks on one: it is somehow only the good moments from
the past that remain, the happy times at Auschwitz rather than the
horrific... I can remember with extreme clarity the time I taught an
Italian folksong to a Hungarian friend, and how he taught me a
Hungarian folksong in return. And I can still recite it, word for
word. It's because that particular moment was so *exceptional*: for
just a few minutes we were ecstatically happy.'

Was Auschwitz, I wondered, all the worse for Western Jews, who
had not already suffered in the ghettos?

'Of course the shock of entering Auschwitz for the first time was
less... severe for the Russians and Poles. For us Italians it was quite
literally a case of having been plucked straight out of our beds at
home to a death-camp. One of the first things I noticed at Auschwitz
was a strong discrimination at the linguistic level: almost all the Poles,
Hungarians and Czechs spoke a little German, whereas the Italians
did not. And you were at a considerable disadvantage if you spoke no
German. I myself knew a little, but I soon realized that I had to know

an awful lot more if I was to have any chance of surviving. I even took private lessons in German, for which I paid with my bread rations. I didn't know, of course, that what I was learning was an extremely vulgar sort of German, full of savage imprecations, insults, blasphemies and imperatives: a *Lagerjargon*, as I now call it. Elsewhere it has been termed a *Lingua Tertii Imperii*, a language of the Third Reich: L.T.I. It was certainly not the German of Goethe or Heine![4]

'But this didn't matter at the time. Because he who spoke no German was by definition a barbarian. You were not a proper *Mensch*, a human being... The Poles were in fact the most numerous at Auschwitz, and the majority of them had already escaped the gas chambers by 1944, when I arrived at Auschwitz, had already learnt the rules of the game. They were incredibly canny people. And robust: robust in both mind and body. Partly this was because Polish anti-Semitism, which has always been very pronounced, gave them a certain... identity, made them tough as nails even before they had been deported to Auschwitz. This was never the case with the Italian Jews: most of us felt more Italian than Jewish, so it was hard to come to terms with being persecuted for one's religion. The Italians have never been particularly anti-Semitic anyway. When the Ministry of the Interior introduced the Racial Laws of 1938, most Italians thought them absurd. But there were exceptions, of course: my uncle, for instance, was betrayed as a Jew to the Nazis by a fellow Italian. I myself was arrested by Italian Fascists, not by Nazis. But one's Judaism counted for very little before the last war: my parents had a maid here in this very flat who never realized that she was in the pay of a Jewish family. She was perhaps puzzled by the absence of the Madonna above their bed, but she otherwise presumably took us for a Catholic family.'

Levi never practised the Jewish faith. In fact he professed no religion at all. He admired the importance given to literacy and education by Orthodox Jews, but rarely went to synagogue. In 1982 he publicly condemned the Israeli invasion of Southern Lebanon. I asked him whether he had any desire to settle in Israel after Auschwitz, like the Jewish partisans in his novel *If Not Now, When?* (1982)? He appeared slightly annoyed, and gave a categorical 'no':

'My home has always been in this flat where I was born. There was no need to look for a new home. Only 500 or so Italians settled in Israel after the last war. Hardly any, in other words.'

Levi's most hostile critics have in fact been Jews, particularly American Jews. Levi told me how 'an absolutely crippling' article had recently appeared in the US Jewish magazine, *Commentary*, where a critic accused Levi of having a 'tin ear' for religion, that he was 'an assimilated Jew'.[5] Levi continued: 'I have given some twenty-five interviews in America, and journalists always ask the same old question: "What does it mean to be a Jew in Italy?" Not an awful lot, I reply. The only language I speak at all well is Italian. My best friends are Italian, few are Jewish. There are only 40,000 Jews in Italy today. Not many, really.'

Levi never used his writing to take revenge on his would-be murderers. 'It has not been written', he wrote in the Introduction to *If This is a Man*, 'to formulate new accusations; it should be able, rather, to furnish documentation for a quiet study of certain aspects of the human mind.' I asked him about his remarkably forgiving attitude to Dr Müller, former SS officer at Auschwitz, whom Levi tried to track down in the 1960s.

'Dr Müller, you see, was in charge of the Buna rubber factory, so I was not surprisingly fascinated by him. And by Germany too: for five years I attended the Goethe Institute here in Turin to learn the language which I had learnt so imperfectly at Auschwitz. But this curiosity of mine . . . I'd say that it even kept me alive in the *Lager* – a place where it was extremely easy to die spiritually. I am interested in men like Dr Müller as human beings, as ordinary *Menschen* – which is of course what they are: ordinary men, made of flesh and blood like yourself.'

Levi's honesty in *If This is a Man* is sometimes quite shocking: there was no point, he says halfway through, in befriending the weak and helpless at Auschwitz, because 'they have no distinguished acquaintances in the camp, they do not gain any extra rations, they do not work in profitable Kommandos and they have no secret method of organizing. And in any case, one knows that they are only here on a visit, that in a few weeks nothing will remain of them but a handful of ashes in some nearby field and a crossed-out register.'

'Horribly cynical, you think?' he asked. 'Well, yes: but cynical by your standards, by those of "society at large". Auschwitz was hardly society at large: a microcosmic form of all the evils in the world, to be sure. But it was not "normal" by anyone's standards. I myself occasionally fraternized with the "drowned" at Auschwitz. But not often. Usually one just let them drift by on their way to death. There was no point in lending a helping hand to those beyond help. The Good Samaritan ethic had no place in the *Lager*. Nor does it have much of a place in contemporary Manhattan. But, no: very little of one's moral world could survive behind the barbed-wire fence of Auschwitz; one had to be a martyr not to renounce or . . . compromise it in any way.'

Shocking, too, is the episode where Levi and a French companion ignore the cries for water coming from the patients in the room next to the Auschwitz scarlet-fever ward, where they had taken refuge after the departure of the Germans.

'Also cynical?' wondered Levi. 'I'm not so sure. You see, it went something like this: we were boiling some soup – a wonderful moment for us because it was the first time we had invented anything for ourselves: how to make the soup, how to construct a stove, how to fetch water – and there was enough soup for eight people. But not for 300. And so we shut the door on the patients next door. What else could we do? If we'd shared the soup among 300 people, we would all have perished: as it was, we succeeded in saving a few lives...

'I repeat: one simply cannot apply ordinary moral standards to the *Lager*...When it comes to something like the Auschwitz "Special Squad", the group of prisoners to whom the SS bequeathed the task of managing the crematorium – transporting prisoners to the gas chambers, removing the corpses, extracting any gold teeth, raking out and getting rid of ashes – it is best to suspend moral judgement altogether. The "Special Squad" performed their duties under duress. It was not something for which they volunteered. Anyway, once physical exhaustion and hunger took their toll, they too were sent to the gas chambers.'

The suspension of moral judgement was the theme of Levi's last book, *I sommersi e i salvati* (1986), a collection of essays on the Nazi concentration camp system. *The Drowned and the Saved* is not simply another addition to what is known in Italy as 'la letteratura concentrazionaria'[6] – quite a lot of which Levi considered 'bad literature'. (And not only the literature: he disliked *Sophie's Choice* with Meryl Streep.)[7] It is a warning, rather, to those who deliver facile judgements of condemnation: only those who have survived the death-camps can judge. And even they are not properly fit to forgive or condemn, for [in Levi's words] 'the story has been almost exclusively written by those who have not fathomed the depths of human degradation. Those who did have not come back to tell the tale. Or their powers of observation have been paralysed by suffering and incomprehension.'

But how much of Auschwitz was quite simply beyond comprehension? I mentioned the episode in *If This is a Man* where a fellow *Häftling* shows Levi the words carved at the bottom of his wooden bowl: 'Ne pas chercher à comprendre.'

'*I tried*', said Levi. 'I tried to understand. Not that it was easy: one's powers of observation were severely limited. None of us even knew where Auschwitz was geographically situated...And it was only months after my escape that I had any idea as to how the *Lager* functioned, how extensive the connections were between slave labour and German industry. Buna was the product of a contract between the SS and a chemical company, as I later discovered: "We'll help build a death-camp, you supply us with labour for our chemical factory." Buna still exists: it's the largest rubber factory in Poland.

'I've been back to Buna twice, in an effort to "understand" things a little better. Strangely enough, I felt little emotion returning there. Today, Auschwitz has the cold impersonality of a monument: not as I remembered it at all. Birkenau, on the other hand, is much more impressive, surrounded by an enormous wasteland of broken-up barrack huts, with just dust and mud all around. Not a blade of grass . . . An odd thing happened to me a year ago, when I was invited by a German pharmaceutical company to visit their plant at Leverkusen. On a strictly professional basis, you understand. "Where did you learn your German?" the management asked. "It's rather rare for an Italian to speak our language." And I said: "My name is Levi. I'm a Jew. And I learnt your language at Auschwitz." Naturally, this caused a little embarrassment . . . But most interesting was the fact that the Leverküsen factory almost exactly resembled the Buna factory at Auschwitz. How little things seem to have changed, I thought.'

Auschwitz remained Levi's great theme; he even admitted that without his experience of the *Lager* – concentration camp – he would never have been a writer: 'Or I would have been a failed writer.' Furthermore, Levi believed the *Lager* was a paradoxical 'godsend', since it gave him his subject 'on a plate': 'But then one could say the same about my great hero Conrad: would he have been a great writer without the sea?'

When *The Truce* first appeared in English, Philip Toynbee gave voice to what Primo Levi regards as a common misconception: 'Whenever this subject [Auschwitz] is put before us again we find that our vocabulary, and even our normal grammatical structures, have begun to fail us . . .' (*The Observer*, January 1965). And George Steiner, too: 'the world of Auschwitz lies outside speech as it lies outside reason.'

'It is true that in one or two chapters of *If This is a Man* I remarked how our language lacks words to express the . . . demolition of man,' admitted Levi. 'And it is true that the witnesses at the Eichmann trial said "You cannot understand! Who was not *there* cannot imagine." But both *If This is a Man* and *The Truce* are written in a language that everyone can understand, in everyday speech. I believe it is the task of every writer to describe what he sees in plain language, and I hope I have achieved this. Not that it is impossible to write about the death-camps in a highly experimental prose with all manner of linguistic pyrotechnics (although I think, *a priori*, this would be somehow indecent): André Schwartz-Bart described the Holocaust in *The Last of the Just* using a rather unconventional prose; Paul Celan, too, wrote about Auschwitz in some extremely obscure, not to say hermetic poems[8] ...

'But I'd say that our everyday language is more inadequate when it comes to describing scientific phenomena: the planets, the galaxy, the world which is invisible to the naked eye. Ours is a language which fails to go beyond what our senses are capable of comprehending. It falls short of the mark. If I say you're tall, I mean you're over six foot, not half a millimetre. And yet half a millimetre is an extremely "tall" measure in the world of atomic science. And the expression "light year" is almost meaningless when describing not only the universe but also the galaxy... Italo Calvino was the only Italian writer to have bridged the gap between our earth-bound language and a science-fiction language adequate to describe the stars...'[9]

Levi, who considered Jules Verne 'a great writer', himself wrote science fiction of a sort: the short stories based on chemistry, astrophysics and molecular biology contained in his *Storie Naturali* (1966) and *Vizio di forma* (1971) make up a satire on futuristic technology, or rather on man's indiscriminate and potentially destructive misuse of such technology. Whimsical *novelle*, similar to the sort of thing Calvino wrote in *Cosmicomics* and *Time and the Hunter*, Levi believed the stories to have 'suffered the fate of all science fiction', which is 'to undergo a rapid ageing process'. He was not particularly proud of them.

'But one cannot *not* communicate,' said Levi, his Piedmontese accent becoming markedly more pronounced as he returned to the subject of Auschwitz and language. 'Even silence itself means something. If a husband speaks and his wife remains silent, her silence is positively loaded with all sorts of meaning. But silence is a poor way of communicating... I can't stand writers like Samuel Beckett: it is the duty of every human being to communicate. The same goes for the likes of Ezra Pound: writing in Chinese simply showed a disrespect for the reader. Writing should be a public service: so-called "incommunicability" (such an *ugly* word!) went out with the 1960s...'

Levi drew the line at Kafka, however – even though he acknowledged the influence he had on Beckett: 'With *The Trial*,' he said, 'Kafka predicted the time when it was a crime simply to be a Jew. I was in fact commissioned by Einaudi to translate the book into

Italian. Looking back, I wish I hadn't: the undertaking disturbed me badly. I went into a deep, deep depression... And so I haven't read any Kafka since, he involves me too much...'

Levi remarked that 'precision and concision are the two hallmarks of the chemist', and that these have their counterparts in writing itself:

'When one writes a "weekly report" in a chemical factory, it must be brief and succinct, and it has to be read by everyone, from the men on the shopfloor right up to the directors. Both Goethe and Leopardi said that a book is valid only once it has been accepted by an intellectual élite, followed by a vast public. If it fails on one or the other count, there's something wrong with it. Now, without wishing to sound pompous, I'd like to believe that both *If This is a Man* and *The Truce* conform to this criterion, since they were read by at least a million people in Italy, from high-powered intellectuals to secondary-school children. Naturally the books were read in different ways by different people, but I hope they had something to say for everyone. And I truly believe this is to do with my factory days... *La chiave a stella*, you know, was read by people who would never otherwise touch a book – labourers and factory hands...'

La chiave a stella (1978) just published in Britain as *The Wrench* (Michael Joseph), concerns the picaresque adventures of one Tino Faussone, a construction worker on bridges, cranes and oil rigs. It has sold well in Italy, although Primo Levi worried about its reception in the English-speaking world: the novel, partly written in Piedmontese dialect, must be something of a translator's nightmare. At any rate, one hopes the almost Rabelaisian humour of *La chiave a stella* will not be lost in translation, since the novel admirably conforms to Levi's belief that 'human beings suffer unjustly; man is great notwithstanding; he is saved by understanding, and by laughter'.

Notes

1 'We may not have the weapons, but we have the courage.'
2 Büchner's unfinished play *Woyzeck* has a down-trodden army private as its hero.
3 'Giustizia e Libertà' was a small, intellectual and liberal anti-Fascist movement which was particularly active around Turin.
4 The phrase 'Lingua Tertii Imperii' or LTI was first used by the German linguist Victor Klemperer, *LTI* (Berlin: Aufbau-verlag, 1949); *The Language of the Third Reich: LTI, lingua tertii imperii* (London: Athlone Press, 2000).

5   The article in question was F. Eberstadt, 'Reading Primo Levi', *Commentary*, October 1985. Levi's reply, 'Italian Jews', was published in *Commentary*, February 1986.
6   'Concentration-camp literature.'
7   *Sophie's Choice* (directed by Alan Pakula, 1982, from the novel by William Styron) is about a Catholic woman who looks back on her time in a concentration camp from postwar America.
8   André Schwartz-Bart (1928–) wrote the prize-winning novel *Le Dernier des justes* (*The Last of the Just*, Paris: Editions du Seuil, 1959; English translation, London: Secker & Warburg, 1961) about a line of just men for each generation of the Jews, the last of whom is engulfed in the Holocaust; Paul Celan (pseud. Paul Anschel) (1920–70) was a poet, born in Romania, deported to the camps, who wrote his extraordinary and difficult poetry in German whilst living in France. He committed suicide in 1970. Levi wrote more than once of his difficulty in accepting Celan's obscurity and darkness, but also of his (partial) admiration for him.
9   Italo Calvino (1923–85), the most important Italian writer of his generation, was close to Levi, working with him through the Einaudi publishing house and sharing an interest in the literature–science frontier, as noted here and in the following paragraph.

Part II
Life

The Little Theatre of Memory
(1982)

(A popular Piedmontese song)

This song is called 'O dì-mi ün po', bel giuvu, da lu capè burdà...';
let me translate the beginning: 'Oh young boy, oh beautiful young
boy with the rimmed hat / what news of my loved one?' I have to say
that in my memory of it, the tune is not quite the same as the one
we've just heard, it's slightly different. It's a popular song, here sung
by the La Grangia choir with words compiled by Costantino Nigra.[1]
My memory of it doesn't come from any high-flown, erudite source,
though. My mother used to sing it to my sister and me when we were
children and her version was different. She'd heard it from her
mother and she from her own mother in turn. My mother still sings
it, she sang it to us and we sang it to our children; so these are very old
memories, from a time when mechanical or mechanized music,
music transmitted over the airwaves, hadn't broken into homes,
when a song really could be the soul of the place, of a generation,
and the thread linking one generation to the next.

('Che farò' from Offenbach's *Orphée aux enfers*)

From a radio programme, broadcast on 10, 17, 24 November and 1 December 1982,
called *Il Paginone (Il teatrino della memoria)*, in which guests choose and comment on
favourite pieces of music. Primo Levi's selections are given in brackets, followed by
his commentary.

If the first memory was linked to my mother, this piece from Offenbach is linked to my father, who died almost forty years ago now... in fact, forty years exactly. My father had taken his studies seriously and he took his career as an engineer seriously too, but culturally he was self-taught, an autodidact. He had built himself a parallel culture over the years; he was a disordered reader of everything the culture industry of the time had on offer. He had also studied music, and this too he took quite seriously, although not on his own this time. He wasn't self-taught in music, he had studied piano formally, and then his work as an engineer led him to spend long periods in musical countries, Austria and Hungary, so in a sense he was steeped in music. All his free moments – which in fact were very few because he was an active man – were filled with music. While he was shaving, he would sing this or some other tune, not always Offenbach of course, many others too. Music filled his empty spaces, you could say. He played too, he would play the piano in the evening; just like we listen to or watch television nowadays, he would go off into his private drawing room, let's call it, where he had his piano and he would play, not that well but with enthusiasm, with joy. And these arias, these themes from Offenbach were part of his repertoire. He was like Offenbach himself, as a person; he was in love with life, he took pleasure in living, had fun, tended to avoid trouble and danger. Unfortunately, this was also true of his final years, to the last he tried not to see what was happening all around him and us. Another piece in his repertoire was the concerto coming up next, Concerto No.5 for piano and orchestra, the *Emperor Concerto*.

(Beethoven's *Emperor Concerto*)

And now for something very different, although still from those same years. Here we move from the private to the public sphere, you might say.

(The Fascist hymn, 'Fischia il sasso')

'The rock whistles, it rings out the name of the boy of Portoria...'[2] Well, these aren't very happy memories! Like everyone else, with very few exceptions, perhaps fewer than 1 per cent, I was in the 'Balilla' too.[3] I had to dress up in that nasty uniform, which I disliked not for any ideological reasons, because I had certainly not yet reached that stage, but because it was so uncomfortable, because it was tight all over, because it was so ugly, it had a sort of... it was called a 'pasta thread', I think, a lace white cord that went across your chest and had to stay in place. The shoes weren't our normal shoes, and the stockings had to be pulled right up, and then there was the fez with the little tassel that always flapped on your nose, and the meetings, all extra, over and above our already dull school day, out of school hours; and then there was the marching too. Not that it was all so difficult; it just seemed to go against the grain, to be unnatural, marching in step; as long as it was just a bit of exercise, you could accept that it was reasonably enjoyable, but gallivanting all over the city like that, pretending to be soldiers, was not something I enjoyed at all, it bored me, even made me cry. I was certainly not destined to become a good soldier, and indeed I never did become one.

('La mia canzone al vento')

I don't remember the name of the film that launched this song, but it was certainly a famous one. I remember hearing it very early on, probably in '37–38.[4] I had finished school and enrolled at the university and the Racial Laws were already hanging in the air.[5] For some reason that I'll try to explain, this song became the theme tune of those years . . . yes, I think I know why; there was a parody of the song going around with the line 'Wind, oh wind, take him away with you'. I can't be sure that the parody is why it has stuck so firmly in my mind, but it certainly brings back for me a time that was strangely not as unpleasant as it could have been, indeed, that I look back on willingly and with affection: my time at the university. I was already marked, catalogued, along with some fellow students, as an 'Italian citizen of the Jewish race'. There were no grave dangers yet, or rather we hadn't realized they were there, but we had been marked out. All the same, the environment we were living in, that of a Fascist university, was not hostile, or at least we felt no hostility around us, I didn't see it. My Aryan friends, as they were called, would sing this song in the lab, and the lab of the Chemistry Faculty was truly a sort of ideal community, a place for socialization, for forging friendships which have lasted until today. We worked hard for five hours a day in the laboratory, from two until seven, and in the midst of the ammonia and hydrochloride fumes the words of the song hung in the air: 'Vento, Vento . . .'

(Another extract from 'La mia canzone al vento', followed by a German military march that continues while Levi talks.)

The official title of this march or Nazi hymn – it was the anthem of the National Socialist Party – was 'Die Fahne Hoch', 'The Flag on

High', or 'Fly the Flag High'. But the German people knew it as 'Horst Wessel [Lied]' or the 'Horst Wessel Song'. The story is a strange one: Horst Wessel was a pimp, a man whose profession was to be kept by his women, who enrolled in the National Socialist Party at its founding and was killed in a street scuffle with the Reds, I don't know exactly by whom or when. He became a martyr, the very symbol of National Socialist suffering in Germany. In any case, it's not an ugly song, it's a beautiful marching tune, very beautiful, and this is instructive. For us, at least for me and my generation, this music makes our hair stand on end, but not for those who heard it at the time. This gap, this split between the musical or artistic level of a piece, the effects it can produce and its power to carry its listener away, the manner in which one or other group of listeners uses and interprets it, seems to me very instructive indeed.

(The march continues and merges into a more light-hearted tune.)

This polka is known all over the world as 'Rosamunda', although I see that on the record-sleeve its official title is different, 'The Beer Barrel Polka'. I don't understand what these words mean here, perhaps it's been poorly translated. For me it is important for at least two reasons: when I was deported to Auschwitz [in February 1944], our arrival in that fearful and unknown world was accompanied by marches, by music played by the camp orchestra. We didn't know then that the orchestra played every morning and every evening as the work squads left and returned. And so it was completely incomprehensible to us how this tragic scenario – a bloody sunset, the freezing cold of an unknown country, the screeched orders in languages we could not even guess at, in Polish or in barracks German – could be accompanied by tunes like 'Rosamunda' that we all knew so well. In Italy, we often used to sing it, it was a dance-hall song, we danced to it; here it produced an effect of what is called estrangement or alienation, of not understanding anymore, of not understanding why the entrance, the threshold of Hell went together with a dance. Then, as the days passed, we realized that it was all much less mysterious than it seemed; not every morning, but often, this 'Rosamunda' was alternated with other songs, some military some not, as the sinister ceremony was played out of squads of ghosts limping out to work in the morning and limping back more heavily still in the evening. But the story does not finish here. In 1964, that is, several years after the publication of my book *If This is a Man*, RAI suggested producing a radio version of it.[6] For me, the experiment, my first experiment with radio, was at once exciting, very enjoyable and sinister, because the recordings were made in the open air to reproduce better the acoustics of the camp setting and to avoid studio sound, and at night, to minimize daytime noise, in Brozolo, a small town in the hills outside Turin. Through my choosing, the accompanying motif, the dominant motif or leitmotif, was this same 'Rosamunda', not in the version you've just heard, but played, I think, by the band of Bolzano, *zackig* [in broken rhythm] – I can't think of the Italian word – in a hard, military, even warlike manner. The effect was very powerful. It's a pleasure to recall, by the way, that the sound technician that day was Pierino Boeri, who is also the technician on the other side of the glass today.

('1812' Overture by Tchaikovsky)

You have just heard the last part of the 1812 Overture by Tchaikovsky. Perhaps you noticed a quotation from the 'Marseillaise'. If I'm not mistaken, Tchaikovsky wrote it in memory of the Russian victory against Napoleon, in 1812: the 'Marseillaise' represents the routed French army. It has stuck in my mind for other reasons, however. After our liberation from Auschwitz, when I was wandering around Poland looking for a bed and a roof, I ended up one day, in the middle of the snow and polar cold at Crakow railway station. The loudspeakers throughout the city were playing this very overture. For me and others, a musical sequence like this, as happens sometimes with smells as well, was etched into our memory and is now like a sort of trigger. Even though it's an heroic piece of music, for me it evokes a period . . . a week of begging, when I was drifting from one mess hall to the next, from one hospice to the next, searching for a warm spot and a bowl of soup.

(A Russian popular song, 'Kalinka Kala', plays in the background as Levi talks.)

This is 'Kalinka Kala', a popular Russian song. It's very beautiful, isn't it? And like the Tchaikovsky it brings back strong memories. In the summer of 1945 I was in the heart of a forest in a half-ruined Red Army barracks, together with a thousand other Italians waiting to be repatriated, although it was proving so difficult to achieve that we hardly ever spoke about it.[7] The Russians told us 'take it easy, your time will come, we haven't been sent home either; we've been fighting in the war, and you haven't, you're Italians, Fascists, so why are you complaining? We're Russians, we beat the Germans and we're still here, we haven't seen our homes yet.' Now, during that long and not unhappy wait – it was summer, it was hot, there was no work to do and enough food to eat – the only unhappiness we felt was the uncertainty. We would hear on the horizon, far far away in the distance, the notes of this and other Russian songs, coming from squads of Soviet soldiers who had been demobbed in the crudest, simplest fashion: their commanders had said to them: 'You've finished fighting the war, now go home'; and home they went, on foot. Now anyone with any idea of the size, the distance along the parallels within the Soviet Union will realize what sort of a repatriation this was. There were squads, on foot, some even barefoot, carrying their boots over their shoulders so as not to wear them out. Others had found the most incredible means of transport, clambering up onto lorries, onto Berlin buses towed along like trains. We saw one motor unit towing two or three Berlin city buses, still with the Berlin signs on them, carrying wildly happy passengers who greeted us with gusto as they travelled east, homewards, with still another thousand, two thousand, three thousand kilometres to go, perhaps into the heart of Siberia; and they sang 'Kalinka Kala' as they passed by in front of us, this and other songs, waving to us all, survivors and the rest.

(The Russian song again)

('Amado mio', from the film *Gilda*)

The song you've just heard is 'Amado mio' from the film *Gilda*, with Rita Hayworth (1946). In fact I remember next to nothing about the film, and very little about Rita Hayworth either, but 'Amado mio' has entered into my blood. For me it coincides with a very abrupt change in my life, my return from the camps, from my long wanderings around war-torn Europe, my homecoming to a shattered, unhinged Italy, reduced to tatters, still hungry, ration-restricted, but with a vital fervour that amazed me. 'Amado mio' is the linking thread, for no good reason, of course: for all of us a tune, a song, takes on an aspect that need not have anything to do with the intention of its composer or its singer. This song coincides with that abrupt re-entry. I was twenty-eight years old, keen to work, very curious, I had four lost years to make up, years worse than lost, four years of imprisonment, suffering and wandering. This song was on every corner and every street, everyone was whistling it, singing it, some in tune, some not. It coincided for me with my engagement and then marriage, and the honeymoon too . . . yes . . . that's why . . . at the heart of my memory of 'Amado mio' are those days and hours of my rather rash marriage, with no means to support us, at just the wrong time to be thinking of raising a family. But we made it all the same, as was the way at that time: it was a matter of turning your back on the past and beginning afresh. My engagement lasted two years, as was the custom in those days, while I waited to find a steady job and a salary. It was a long-distance affair [*he laughs*]; my future wife lived in Turin and I was living in Avigliana and working there in a half-destroyed Montecatini factory where I learned to make paints. In the factory, in the lab too, they sang 'Amado mio', because in labs you sing, that's always the way: whenever we can, we sing as we work. I used to go to Turin as often as possible, sometimes in the goods trains they had then, some-times by bicycle; it was twenty kilometres, which didn't seem too far, it felt natural to go to Turin by bike and go home again at dawn pedalling all the way uphill. I had already worked once as a chemist for about a year, the first serious job of my career, after graduating and before being deported, but to me and to everyone there it felt temporary, not for us. Now I had a job that I felt was for me, and for the others there too, a job to be taken seriously. They gave me technical problems and I would try to solve them as best I could. Sometimes I didn't manage it, I couldn't solve them at all, but nevertheless I gave myself body and soul to the task, as I did to another task, because – it amazes me now to think that I could do three so very different things all at once, but when you're young you can do many things at once – at the same time as I was the fiancé and the chemist, I was also writing a book. My memories of 'Amado mio' are also interwoven with hours spent in front of blank pages, and on occasion a typewriter, writing *If This is a Man* without any clear idea of what I wanted to do with it. I felt as if I were dictating, leaving a trace of my memories for future generations. The core of the book was coming into being.

('La femno luerdo')

This is 'La femno luerdo' sung by the Waldensian Choir of Torre Pellice and it is part of the extremely rich and beautiful repertoire of Waldensian music.[8] I used to sing it, badly as always, along with others from the same repertoire, to my new-born daughter in 1948. I had first learned it a few years before then, although it felt as if an abyss separated me from that time, in Milan in 1942–3, after gradu-ating and before being deported, when I spent a lot of time with a group of Turinese friends, who were not Waldensians themselves but were friends of Waldensians, and had inherited from them this corpus of songs that I loved dearly and still do. They were our songs; we would meet between air raids, between evacuations, and it felt natural to sing songs. Today it doesn't seem so natural to sing at the edge of the abyss, for that is what we were doing, not just us but the whole of Europe.[9] But still, it was a refuge, an escape, and it was also, you could say, a sort of compensation or revenge, expressing ourselves in this way.

(Extracts from *An American in Paris*)

Those were extracts from Gershwin's show *An American in Paris*; and if the other pieces we've heard represent some sort of conditioned reflexes, evoking in me particular times and places or circumstances, Gershwin is much more diffuse; he brings back an entire epoch, the epoch when we were going back to work, struggling to build ourselves a present and a future, and I can't even tell you precisely why I like Gershwin. My musical education is minimal, in fact non-existent, I just follow my nose, go by instinct. This music satisfies me, makes me happy, fulfils me, gives me peace and so I could put it down as the music of the 1950s, a time when the future wasn't so precarious any more, when I was at peace with my own conscience, having written a book and when I had no thoughts of writing any more.

(More Gershwin)

(A march, in crescendo)

This is the marching song ('Colonel Bogey') from the famous film, *The Bridge on the River Kwai* (1957) with Alec Guinness. The opening scene of the film is epic. You see a group of English prisoners-of-war in the hands of the Japanese, almost all wounded and maimed, dragging themselves from the battlefield to a collection camp, a concentration camp. They're limping along but one of them begins to whistle this tune and soon all of them rediscover their strength, their courage, even the maimed, and this band of derelicts begins to look like a squadron of soldiers again, defeated but not bowed, defeated but not crushed, who show their steadiness, their *sturdiness*[10] in this way: whistling a march that isn't a military march, it's a comic march, to show the Japanese victors that the battle isn't over.

(An extract from the *New World Symphony*)

That was part of the *New World Symphony*, Symphony no. 9 by Dvořák, conducted by Bruno Walter. As I said before, my musical education is non-existent; and yet this piece has been my lifelong companion, I don't know why; it could be something to do with the title, because if for Dvořák the New World was America, for us the New World is something genuinely new, that doesn't yet exist, is to come in the future; and it may be that, indirectly, the title influenced me and led me to choose this from a thousand others as a piece that I hold dear. Or perhaps it's some quality of the music, because there's no reason for music to be enjoyed only by cognoscenti, that would be terrible. I can't even talk here, as for other extracts we've heard, of conditioned reflexes or the like. We are lucky not to be living in a time when life takes sudden, brutal and unexpected turns, marked in some way by a symbol, a tune. The texture of my life today – at least since we have been living in peacetime – is fortunately less tragic, less dramatic, there are no such sudden twists. It's more relaxed, and perhaps that's why this work, in its own way a music of happiness, at least as I see it, is a good companion for the road.

(Extract from *Pictures at an Exhibition* by Mussorgsky)

That was an extract taken from Mussorgsky's *Pictures at an Exhibition*. My link to it is not immediate, in fact it's extremely indirect and again related to RAI. Four years ago here, we worked together for two months to record and edit the radio version of my second book, *The Truce*, and we used parts of *Pictures at an Exhibition* for the breaks between acts.[11] And I'd like to talk a little about this experience that for me has been an extra, on top of my experience as a writer. I can say without fear of exaggeration or flattery that the television and especially the radio versions of my work have been of great importance to me, because they filled a void that I had never filled before, the space of live representation, of the theatre, that I have scarcely touched on, of cinema that I have never encountered.[12] The experience of reaching an audience directly, not through the medium of the pages of a book, but through the eye and the ear, was extremely stimulating for me. I can honestly say that the hours and days spent here, working in a team, were amongst the happiest of my postwar career, of my career as a writer – and that was new for me too, working as a team, with others, not the lone writer at his desk, producing together, as in a big game, something that began life so alone, the solitary birth of the writer's craft.

Notes

1   Costantino Nigra (1828–1907) was a diplomat, scholar and poet who also collected Piedmonese popular songs (*Canzoni popolari del Piemonte*, 1858).

2   The Fascist song 'Fischia il sasso' tells the story of the boy Giovanni Battista Perasso, nicknamed 'il Balilla' (see note 3), who threw a stone at an Austrian official in 1746 and thereby started the uprising that liberated Genoa from the Austrians.

3   The Opera Nazionale Balilla was a Fascist youth organization, named after the Genoese boy referred to in note 2, for children of elementary school age.

4   The film, directed by G. Brignone in 1938, was also called *La mia canzone al vento*. The song was written by the team Bixio and Cherubini and sung by Giuseppe Lugo. In the popular parody of the song mentioned by Levi below, the wind was begged to carry 'him' (i.e. Mussolini) away.

5   See note 3, p. 22 above.

6   A radio adaptation of *If This is a Man*, directed by Giorgio Bandini, was broadcast by Italian state TV and radio network RAI's Radiotre, beginning on 24 April 1964.

7   Levi's difficult return journey is recounted in his 1963 book *The Truce*.

8   The Waldensians are a small Protestant community concentrated in Northern Italy, which began as an heretical sect in twelfth-century France. There is a certain affinity between the Waldensians and the Jewish community in Turin as both are small, non-Catholic groups.

9   This period is described in some of the chapters of Levi's 1975 book, *The Periodic Table*. Levi and his friends jokingly, and indeed prophetically, labelled their group 'The Orchestra on the *Titanic*'.

10   Levi uses the English word here.

11   The radio adaptation of *The Truce*, from Levi's own script, directed by Edmo Fenoglio, was broadcast on RAI Radiouno, beginning on 25 April 1978.

12   Apart from the adaptation mentioned earlier in the interview, several of Levi's science-fiction stories were either born as dramas or adapted for radio, television and theatre. *If This is a Man* was staged as a play in Turin in 1966, and published in book form in that year. Francesco Rosi's film adaptation of *The Truce* appeared in 1997, although Rosi had spoken to Levi about the project and had received his approval ten years earlier in 1987.

Turin (1980)

Giovanni Tesio

How did Turin seem to you after the hell of the camps and the odyssey of your return home?

First of all I'd like to say something that I have never put in my books. Before my actual deportation to Auschwitz, I was first deported from Aosta to Fossoli.[1] When the train reached Chivasso [near Turin], it was sunset, in February. The sky was gloomy but from the station I managed to make out the Mole.[2] That was the wrenching moment for me, a farewell that broke my heart. I came back to Turin after the war early one morning. The train had left us at Porta Nuova. I was with a friend. From the train my friend saw a building on corso Sommeiller where some of his relatives lived. It was intact. He said to me, whatever happens, we'd find a place to stay the night there. The city had been seriously damaged by bombing and then by the insurrection, but I remember being struck by the extraordinary vitality I found in my friends. They were all victors. I was not.

To which parts of the city do you feel closest?

The places that appear here and there in my books. The area around my home, my school, liceo Massimo D'Azeglio, the University, parts around the Valentino and via Po, where, among other things, my father's mother lived. Also the old via Roma, although I only have

From 'Intervista con lo scrittore', *Nuovasocietà*, 167, 22 March 1980.

vague memories of it. One of my legendary grandparents had a fabric shop on old via Roma, and at carnival time we could go out onto the balcony of the mezzanine to watch the procession go by. I'd also include in my list the route of the journey I took daily into work over twenty years of commuting from Turin to Settimo and back. It was during one of those that I happened to see a shop sign with the name that I took as a pseudonym [Damiano Malabaila] when I wrote *Storie naturali* ['Natural Histories'].

Has being from Turin influenced your formation as a writer?

I'm not sure how to answer that question, just as I never know how to answer when I'm asked if I would have been a writer even if I hadn't been in the camps. My being Turinese certainly didn't influence my decision to be a writer. But it did influence my way of writing. Today, I can say this: the city is changing very rapidly. I think it would be worthwhile to help preserve the image of what it was before it disappears completely.

In creating Tino Faussone [the central character in The Wrench] *did you have in mind a tradition of the Turinese worker who is especially industrious and alert? I'm thinking, specifically, of Gobetti's visit to Fiat and perhaps of the factory occupations.*[3]

Absolutely not. Faussone is blind to syndicalism. He's on his own. He has other values. That is his character.

Notes

1   In December 1943, Levi was arrested as a partisan by the Fascist militia in the mountains in Val d'Aosta and spent two months in prison in Aosta before being sent as a Jew to the holding and prison camp at Fossoli in central Italy, from where he was deported to Auschwitz in February 1944.
2   The large structure of the Mole Antonelliana is one of the dominant buildings in the Turin skyline. It was begun as a new synagogue in 1863 and completed in 1897 as a civic monument.
3   Piero Gobetti (1901–26) was a brilliant young Turinese liberal intellectual of the period after the First World War. He visited the Fiat factory and wrote about it in 1923. The factory occupations referred to are those of the years 1919–20, when Antonio Gramsci took the lead in creating Soviet-style factory councils in Turin.

Mountaineering (1984)

Alberto Papuzzi

The climb up to the Torre del Gran San Pietro by the south-west ridge has one alternative route still cited in the *Guida del Gran Paradiso* by Andreis, Chabod and Santi: it is the route followed by Alessandro Delmastro with his sister Gabriella on 11 July 1938. Delmastro is the Sandro to whom Primo Levi dedicated the chapter on iron in his book, *The Periodic Table.*

'He was a boy of medium height, thin but muscular, who never wore an overcoat even on the coldest days.... He had large, callused hands, a bony, rugged profile, a face baked by the sun...' Sandro, Levi relates, seemed to be made of iron, and together they lived some of their happiest adventures climbing in the mountains.

At that time, Primo Levi was a chemistry student who would spend his Saturdays and Sundays clambering up on the peaks of the Gran Paradiso, getting soaked in the snow with his skis in winter, in spring and autumn taking on the rocks of the Picchi del Pagliaio, the Denti di Cumiana, Roca Patanüa, the Plô and the Sbarüa, all Turinese training grounds, some of which later became classic climbs, others now forgotten, but all at that time only attempted by a few brave or eccentric types, in knickerbockers and old boots.

That was then... Today Primo Levi is famous throughout the world as a writer, and within the four white walls of a room at the publishing house Einaudi (which publishes all his work) he looks at us with a gentle smile, not without a glimmer of irony, no doubt because he is rather surprised to be interviewed, for the first time, on

From 'L'alpinismo? E' la libertà di sbagliare', *Rivista della montagna*, 61, March 1984.

his experiences and exploits as a mountaineer. They are not in the least unusual except as part of his own history, the history of a man.

'I began going up into the mountains when I was thirteen or fourteen', Levi explains. 'In my family there was a tradition of seeing the mountains as a source of strength, something like the world Natalia Ginzburg describes in *Lessico famigliare*.[1] Not mountaineering as such, no climbing rockfaces... You just went up into the mountains, for some contact with nature...'

Straight away, on his first time out, he ran into a 'negrigura' as another Levi, Natalia Ginzburg's father, might have said.

'I was at Bardonecchia and we had decided to set off on a trip, myself and a friend who was fourteen like me and a boy of sixteen who declared himself in charge. The idea was to reach Valle Stretta by way of the Catena dei Magi. Only we left in the afternoon, with no food and no backpacks. It was already almost dark when we reached the summit. Before us lay a treacherous descent, and far away the faint light of a shelter, I can't remember its name. We started shouting, and a team of mountaineers came up to get us. They shouted back down: "son solo dei gagno brodos..." [it's just a bunch of crying kids...] and then they tied us up like salamis and winched us down in the night, by lamplight.'

Levi's first climbs were at the age of about eighteen or nineteen, born of a desire for adventure but also for independence, to give it a go, to do it himself: 'I wanted to go into the mountains properly, but not with a guide.' A desire that chimed with the times, those of the Fascist regime and for Levi, as a Jew, those of the Racial Laws.

What did it mean, then, to go climbing and to go climbing alone, for that young Jew from Turin at the end of the 1930s?

'It was an absurd form of rebellion,' Levi replies. 'You, Fascist, you discriminate against me, you isolate me, you say I am worthless, inferior, *unterer*: well, I'll show you that it's not like that. I promoted myself straight away to the rank of lead climber, even though I had no experience and had taken no lessons. Indeed, being rash was part of the game. The first time I went alone was at Herbetet, by the east ridge. We weren't even in touch with CAI, our group, since it was a Fascist organization and we were anti-institutional.[2] The mountain represented freedom, a small window of freedom. Perhaps, too, in some obscure way, we felt a need to prepare ourselves for future events.'

This need to prepare themselves, Levi explains, was crystal clear in Sandro Delmastro. His was a rough, working-class mountain. His family were anti-Fascist, with a real ideological hinterland, whereas Levi was a nice middle-class boy. Delmastro had no doubts as to how things would all end: 'in tears', as Levi puts it. By contrast, the bourgeois Jews refused to look the future in the face, and remained prisoners of a lazy, fearful pacifism.

Delmastro becomes the retrospective projection of all the tensions and ideals that Levi felt, at the time only as a confusion but today with a lucidity verging on abstraction. And Delmastro's mountaineering, seen in hindsight, as if in a silent, slow-motion sequence, is a living metaphor of that projection, with his rejection of comfort, of fashion and consumption, 'already of another time, even then' . . .

'We never went to Sestriere, because they had lifts, and lifts were worse than the devil! No padded coats, no new shoes, the CAI guidebook only to do the opposite of what it advised. Our equipment was minimal: my sisters gave me a hammer, a pair of springhooks and three nails. That was all the equipment I had. The rule, though, was to stretch our physical and technical strength to its limit every time. I remember one Easter, when Daladier had said "Never" to Mussolini.[3] This meant war, but we had our mind on other things. I went off with Delmastro and Alberto Salmoni, walking one night from Bard to Champorcher: the day after, on skis, and with thirty kilos each to carry, we wanted to cross over to the so-called Champorcher Window, then descend, climb back up Valeille, reach Piantonetto, and head for Gran Paradiso . . . It was Delmastro's idea: the more tired he got the happier he was. I gave up as early as Cogne.'

This was the mountaineering philosophy of Lammer: a euphoric disdain for danger, the mountain as an introduction to suffering. 'Yes, I had read Lammer too,' Levi says, '*Fountain of Youth*, and also Whymper and Mummery.[4] From those pages had filtered through to us the idea of always measuring oneself against extremes, that the essential thing was always to give your all.'

And yet, this Romantic ideology went hand in hand with a positivist attitude. Levi's and Delmastro's motivation in taking on the mountains was double-edged. Lammerian Romanticism was mixed in with a secular, scientific interest in the mountain as a setting for the study of the world at its origins. Both Levi and Delmastro shared a passion for chemistry.

'I was convinced that in chemistry I could find the answers to the questions that philosophy left unresolved. With chemistry, I was searching for a vision of the world more than for a profession. Now, my passion for the mountains was intimately connected with my passion for chemistry, in that I could find in the mountains the very elements of the "periodic table", caught between the rocks, frozen still within the ice, and I could use them to unveil the very nature of the mountain, its structure, the reasons for the shape of a single gully, the history of the architecture of a sérac...Once, at the Pagliaio peaks, Sandro hooked onto a crystalline hold but it came away in his hands. He showed me the rock without getting ruffled and said: "001 cleavage", using the terminology of stereographic projection which identifies crystals according to the planes along which they split.[5] So the mountain was also exploration for us, a substitute for the journeys to discover the world and ourselves that were not available to any of us, the journeys narrated in our books of that time, by Melville, Conrad, Kipling, London. Our homespun equivalent of those journeys was the Herbetet.'

Primo Levi continued to take trips into the mountains after the war, after his return from Auschwitz, after writing a book, *If This is a Man*, which is the highest literary testimony we have of the human condition in the face of the violence of mass extermination. He went walking or skiing, but he only went climbing again once, on his own, when he tried some third-grade passes on one side of the Testa Grigia above Gressoney: 'I wanted to prove to myself that I could still do it, even if I was over forty by then...' But his relation to the mountains is firmly rooted in that distant, youthful season; in the intellect of a citizen who looked to the mountains, went up into the mountains for clues and answers he could not find in his life, or rather in the stifling atmosphere of his Turinese life, which seemed devoid of both past and no future. He had no contact with the generations of intellectuals that had preceded his, with names like Monti, Mila or Foa,[6] as though a stark divide had been scythed out between them, and the future was cloaked in the impenetrable conformism of mass rallies and the myth of race.

'I had even tried at the time to write a mountaineering story,' Levi now remembers, with a touch of amusement. 'I never finished it, it's never been published and it never will be, because all in all it really is very bad. I filled it with all the epic grandeur of the mountains and the metaphysics of mountaineering. The mountain was the key to everything. I wanted to describe the sensation of climbing up with the horizon filled by the line of the mountain: you climb, you see nothing but this line, nothing else at all, and then all of a sudden, you cross over it and you are on the other side; within seconds you see a new world, you're in a new world. There it is: what I had tried to capture was that moment of passage. Then I read the story to my friends. It was no good.'

After 8 September 1943,[7] Primo Levi went up into the mountains once again, to find *his* moment of passage, and this time it was not metaphysics at stake but the side he had chosen and the battle yet to come. As is well known, he was captured almost straightaway and sent to a concentration camp. His friend and climbing companion Sandro Delmastro was the first casualty of the Piedmont military command of the Partito d'Azione in Cuneo.[8]

One of the best adventures Levi had shared with Sandro had been in a bivouac at altitude, in the depths of winter, with their feet in their sleeping bags and 'their shoes so frozen solid that they rang like bells'. 'And how do we get down?' Levi had asked his friend, when the shadows of dusk had begun to gather just as they were finishing their ascent.

'We'll think about getting down when the time comes,' Delmastro had replied, adding, 'the worst that can happen is that we'll get a taste of bear's meat.'

They did indeed get a 'taste of bear's meat' that night, forced to bivouac in the freezing cold. Remembering the episode in one of the best and most moving passages of *The Periodic Table*, Levi writes: 'Now that many years have gone by, I regret that I ate so little of it, since of all that has been good to me in life, I can think of nothing even remotely resembling that taste, the taste of being strong and free, free even to make mistakes, of being master of your own destiny.'

Many, many things have been written and said on the significance of mountains and mountain-climbing, but none has been more simple and true than Levi's words: the freedom to make mistakes, to be master of your own destiny.

Notes

1   *Lessico famigliare* (Turin: Einaudi, 1963; English translation *Family Sayings*, Manchester: Carcanet, 1984) is Natalia Ginzburg's autobiographical memoir of her childhood as a member of an active anti-Fascist family in Turin. One of her father's eccentric sayings was the word *negrigura* (from 'negro', so meaning something like 'negro stuff') that Levi mentions below, used for anything or anyone that was gauche or foolish.

2   The CAI is the Club Alpino Italiano.

3   Edouard Daladier was French Minister of Defence in 1940 when Germany invaded France and Italy entered the war.

4   Eugen Guido Lammer (1863–1945), Edward Whymper (1840–1911) and Alfred Frederick Mummery (1956–95), the first Austrian and the latter two English, were three of the most famous mountain climbers of the late nineteenth century.

5   '001 cleavage' refers to parameters known as Miller indices which define intercepts between crystal surfaces and the three crystallographic axes. It explains why the rock broke off in thin slabs.

6   Three members of a famed generation of Turinese liberal and left-wing anti-Fascist intellectuals: Augusto Monti (1881–1966), who taught several of this generation at the famous liceo Massimo d'Azeglio; the musicologist Massimo Mila (1910–88); and the trade unionist and writer, Vittorio Foa (1910–).

7   8 September 1943 was the date of the Armistice between Italy and the Allies, following the fall of Mussolini weeks earlier. After that date, the Germans occupied central and Northern Italy and many Italians including Levi chose to join the Resistance at that point.

8   The Partito d'Azione grew out of the anti-Fascist movement, Giustizia e Libertà (Justice and Freedom), and was a small liberal party involved in the Resistance which included a large number of the Turinese liberal intelligentsia.

Chemistry (1983)

Enrico Boeri

Dr Levi, this must surely be a rather unusual interview for you: you are in the Technologie chimiche *armchair not only as a writer of successful and prize-winning books, but also and above all for your long professional career as a manager of a chemical industrial company. What can you tell us about your experiences in this field?*

I began my professional career as a chemist immediately following my return from imprisonment in Auschwitz, in 1946.

Even during the war (after graduating in 1941), despite the Racial Laws, I had found semi-clandestine work as a chemist in Milan in a pharmaceuticals company, and then also in the laboratory of a mine where I searched desperately to enrich an extremely poor nickel-based material. These are the experiences that I described, with just a few minor changes in the details, in my book, *The Periodic Table*. The 'lieutenant' of the story was a dear friend of mine who later became President of the Piedmont League of Chemists, the late Dr Mariotti.

In the same book I described my attempts to become a manufacturer of chemical products which I and a friend managed to extract with parlous economic return: stannochloride and vanillin. In 1948, I finally heard that a paint company near Turin, SIVA, was looking for a young chemist. I was taken on first as a lab chemist, and later I became their technical director and finally managing director. I stayed with SIVA for twenty-nine years, until 1977. In 1975 I had

From '4 chiacchiere con . . .', *Technologie chimiche*, December 1983.

already warned them of my impending retirement: it felt wrong, because of the bond of friendship that linked me then and now to the owner, to up and leave without any notice. So I gave them two years to find a replacement and they did. I've written about this time as well. My journey to Russia in *The Wrench*, for example, is auto-biographical, even if the reason for the journey wasn't the one I invented for the book (paint for the inside of tins of anchovies). I changed a lot of details because, here again, it seemed wrong to use facts from the company's own cases.

Since then, as a chemist, I've retired; but your magazine has brought me a tinge of nostalgia for a profession that saved my life at Auschwitz and then gave me a living for many years.

A profession which, as you have written, is 'a special case, a more strenuous version of the business of living' and which has provided you with the material for some of your most beautiful and successful works. What else do you remember of that time?

The episode of the 'sick tower' [in *The Wrench*] is also entirely autobiographical. The acetic acid extractor column belongs to SIVA, you can see it from the Turin–Milan motorway, just after the toll-booth on the right. I set the tower up, I taught the workers to operate it and I spent several nights there watching over it.

Originally it had been designed by a Milanese engineer, on the basis of the design of another working tower. But it's possible that that tower had a filling of metal rings. Whether that's true or not, in the SIVA tower the lower rings, made of ceramic, were too weak to take the load and they shattered. When it filled with fumes, the tower overpressurized.

Creating that pitiful image of 'a sick man trying to throw up, but all to no avail', an image described by your character, the rigger Faussone, that any chemist who has worked in distillation plants will doubtless know well.

Precisely. And to sort the problem out we really did have to rig up distillation plates one by one, as described in the book, replacing the filling, so that the tower could start working again.

But Faussone is a real person, and he really is a rigger. I'd never have believed it when I invented that slightly silly surname (Faussone can mean 'false', like the typical Piedmontese character, or a large sickle, 'faussôn' in Piedmontese dialect). And yet when I was invited to speak at a conference at San Mauro Torinese, an elegant young man introduced himself to me at the end in his pure Piedmontese accent, saying: 'May I? I am Faussone.' And when I began treating him like a practical joker, he took out his identity card. Then he asked: 'Guess what job I do,' and I said 'you must be a rigger'. 'Propi parèi' – quite right.

The book had just come out and I suggested that we could appear together, the Author and his Character, on a television programme that had invited me as a guest. But he preferred not to, saying, and I quote, 'that it wasn't a serious business, whereas his work, that was serious'.

Is there any other episode from your life in the chemical industry that you could tell our readers about?

Here is a story. All chemists know about the dangers of static electricity, so that, say, even systems for drawing grain out of ship holds have to be earthed.

Well, at SIVA, we had a system for pouring out a synthetic resin and we had indeed earthed it. But I didn't know that the same danger exists for liquids: a hydrocarbon running along an iron tube can spark and catch fire because of the static, and the purer the liquid the easier it catches fire.

In the factory we had large tanks full of solvents: toluol, xylol, hexane etc. What happened was down to my professional error. For convenience, to speed up the frequent small extractions we made from a 10,000 litre tank of toluol, I had had a tube built over the container wall. For years nothing happened: workers would go with their empty buckets and fill them up. But once, in the middle of one summer, the toluol caught fire as it was coming out of the tube. The worker fled in terror, but luckily the section chief was nearby and he leaped over the wall to shut off the main tap.

Only then did I learn that there's an extensive literature on precautions and risks of such fires and also that there is an antidote, a metallic soap that makes the hydrocarbon fairly conductive, which we hurriedly added into our solvents as soon as they entered the factory from that day on. As an aside, this is also the reason why the same danger doesn't exist at petrol pumps, thanks to tetraethyl lead and other additives which make the petrol conduct.

Episodes like this make me think that chemistry should be taught in schools and universities by people who have had some sort of work experience.

On the question of additives, though, it would be fascinating to look into why there are so many formulations with additives whose origins have been quite forgotten, but which are kept because 'we've always done it like that'. For example, in my area of work, the paint industry, there are additives which I'm almost convinced are quite useless, but who would ever dare to remove them, knowing that the negative effects could come to light only years later?

Looking back over your life, which career is closest to you, that of the chemist or the writer?

They are two difficult professions. In industry, your productivity can vary by a maximum of about 20 per cent. With writing, there are days spent sitting in front of a blank page without achieving anything. On other days, maybe in your car, sitting in traffic, wonderful ideas come to you: productivity is completely unpredictable.

On the other hand, another point of comparison is that in working as a chemist you only very rarely sign your work as your own, or if you do, it's as part of a team. Managing a factory means depending on a wide array of external factors: colleagues, clients, the boss, suppliers etc. The work of a writer, by contrast, is terrifyingly autonomous; if you do it badly you have no one to blame but yourself, although of course, by the same token, the pleasure you get from doing it well is all the greater.

What are you working on at present? Will chemistry inspire any more books?

At present I am only working on a translation from German.[1] Just to keep up to scratch.

The logical follow-up to my book of stories *The Periodic Table* would of course be something about the world of organic chemistry. I even had a title ready for it: *The Double Bind*, a suggestive title. But I didn't take it any further, because much of the material for it was channelled off into *The Wrench*. For the moment I have nothing else in mind.

A classic question: can you name one virtue and one defect?

My virtue is that I stick to reality: a debt that Primo Levi the writer owes to Primo Levi the chemist. My defect is lack of courage, fear for myself and for others.

A lack of courage that certainly hasn't been apparent in your life up till now, either in your choice to become a partisan or in Auschwitz...

What I mean to say is that I am afraid of people, not of things, that my response to raised voices is to take it and then leave, to avoid all argument. And that is not right.

Note

1   Levi was translating Kafka's *The Trial*. See the interview 'An Assault Called Franz Kafka', below, pp. 155–60.

The Sinister Power of Science
(1987)

- *Given that we all share a belief in the necessity of peace, do you think it is possible to make a specific and constructive contribution to the progress of peace movements, in our country and throughout the world?*
- *What scientific or cultural contribution do you think can be made from within your specific field of expertise?*
- *What lines of research and study are you already pursuing to further the aims of peace, or what work of this kind might in your opinion be pursued to such positive ends?*

I think I shall need to split my answer into two parts: peace movements have and will continue to have quite different destinies in our country and in the wider world. Here, pacifism has by now been accepted by almost the entire population. We no longer have any disputes over borders, we have no aggressive neighbours, we have immense internal problems to tackle, but no problem with hostile minorities or with minorities who are victims of the hostility of the majority. No Italian wants war, even if we have, regrettably, joined NATO.[1] Military service is seen as a sad and unnecessary evil; our armed forces are by no means war-mongering, even if they are faced with terrifying instruments of death.

And yet we harbour arsenals of horrifying power, in the hope (perhaps unfounded) that we will never have to use them. We live

Reply to a questionnaire set by Fiora Vincenti, Roberto Guiducci and Mario Miccinesi, *Uomini e libri*, n.112, January–February 1987.

in a world that is preparing for war and that, at least for now, far away from Europe, is waging war every day.

It is thus indispensable that, as Roberto Guiducci suggests,[2] a culture of peace should be imposed and should prevail, but there is not much to be done in a country such as ours. Nevertheless, what little can be done should be done. Italy must set an example: our Constitution sanctions a culture of peace and rejects war as a solution to international problems and this fact should be underlined in all our schools and at every level.

Furthermore, the military all over the world, and especially in the quarrelsome Third World, would be impotent were it not for the continual flow of war-directed innovations and refinements issuing from scientists and universities in the service of political power. Throughout the world (but why not start at home) physicists, chemists and biologists should become fully aware of their sinister power. I am sure that science can be hypothetically neutral, but I am equally sure that there is another science which is far from it: it is this other science that must be stopped. A precise moral consciousness should be encouraged, above all in university science faculties: 'I accept this task, but I do not accept that other one. I will work on a new antibiotic, not on a nerve gas. I will dedicate myself to fusion energy, not to the neutron bomb.' In each instance, the young scientist must demand to know the aim and use of the work he is undertaking and he must have the courage to say no when the aim appals him, to refuse to work for forces of destruction. Believers could be bound by a sort of Hippocratic oath, non-believers by an oath on their honour. Every science faculty should provide a course, or at least some lessons, aimed at awakening this moral consciousness that we all have within us.

Of course, there will always be cynics and perjurers, but there will also always be some conscientious objectors, and who is to say that an example from Italy might not find imitators elsewhere, perhaps even in those countries where science is most alive but also most indebted to power.

Notes

1   Italy was one of the original signatories to the NATO treaty in 1949, although relations between Italy's left and the alliance have consistently been tense.
2   Roberto Guiducci, a sociologist and writer and one of Levi's interviewers here, had founded the 'Club per le scienze della pace' (Club for Peace Sciences).

Poetry and Computers (1985)

Is poetry compatible with computers?

Poetry certainly existed before writing and when one sees the close links that bond the poetry of our own civilization to that of other civilizations, remote in space and time (Aztec, Indian, Ancient Egyptian), one is struck with a feeling of reverence. Poetry has come down through dozens of centuries and has garbed itself in as many different techniques of writing, from stone or clay carvings to parchment and papyrus, from Chinese brushes to wax tables, goose-quill, ink or ballpoint pens, all the way to the typewriter. It doesn't seem to depend a great deal on the workings of the hand: poetic imagery is born in some part of our brains and it makes its way towards 'recording' via various obstacles none of which has much weight or importance. So, if we are just talking about the computer as a tool for writing, about various kinds of word processing, I don't see any incompatibility. On the contrary, the ease with which you can erase, correct, add and replace makes the passage from mind to paper smoother. Perhaps it even makes it too smooth; the lack of obstacles (writing on screen is much less tiring that any other method) can lead to verbosity, it can damage the pithiness of the writing, although the converse is also true: cancellations are instantaneous and leave no scars behind on the paper, draining off excess couldn't be easier or less painful.

Primo Levi's written response to 'Una domanda a Primo Levi', *Genius*, 4 January 1985.

Computers, as we know, can do much more than this. They have already proved to be precious instruments for so-called quantitative linguistics, saving scholars from the massive task of counting the frequency with which a certain writer or a certain timespan uses particular words. In this way, there is some hope, whether well founded or not, of finding a reliable method of attribution of disputed texts. Hovering patiently in the wings, waiting to pounce on their prey, are the psychoanalysts, keen to find out how many times Dante, Leopardi and Montale each use the word 'water', and how this might relate in each case to their birth or childhood traumas. Computers are ideal for this grey business, although this is no way to create poetry; on the contrary, it is a way of performing an autopsy, a post mortem on poetry itself.

During the creative process, computers can indicate rhymes, repetitions, alliterations, anaphora, deliberate or otherwise; they can instantly change one term for another, a synonym or an antonym, or correct its spelling; they can work as a warehouse of ideas, as a bridge between ideas, and no doubt perform many other miracles which I, as a novice – I've only recently bought my first electronic word-processing machine – cannot even begin to imagine. And yet, in my view, all these services are marginal, they will never make a poet out of an amateur, nor could they enhance the qualities of a real poet. Nor indeed, I should add, will they do the poet any great harm. As I see it, the slight rash that breaks out in many quarters whenever poetry and computers are mentioned in the same breath is in large part caused by the ugly sound of the word 'computer' in Italian. Computer – *computisteria* [book-keeping] – bills – VAT – bank statements – debits – credits – banker's drafts: the chain of association is immediate, both consciously and unconsciously. Nor is the more specific term (word processor, in English or Italian) any more enticing, but these are merely problems of nomenclature. Clearly the question in hand is double-edged, it is a trick question in a way: the computer has been with us for forty years, and in that time it has made more rapid and astonishing leaps forward than any other invention. It has taken over from the human mind in calculation, planning, storing memory, organizing information. Today it can play chess and bridge, even if not very elegantly. It can simulate the flight of an plane or a car journey. It drives spaceships in search of 'truths that earn envy'[1] and missiles in search of trouble on our planet. These days, there isn't a single bar without its groups of adolescents messing about with video games. *Ergo* it can do anything; *ergo* it could also write verse.

I'm well aware how inadvisable it is to make negative predictions: illustrious scientists declared with confidence that experimentation with flying machines 'heavier than air' was absurd, only ten years before the first aeroplane; others, only a generation back, predicted that an electronic computer, even if it were possible to construct one, would be as tall as a cathedral, use the energy of Niagara Falls and cost more than an aircraft-carrier. Nevertheless, although I am almost entirely ignorant of computer theory and of poetic theory, and without wishing to speak nonsense, I am prepared to state that there will never exist a computer that secretes of its own accord original and genuine poetry. Bad poetry, certainly: it would be easy (even today if only someone would turn their mind to such a futile enterprise) to compose hendecasyllables[2] with the right stresses and with some meaning or even hexameters in line with the rules of Latin prosody. They might even cause wonder and/or laughter with their parodic resemblance to human poetry, but they could not create poetry in the strong sense of the word, ever.

Why? I have no rigorous proof, but I suspect that computers can only ever perform logical operations, or (if they've been programmed to do so) arbitrary ('randomized' to use the jargon) choices. Poetry is greater than logic and chance. It can contain both of them, but its scope is broader. It has something else: deep or subtle associations that are necessarily also new, echoes of archetypes, ill-definable correspondences between signifier and signified, between music, vision and word, premeditated or instinctive references to illustrious predecessors, so that, using a lovely title of Paul Eluard's, we can truly speak of an 'uninterrupted poetry'[3] moving down the centuries and across geographical borders, an essentially unitary poetic heritage that accompanies humanity in its history and in its anguish.

The computer is a superb instrument for clear, distinct tasks, and poetry is neither of these: it is fluid, oblique, continuous, suffused with auras and shadows. It is not chance that, although poetry has been with us for millennia, no one has yet come up with a definition, with a universally accepted 'specification' for poetry. In short, poetry is indeed compatible with computers, but it has little to gain and little to fear from them.

Postscript: I have made my oracular pronouncement and now I am more and more worried that I spoke out of jealousy and fear. Out of Luddism: with the same spirit as the working-class men who followed Ned Ludd in the early nineteenth century, destroying the new textile machines for fear they might lose their jobs. Well, let me say it loud and clear: if I am present at the birth of a poetry machine with a reasonable output in terms of quantity and quality which does not cost the Earth, I will buy one myself, although not without consulting a lawyer (man or machine) to check whether I could then sign the machine's work as my own and whether it or I would be entitled to the royalties.

Notes

1 Levi is quoting from Dante's *Paradiso*, canto 10, l.138 ('invidiosi veri').
2 The hendecasyllable, an eleven-syllable line of poetry, is the standard 'heroic' verse in Italian, equivalent to the iambic pentameter in English or the French 'Alexandrine'.
3 Paul Eluard, *Poésie ininterrompue* (Paris: Gallimard, 1946).

Me, Old? (1982)

Sixty years old: retirement age. And along with retirement, empty time to fill. Uselessness as a synonym of old age. Is there any truth in all this?

Me, old? Absolutely yes: my date of birth, my long-sightedness, my grey hair, my adult children all go to show it. Last week, for the first time ever, someone gave up their seat for me on the tram, and it left me feeling very strange.

In myself, as a rule, I don't feel old. I haven't lost my curiosity for the world around me, nor my interest in other people, nor my competitive instinct nor my taste for playing games and solving problems.

I still like interacting with nature, I take joy in encountering it through all five senses, studying it, describing it in speech or writing.

All my organs, my limbs, my memory and my imagination are still in working order, and yet I am all too aware of the grave ring of that terrible word I have just written down twice: 'still'.

From *Stampa sera*, 15 September 1982.

Part III
Books

The Truce (1963)

Pier Maria Paoletti

He is wearing a petrol-green summer suit and thin short-sleeved shirt. Out of the sleeves stretch two thin bright, nervous arms, an outdated watch on the wrist, and just above, in slightly faded blue on the tanned skin, a number: 174517. To look at and to listen to, *Häftling* [prisoner] Primo Levi is captured perfectly in this picture: a delicate small man, much more frail than you might imagine from the familiar photo on the back of his books, with his army sweater and his partisan look. That number, which destroyed his youth and marked out his destiny as a writer. His harsh, punctilious moral rigour softened by his modest and mild aspect and by his calm, polite conversation, full of deeds, people and things, straight, free from violent resentment and always filtered through his sense of irony, his amused taste for penning grotesque, outrageous caricatures of the monstrous, clean-cut, supremely confident 'Aryans', the zoological samples (as he puts it) encountered in his horrendous past life.

Of course we talk about *The Truce*, his odyssey home from the concentration camps, the real 'discovery' of this year's Premio Strega,[1] following on from the translations and the plaudits from abroad lavished on his first book, *If This is a Man*, written in a rush, to 'make others share', and published after his miraculous return from Auschwitz, in times when literary events made less of a splash. 'I wasn't upset, you know, about the Premio Strega,' he says, speaking in his heady voice, with rather a strong Piedmontese accent. 'Of

From 'Sono un chimico, scrittore per caso', *Il Giorno*, 7 August 1963.

course, I'd have been happy to win it, but I was happy not to win also; after all, I had said what I had to say. In any case, it was my first taste of the literary world in flesh and blood.' He pauses, one of those pauses to take time to smile to himself, absorbed in his thoughts, and his eyelids flutter in a nervous tic, before he completes the sentence: 'but I realized I was a foreign body'.

'Why did I write this book?', he continues, asking and answering the question himself. 'The history of *The Truce* is the history of all the tales I've told for years, without changing a line, to my friends, the few close friends I have here in Turin, you know, old school friends, when we meet in cafés, at home, walking along the Po. And they used to say to me, why don't you publish them?' Another pause: 'Until the day came when the equation in my life between free time, my own desire and the pressure from others reached the perfect balance.' Foreign body, equation. His precise, scientific language. Again: '*The Truce* cost me two hundred hours of work, one chapter a month. If you think that I could only write in the evenings, after work at the company, and that I need on average an hour or so to change skin each time, you could say that the book was born in three or four hundred days, in other words in one year.'

The obligatory question. What are you now, after the sudden success of *The Truce* and the reprint of *If This is a Man*: a writer who also works as a chemist or a chemist who has written a couple of books? 'Oh, a chemist, no doubt about it, let's not get confused. And those two books of mine, I wrote them both by chance.'

Primo Levi, as is well known, is the technical manager of a resin and paint factory at Settimo Torinese [outside Turin]: there, as a manager, he receives customers, shows them round the factory, demonstrates the equipment. And he doesn't much like it. Even if, every now and then, at the factory or during his frequent trips to the Rhineland, he has the pleasure of showing the tattooed number on his arm, 174517, to some German industrialist who collaborated with IG-Farben,[2] introducing himself, 'Levi, how do you do' (articulating the words carefully, the surname first, to make sure he hits the target). It is a pleasure no one can deny him.

In his work as a scientist Levi enjoys himself much more. His real métier, as he calls it, fascinates him. A client might ask him, for example, for a particular resin that fulfils certain mechanical, technical and electrical criteria; he might, say, request a paint for radiators on transatlantic liners, that would be resistant to the saline atmosphere at sea at certain temperatures and for a certain number of years. It's his job to study the case. Then he goes home, each evening, along the old Appian Way, to his large art nouveau building on corso

Re Umberto, where he grew up as a child (the clean, fresh study, with all his many favourite books lined up in order, a lot of them para-doxical fantasists and rebels – Villon, Rabelais, Swift, Conrad, a few Italian classics, Dante and Ariosto but no Foscolo or Leopardi, 'blocked out' in his memory forever by his schooldays) and he changes skin, as he puts it again, he becomes a writer. Not an occasional writer, though. A real writer, born and bred. And he knows it well, even if he feigns modesty.

He can be allowed a touch of coquetry, after all, for all his Piedmontese rigour and intransigence. He can allow himself to reply, at once, that he is no more than a humble chemist who has written two books by chance. Then, as he warms to his theme, he comes closer to a true answer. With a little speech, clearly the product of some careful thinking.

'Look, today perhaps I have more fun writing than being a chemist, but my real ambition, what I dream about in secret, is to find a point of coincidence between the two. Let me explain: I'd like to tell the wider public the story of what scientific research means, a fantastic record, not too far from the truth, of what happens in the secret world of the laboratory, which is nothing other than a modern-day version of the most ancient, the most mysterious emotions known to man, the moment of uncertainty – whether to kill the buffalo or not, whether you will find what you are looking for or not. I mean, there are entire narrative traditions based around, the lives of miners, doctors, prostitutes, and yet there is next to nothing about the spiritual adventures of chemists.'

He looks up and smiles. He hasn't quite finished. 'Science fiction?', I ask him, thinking of his own short stories. 'Yes, science fiction. Many of its themes amuse and fascinate me. I see science-fiction stories as moral tales dressed up, in disguise. I scribble several at a time in gaps, or rather, in time carved out as best I can in my manager's schedule.' I ask him if he has plans to put them together as a book. 'I would really rather like to, in a few years' time, of course. At present, with *The Truce*, they would be rather baffling bedfellows.' The usual pause. 'Naturally, only if they agree to publish them', he adds.[3]

'So you're all done with the experience of the camps?' 'Absolutely, not another word. Nothing. I've said everything I had to say. It's all over.' Perhaps it is all over as a theme for future work. But the characters remain, the questions remain, why all this happened, why 'blue eyes and blond hair are essentially evil' is a mystery, as he says, that has not yet been explained. Dr Pannwitz of Kommando 98 – he of the 'chemical examination'[4] – was searched for by Levi for years after the war, carefully, tenaciously, untiringly, all over Europe, not in order to exact revenge but rather to carry on with unfinished business, to understand him 'at the innermost workings of his humanity'. Or of his non-humanity. Finally, he discovered that he was dead.

And the extrovert, crazy, picaresque people in *The Truce*? They keep coming up as he talks. Cesare, for example, that 'child of the sun, everybody's friend', the charlatan, trickster, all at once fickle, merry, rash and innocent. 'Of course, his real name isn't Cesare, but don't write what he's really called, please; he lives in Rome now and has a position of some moral and financial responsibility. My book could do him damage. Once, he wrote to me saying that Romans are too shrewd, that you can't work anything in Rome, you know, "work" in his sense of the word, and that he wanted to move up North and was wondering if I could find him a wife. After *The Truce* he hasn't written to me any more. Maybe he didn't understand what I was trying to do, maybe he's upset. But please don't put his name in, I wouldn't want to cause any offence.'

He wouldn't even want to upset the Greek, Mordo Nahum, a character sketched out in twenty pages, who already holds his own alongside some of the most famous in all literature, a super-Greek, an astute barterer, anarchical and intransigent in his strange code of manliness, with the rapacious look of a night-hawk caught in the moonlight. He lives in Salonika and of course his name isn't Mordo Nahum, 'but please don't put his in either, perhaps he's quite respectable now'. He would like to go to Salonika and meet him, but he fears he would not recognize him, would find him grown pale with 'all the trappings of civil existence'.

No, he will not write anything more on the concentration camps, all that there was to say has been said. With fearless detachment. Now *The Truce* is in the running for the Campiello Prize; in fact, it has already all but won it. Levi is almost shocked, he is afraid of offending figures like the Belloncis,[5] that they might take it as an insult, 'after they have been so kind' to him. 'It was nothing to do with me, you know. All the work of others. Everything happened without my assent, without even my knowledge.'

Now Dr Primo Levi gets up, does up the jacket of his summer suit, says his thanks, apologizes for any inconvenience; he has to get back to the factory, to study his troublemaking resins and paints, to show important clients around, maybe one or two of them blond and elegant, once upon a time model workers in IG-Farben.

Notes

1   The Premio Strega is Italy's top literary prize. In 1963, the prize went to Natalia Ginzburg's *Lessico famigliare* (*Family Sayings*).

2   IG-Farben were the owners of the Buna plant that Levi and other slave labourers worked at in his time at the Auschwitz-Monowitz camp.

3   Although Levi's science fiction only began to appear in book form in 1966 (*Storie naturali*), he had published several stories in various newspapers from 1960, and indeed, had been writing them sporadically ever since 1946, that is, weeks after his return from Auschwitz.

4   Pannwitz is the German officer who puts Levi through a mock chemistry exam, recounted with great power and indignation in the chapter entitled 'Chemical Examination' in *If This is a Man*.

5   Goffredo Bellonci (1882–1964) was a critic and journalist who, together with his wife Maria, established the Premio Strega prize in 1947.

Science Fiction I
Storie naturali

Edoardo Fadini (1966–1971)

As many of his readers are aware, Primo Levi, the well-known writer, works by profession as a chemist in a factory on the outskirts of Turin. Later this month, the Teatro delle Dieci in Turin is putting on, under the direction of Massimo Scaglione (who also runs the theatre), three single-act plays by Levi, together entitled *Storie naturali*. They are science-fiction stories: 'La bella addormentata nel frigo' ('The Sleeping Beauty in the Fridge'), commissioned by RAI, 'Il Versificatore' ('The Versifier'), recorded by RAI radio in September–October 1965, and 'Il sesto giorno' ('The Sixth Day'), planned in 1946–7 and finished in 1957.

What did the author of *If This is a Man* and *The Truce* (two of the greatest expressions of the tragic experience of the Second World War and the concentration camps) expect from science fiction? Levi's reply is quite calm: 'No, these aren't science fiction, if by that you mean fiction about the world to come, cheap futuristic fantasy. These stories are *more possible* than many others. Indeed, they are so possible that parts of them have already come true. Take "The Versifier" (a commercial poet buys a machine for writing poetry to speed up his customer service; the machine then becomes the author of the very play we are watching): several, quite interesting attempts have already been made in this direction. So, these are stories that take place at the edges

These two interviews are related to Levi's two major collections of science-fiction short stories, *Storie naturali* (1966) and *Vizio di forma* (1971). They are brought together here because many of the stories from both books appeared together in English in the volume, *The Sixth Day*. The first interview, with Edoardo Fadini, 'Primo Levi si sente uno scrittore "dimezzato"', *L'Unità*, 4 January 1966, refers in particular to three one-act plays included in *Storie naturali*.

of natural history – hence the title – but they are also unnatural seen from a certain angle. Clearly the two meanings overlap.'

Is there any link between man in the concentration camps and these stories of machine-poets, women in permanent hibernation and bureaucrat-creators? Here Levi becomes quite sharp: 'I am amphibian', he says, 'a centaur (I've even written stories about centaurs). It seems to me that the ambiguity of science fiction reflects my present destiny. I am split in two. One half of me is of the factory, is the technician and the chemist, but there is another, quite separate half that lives in the world of writing, giving interviews, working on my past and present experiences. They are the two halves of my brain. I live with this paranoiac split (as, I imagine, did figures like Gadda, Sinisgalli, Solmi).[1] They are two parts of me that exist so distinctly that I cannot bring the second – my work with the pen and with my imagination – to bear on the first, the factory world. I have tried to write stories about my factory life. They are the worst I have ever written. No. I'll never manage it, I am quite sure. The world of my books is something quite apart, it is the world of my youth, of racial discrimination, of my struggles not to be set apart from my school-friends, then my reclaiming of the Jewish tradition (Judaism opposed to Fascism, like freedom to terror, because I found out among other things that many principles of liberty are rooted within the core of the Jewish tradition at its most pure), the partisan war and finally, the camps and my writing about that hideous distortion of humanity. My books are all these things, and also the notoriety they have given me, the new encounters, the new dimension of humanity I have encountered. But all this has gone on *outside* my everyday life. Given all this, I think it is natural that I should turn to science fiction. These *Storie naturali* are versions of the ideas of science and technology seen from that other half of myself through which I happen to live.'

Levi tries conscientiously to restrict his comments as far as possible to the terrain of the personal, of individual experience. But it is clear that he means something more too: that in the face of the barbarity he has lived through from within, and which has tainted his deepest self, there seems to be no other way to judge than through this projection into the world of the possible, accepting the inner division within man which must be carefully watched over to avoid the horror of further lapses. It is as though his experience of the *Lager* means that he cannot give any more of himself beyond those first two masterful books. As a man, he has remained modest, upright and ready to fight for the ideas he believes in, but something of the lacerations he went through, a shadow of that strange, horrific distortion that tried to overwhelm him, hangs over his eyes.

In what ways does he think that things must change, even at the level of form and language after those experiences? 'I don't understand the question,' he replies. 'Language is what it is. It serves to communicate. No doubt, for us Jews, in the *Lager*, this was a problem. I have a sort of unrequited love for linguistics. I learned German in the camp.[2] With no grammar. But the terrible problem of language in the camp was simply the problem of "understanding". Think of the terror of listening to incomprehensible orders which will lead you straight to the ovens precisely because "you didn't understand". In the camp, there was a caste system amongst the prisoners who "could understand". The Russians used to call the Germans "dumb". Many of us had studied languages at school, but now we were in the midst of an unheard-of barbarism. We had to rebuild amongst ourselves the links that had been shattered by creating a shared jargon. Beyond it lay the "foreigner", "the strange", "the outsider", all three at once. Beyond us were the Germans, the Third Reich, Nazism.'

Many will perhaps not understand Levi's decision now to set himself 'beyond' the real: they will see it as a means of escape from the tragic problems that assail us, then as now. But in reality the decision is proof of Levi's realism and courage. If these *Storie naturali* can be called science fiction, then they show, once again, man's imagination as it has always been: an immense reservoir of possible solutions to the problems of existence, even in the midst of the sinister omens that surrounds us once again. It is, in short, anything but a means of escape. It is a journey to the end of the road, the tunnel, the well. And on the way there are all the elements that make up man, society and history today. Levi has taken on the distortion, the fracture and placed himself at the extreme edge of the springboard with the courage of someone who is perfectly aware, perfectly alert in what he is doing.

Notes

1   All three are examples of twentieth-century Italian writers who were also interested in or worked in science in different ways: Carlo Emilio Gadda (1893–1973), the great Joycean novelist and philosopher, famously worked as an engineer, as did the poet Leonardo Sinisgalli (1908–81). Sergio Solmi (1899–1981) was a writer and critic who published science fiction and translated Raymond Queneau (Calvino later revised Solmi's translation of Queneau's *Petite cosmogonie portative* (1950) with Levi's help on technical matters).

2   In earlier interviews in this book, Levi explains that he had a basic reading knowledge of scientific German before reaching the camps, having studied chemistry at university using the textbook by Gattermann later included in his 1981 anthology of favourite books, *La ricerca delle radici* ('The Search for Roots').

Science Fiction II
Vizio di forma

Luca Lamberti (1971)

After six years of silence Primo Levi returns to the literary limelight [...]. His new book, *Vizio di forma*, is out this week, published by Einaudi. It is a collection of about fifteen stories, all set in a near or worryingly probable future. Science and technology are projected forward in a form of invention always caught between utopia and catastrophe, between certain hopes and sudden, almost grotesque disappointments.

Primo Levi, fifty years old, from Turin, a chemist by profession, describes his stories with a little of that objective technician's interest, but also with his own rash, restless curiosity, like a sort of Ulysses, with the irony of a native moralist and with the niggling concern of a man who has felt in his own flesh what disasters the 'sleep of reason' can bring.

Levi's is an unusual case: a writer who made his name through strictly autobiographical work but who found he had not exhausted his literary vein with that direct private testimony and who has gone on to create his own autonomous narrative world.

The first question I'd like to pose is this: what are the continuities and discontinuities between If This is a Man *and* The Truce *and* Storie naturali *(published under the pseudonym Damiano Malabaila) and* Vizio di forma?

From 'Vizio di forma: ci salveranno i tecnici', *L'Adige*, 11 May 1971. This interview marked the publication of *Vizio di forma*.

All authors find it difficult to judge their own work, I think: and for me it's especially difficult. When I finish books, they intrigue me and disgust me and then, after a few more months, I fall in love with them just like Pygmalion, in a sort of parental, acritical spirit. Having said that, I think I can see, superficially at least, a faultline or a tear between the first two books and the next two. With *The Truce* I felt as though I had finished something, as though I'd plumbed the depths of a group of experiences that were unique, tragic and yet (for me) paradoxically precious. I felt I had completely burned myself out as a witness, narrator and interpreter of a certain reality or let's say a chapter of history. But I still thought I had a few things left to say, things I could only say in another language, a language some might call ironic, but which I see as shrill, oblique, spiteful, deliberately anti-poetic; anti-human [*disumano*] where my earlier language had been inhuman [*inumano*]. Yes, maybe it is a question of that assertion by Adorno, that 'after' Auschwitz there can be no more poetry, at least for those who were there; whilst it was still possible to write poetry 'on' Auschwitz – a heavy, dense poetry, like molten metal, that runs away and leaves you gutted.

There is much talk, perhaps too much, today about the crisis in the novel. What are, in your opinion, the duties, the burdens and the honours that literature must assume in contemporary society? What is the relationship between art and society?

I don't think there is any general rule. No burdens nor honours. Whoever takes up writing does so for a hundred different reasons, some open some hidden, some conscious some unconscious. As for its value, well, 'you will know them by their fruit'. Amongst these hundred different reasons, there is probably also writing in hope of honours and writing through a sense of civic commitment, but in both cases the fruits are unpredictable.

I would have to be just as vague in defining the links between art and society. Art can be a guide or a mirror, an antagonist and a judge for society. It can also ignore society, or at least try to. All we can ask of those who create is that they should be neither servile nor false; that they should have the humility to look around them, to realize that the figure of the artist-prophet, the voice of God and source of all truth, no longer has any currency. Another culture has grown up and is growing rapidly still. The poet has to make room for the physicist, the economist, the psychologist; and if he does so he'll find himself in good company and maybe he'll have even more to say.

In painting a picture of a disquieting near-future world in the stories of
Vizio di forma, *you show an essentially trusting attitude towards the figure
of the 'homo faber', in his ability to turn around even the most compromised
situations, to give a human face to the world and the society around him.
Some might find this trust somewhat surprising coming from someone who
has lived through the ineradicable experience of the concentration camp.
Where does this faith come from?*

I don't know if *Vizio di forma* is a despairing book. Some readers have
thought so, perhaps taking a little too literally the pseudo-prophecies
it contains. In myself, I am not despairing. For eight hours a day, I'm
a technician, a man at war with the obtuse and malign inertia of
matter; and you cannot fight a war in despair, since at least you have
an end in sight. I wasn't even desperate in Auschwitz, for the same
reason. Those who despaired, who gave in to despair, died in the
space of a few days. However, I would not be able to give a full,
explicit justification of this faith of mine in the future of mankind. It is
a faith I would call biological, that infuses every living fibre and that
has led mankind, despite innumerable errors, to the conquest of the
planet. It may well not be rational, but then neither is despair. It
solves no problem, in fact it makes new ones and by its very nature it
causes suffering. Certainly, some of my stories end in catastrophe,
but I intended them to be ironic or what you might call conditional
catastrophes: we'll end up like this unless we do something about it,
but we have the means and the wit and the strength to prevent it.

*I hope you don't mind answering a non-literary question. In your opinion,
can we only hope for a 'restoration of planetary order' to come from
technology, whose effects might supersede 'political questions'; or have
science and technology shown themselves to be faithful and blind hand-
maidens of power? Isn't the problem still and always essentially a political
problem?*

If every problem of priority or choice is a political problem, then
clearly we have to turn to politicians. But we have to choose our
words carefully and understand their meaning. Politicians alone can
do nothing; they have already shown how impotent they are.

It is true and scandalous that in recent decades scientists have
given in to politicians' orders, but this is not the most important
point, nor is it the most profound error they have made. Only people
immersed in the day-to-day minutiae of politics could fail to notice
that the immense transformations going on in the world today, for

good or ill, were all born in the laboratory. New forms of farming, new weapons, new illnesses and new cures, new sources of energy and new contaminations. In my view, the greatest error of the applied scientists (pure scientists are another matter) has not so much been capitulation to power, but rather the undervaluing of their own influence and of the scale of change unleashed by their work. This is their real 'formal defect' [*vizio di forma*]. I don't for a moment think the error is irreversible and I hope that all of the world's scientists understand that the future depends on their return to conscience. I am sure that equilibrium can be restored and, what is more, with the tools we already have, not through some hypothetical new discovery nor, worst of all, through violence.

The Periodic Table (1975)

Giorgio De Rienzo and Ernesto Gagliano

Primo Levi, fifty-six years old, from Turin, graduate in chemistry, author of two famous books (*If This is a Man* and *The Truce*), has just published a new work, *The Periodic Table*. It contains twenty-one chapters, each one dedicated to a chemical element, each inspired by a moment in his life. There is the war, his laboratory research, the Nazi camps, the struggle to return to normality. Alongside the encounters with people, there is the encounter with matter – at times hostile, at others friendly, even salvational. The prose is composed and lucid, a blend of irony and affection. The events (even those which are violent and turbulent) are inserted into a frame where reason seems to reign. We asked Primo Levi a few questions.

Is your book the autobiography of a chemist?

In a certain sense, yes, but any book which has only one face, that you can only read in one way, is, I think, a rather poor book. A good book is necessarily, I won't say ambiguous, but at least polyvalent. In this case, I hoped that hidden beneath the condition of the chemist was an account of the human condition in general.

You have spoken about the struggle between man and matter. What is their relation?

From 'La ragione non può andare in vacanza', *Stampa sera*, 13 May 1975.

Here, too, the relation between man and matter in the book is ambivalent. Matter is maternal, even etymologically, but it is also inimical. The same goes for nature. And in any case, man too is matter and is thus in conflict with himself, as all religions have acknowledged. Matter is also an education, a genuine school for life. Fighting against it, you mature and grow. In the course of the struggle, you win and you lose. At times, matter seems astute, at others obtuse, and there's no contradiction because the two different aspects coexist.

Your prose has no sudden starts: it's lucidly constructed, with calm and detachment. How have you managed still to believe in the triumph of reason after all you've been through, in persecution and in the camps?

To believe in reason means believing in your own reason, it doesn't mean that reason rules the world nor even that it governs man. To have been present at the shipwreck of reason – and here I'm referring not only to Nazism, but also to our own Fascism – must not and cannot lead us to surrender. I would agree with Calamandrei[1] who says that for our generation there is no respite. For reason too there is no respite, we cannot take a holiday from reason. For my part, I am deeply suspicious of any absence of reason. And therefore I consider any métier that exercises reason as healthy, and mine is one of those métiers. It is not by chance that in this book I constantly equate my work with hunting. Man became man through hunting, that is, through exercising his reason.

Do you think that every chemical element can have a specific human meaning?

Let's not exaggerate. Samarium and Gandolinium are for now generally perceived as purely hostile and extraneous to man. But it's a question of time and familiarity, just as with people. Other elements – like iron, gold, sulphur, those which have a long history – undoubtedly have a human physiognomy, an anthropomorphic character and I've exploited this character, for example in the story about lead, but it wouldn't be difficult to do the same for oxygen or for copper. You wouldn't even need to be a chemist to do it.

You believe in the pleasure of work. Why?

Not all forms of work are pleasurable. That is a sad and obvious truth. But it would be good for the individual and thus also for society if they were able to choose a form of work that might give pleasure. Whoever manages this has a good chance of knowing happiness, even if only occasionally.

There is a masochistic habit around these days, which I consider crass and even contemptible, which says that work is a punishment. Even the Bible says so. It then hastily concludes that to work is to suffer and thus that it is better not to work. Well, this is just not true, or not necessarily true. Even today, if you think back to the work in the camps, say, work is much less oppressive that it was forty years ago and it can be less so in all spheres.

In this book, I have tried to bring to light the nobility of my work, its educational and formative value. It is also polemically opposed to other current ideologies in our country which still today see the main route to culture and maturity as Latin, Greek and aesthetic analysis, whilst mathematics and physics are seen as useless obscurities or useful only for jobs, for making a living. You must have noticed how you often hear people quite shamelessly, indeed with a sort of pride, confessing 'I never understood a thing about algebra'. No one would boast that they knew nothing about spelling or grammar, even when in practice they do not know anything. My aim was to show that a science, a technology can not only be the subject of a book, but also a school for thinking and thus for writing. I would be delighted if a physicist or a biologist followed my example. As for doctors, they've been writing stories of their profession for years.

Note

1   Piero Calamandrei (1889–1956) was an eminent jurist and politician who played a key role in the drafting of Italy's postwar Constitution. He edited the influential journal *Il ponte*, which published two stories by Levi in the late 1940s.

The Wrench (1979)

Silvia Giacomini

Primo Levi is a small, reserved man. But you can see in his eyes a glimmer of irony. Counting on that glimmer, I openly confess my difficulty in having to interview someone with so many differing coexisting personae: someone who has given voice to all those who have no voice, almost like a prophet; one of a small Turin clan which to outsiders might seem a little arrogant; an author of books about the world of technical and scientific work, following in an illustrious, if minor Lombard tradition.

As we speak, the irony wins out over the reserve. Levi laughs openly at the name Cattaneo.[1] He exclaims, 'but was I supposed to be the survivor for my entire life? Let's be clear, I am a survivor, but I don't want to write only about Auschwitz. I want to say something to the younger generation also. Look, I have gone and spoken about *If This is a Man* in at least 130 schools, but I have decided not to accept any more invitations of this kind. For some time now, I have come across questions about whether what I wrote was really true. And in any case, I am sure that writing about the camps still shocks but it is no longer a current issue. The danger of a return to that world, at least in Europe, does not exist today; or it is secondary, tertiary even, compared to other threats, other fears, other uncertainties.'

And with The Wrench *you hope to respond to the fears, the uncertainties of today?*

From 'Il mago Merlino e l'uomo fabbro', *La Repubblica*, 24 January 1979. The final part of the interview, which is not about *The Wrench*, has been omitted here.

Yes, I think that the discussion about work is important. The reasons that pushed me into writing this book are not wholly clear to me. I'd like to say that I wanted to fill an ecological niche: literature is full of duchesses, prostitutes, adventurers, so why not include one of us 'transformers of matter'? And further, I thought the attitude of the '68 movements to work was very abstract. I'm thinking of the salon unionists, who saw the world as made up of assembly-line slaves and evil bosses. In reality, the world is more articulated, there is a whole band in between those two extremes where work is neither punitive nor alienating. Like the work I have done for many years, managing a small factory. They haven't been wasted years. In work I found a Conradian view of life, the significance and the positive labour of struggling to reach an end. I saw the acceptance of responsibility, not its rejection, as the route to becoming adult.

And so you invented Faussone, the expert mechanic from Turin who tells the tale of a life spent travelling the world to construct cranes and pylons. Faussone speaks a very particular language, a very amusing Piedmontese-Italian. Why?

I didn't see why, if Pasolini could have his *Ragazzi di vita* speak Roman and if Edoardo De Filippo could have his characters speak in Neapolitan,[2] then the Piedmontese couldn't do the same.

Faussone's Italian exists: it is the democratic, perhaps polluted Italian of the factory workplace. I enjoyed writing in Faussone's language a lot, I've never written so easily, so much so that some journalists have assumed he must actually exist. Probably because the stories he tells are all true, except for the one about the ape. The first one, about the curse, that I set in an unspecified Middle Eastern country, in fact took place in Milan, in a factory where the committee was made up of southerners. I was told the story by a friend of Roberto Leydi.[3]

Reading your book, however, I had the same feeling I remember from when I read a popular science book as a child. It told the story of Merlin the Wizard who woke up a child from his bed at night and took him on a journey through the universe, explaining the laws of magnetics, gravity. And I used to think, but what's Merlin got to do with it, if all this is true? And I understand the fun you must have had with Faussone: but why invent him if all these stories are true?

Because it would be very hard to tell those stories in standard Italian. They have their own language. There are technical terms that no one uses, still less understands, in Italian. Man as maker speaks the language of man as maker. Try saying '*scodimento*' in Italian.[4] You would probably need a periphrasis of two lines. Try making Gioanin Bongée speak Italian.[5] It isn't just a whim that Porta has him speak Milanese. I don't know if '*el mestèe*' succeeded, but I don't think the approach was wrong. And then, even if Faussone is made up, his father, for example, isn't. I borrowed him from a coppersmith who worked in the factory I managed. His father was a smith I'd met years ago. So when I needed to give Faussone a father I asked the coppersmith to tell me the story of his father. He understood at once what I meant by 'telling the story'. Later I showed him the draft of the story and he corrected two or three technical terms.

But whilst you are talking about work, others are sowing doubts about the historical truth of the Nazi camps. Will we end up forgetting them just as we have forgotten the extermination of the Cathars and the Albigensians?

I stopped acting as survivor when I took up writing, but I continue to be one. Next week I am going to attend a meeting to organize an Italian memorial to Auschwitz. But over the last thirty-five years I have accumulated other experiences, and I thought it would be useful to talk about them. Giovanni Raboni[6] has pointed out a continuity between *If This is a Man* and *The Wrench* in their shared treatment of the dignity of man.
[...]

Notes

1   Carlo Cattaneo (1801–69) is cited as an example of the 'illustrious Lombard tradition' described by the interviewer above. Cattaneo was an historian, essayist and journalist who took part in the 1848 uprising in Milan and founded the innovative periodical *Il Politecnico* in 1839.
2   Pier Paolo Pasolini (1922–75) wrote a number of novels and stories in the late 1950s (and then made films in the 1960s) set in the slums of Rome, using heavy Roman dialect or slang. *Ragazzi di vita* (*The Ragazzi*, Manchester: Carcanet, 1986) was the first of these, published in 1955. Edoardo De Filippo (1900–84) was the greatest Neapolitan actor and playwright of the century and many of his works were in Neapolitan.

3   The stories Levi refers to appear in *The Wrench* as 'The Helper' and
     'With Malice Aforethought', the third and first chapters respectively.
     Roberto Leydi was an ethnomusicologist.
4   'Scodimento' is a term for a leak of a certain kind: it is now in the UTET
     Grande dizionario della lingua italiana with Levi as the citation.
5   Gioanin Bongée is the comic hero of a number of works by the nine-
     teenth-century Milanese dialect poet Carlo Porta (1775–1821), includ-
     ing *I desgrazzi de Giovannin Bongee*.
6   Giovanni Raboni (1932–   ) is a poet and literary critic.

La ricerca delle radici ('The Search for Roots') (1981)

Aurelio Andreoli

The latest book by Primo Levi, *La ricerca delle radici* (Einaudi), collects together some extracts of books we might find in a hypothetical universal library. That is, it is an anthology put together as if all literature from Homer onwards, with all its variety of genres from satire to drama to epic, coexisted simultaneously in a single order. Included among others are pages from the Book of Job, the story of a just man that looks forward to Plato, part of *The Odyssey* where Ulysses gives himself the name Nobody, the story of Jacob in the Thomas Mann's reworking of the Old Testament [*Joseph and His Brothers*], *Moby Dick* or the visionary world of Melville, Marco Polo's *Il Milione* with its memory or dreams of his travels, nature according to Lucretius, *Murder in the Cathedral* by T. S. Eliot, or Christian hope in an age of desperation.

Primo Levi, from Turin, sixty-two years old, survivor of Auschwitz, industrial chemist, has already published with Einaudi *If This is a Man* (1958), *The Truce* (1963) and *The Wrench* (1978).

Why a personal anthology?

The idea was Giulio Bollati's.[1] It's an anthology in the sense of a personal collection of the author's own books. So the reflexive element, the author putting himself forward, is present but in the background. A selection like this is indeed a form of autobiography, but

From 'Per Primo Levi questo è un modo diverso di dire io', *Stampa sera*, 21 August 1981.

there's more to me than this. I was not born a writer, my 'roots' are only in part literary: for thirty years I worked full-time as a chemist, with various moments of enthusiasm and dejection, a life within a life.

Why the title, La ricerca delle radici? *Is it perhaps an attempt to analyse that part of your cultural identity derived from books?*

I am incapable of analysing myself. My work is nocturnal, often carried out unconsciously. I would like to have called the book 'Another Way of Saying I'. In the preface I ask how much of our roots are in the books we have read? And in my case, how much of what we write comes from what we read? Now many things come from 'elsewhere', not from books read, but from the experiences of the *Lager* (arrest, journey, deportation) that inspired my first book *If This is a Man*.

Who is your anthology for? Could this book also be a guide to the formation of a personal library of narrative and poetry for your reader?

The book doesn't have any didactic purpose. Although I have thought of producing an anthology of my own works for a series of Einaudi school-books as a variation on the same theme. My readers?...First, my chemist colleagues, readers of my other books, others searching for individual and collective roots, critics (without wishing to aim too high), but above all the young, even though, as I say, I'm far from thinking of it as educational project.

Who would you save for a hypothetical universal library amongst contemporary Italian writers?

I'm a little diffident on this. I certainly don't rush out to read the new books when they come out. I wait to see how long they last. Luckily I am not a professional reader. I don't have to read everything by everyone straight away. I would certainly save Calvino, without a doubt. Then Rigoni Stern, because he is close to me as a writer; D'Arrigo, to do justice to a writer often unjustly neglected; Elsa Morante, Natalia Ginzburg.[2]

Why did you not include the founding classics of our literature in your library?

There's no Dante and there's no Manzoni because *The Divine Comedy* is in every universal library. It would perhaps have been useful to have included Leopardi and Boccaccio, but here too I decided to omit books that were part of any reader's heritage. Although I should add that Leopardi has never been a favourite author of mine, because of the profound difference between us: he sees the world with such despair, whereas I am immersed in the world...

And yet, in your anthology, you include a line of readings that you call 'man suffering unjustly', and you include Eliot and Babel.[3]

Yes, and yet I see in both Eliot and Babel something that transcends despair. In Eliot it is his faith, which I do not share, and in Babel it is that vital impulse which turns him from Jew into Cossack. I think the desperation we see in Babel is posthumous, attributed to him only in the light of his murder. He seems to me rather a man of adventure, an explorer of the spirit. There is pure despair, however, in Celan, and yet I have also put him into my anthology.

Let's move onto another important line in your readings, which you call 'the salvation of laughter', a line you draw from Rabelais to Porta, Belli, Shalom Aleichem[4]...

This dynasty of writers is linked by their joyous and genial use of language. They are all linguistic innovators, conscious or unconscious philologists. In all of them laughter is triggered by the language they use. Swift isn't included here because his is a bitter laughter. Perhaps I should have added Samuel Butler as an ironic critic, a fantastic scientist. The most common question I get from friends and readers is why not this author instead of that one? But it's natural that I should have my own tastes.

Why no Borges amongst the contemporaries?

I know his work very little and I would say I have a veiled dislike for him. I see something in Borges that is alien and distant from me. In any case, it would be ambitious to think I could justify all my likes and dislikes. For some, the reasons are clear, for others much less so. Even my love for Rabelais is apparently inexplicable, and yet he is the one I feel closest to of all, almost like a son. If I could I would choose Rabelais as a father.

Why, as a Jewish author, have you excluded a great writer like Isaac Bashevis Singer?

Because I'm not so convinced that he is a great writer. First of all, he writes too much, and so he seems too thin. As a person he is dear to me, but it would have been a lie to include him amongst the writers I read and reread and that is what this is all about. I don't think he has the 'backbone' to get into the first division of writers. I fear that a generation from now he will be read only by the experts. Put a page of Singer alongside one by another, lesser known Yiddish writer like Shalom Aleichem – who is included – and you'll see the difference between the two at once in terms of 'stylistic vigour'.

And why no authors from that Mitteleuropean tradition: Proust, Musil, Kafka?

I find Proust boring, Musil I don't know well enough and Kafka provokes ambivalent feelings in me. In part, I feel in the presence of works of fundamental importance, in part I feel a repulsion that is clearly of a psychoanalytic nature.

Let's talk further about your literary dislikes...

Dislikes are not always rational, they come from chance causes and circumstances, or because you happened upon the wrong work or the right work at the wrong time. Amongst my dislikes, there's Dostoevsky, whom I tried to penetrate again recently but whose wearisome style stops me short every time. I find his mingling of portentous introspective lucidity and confusion rebarbative. It would be a service to cut his books by a third. Of course, I'm reading him in translation and I know from personal experience that the job of the translator is difficult and dangerous. So, with authors whose language I don't know, as with Dostoevsky and the Russians, generally I feel somewhat diffident. Balzac is someone else I've rejected,

I've only read two of his books and then I gave up. Life is too short to read all of Balzac.

In what ways has your experience as a chemist influenced your reading and writing?

Chemistry wasn't only a profession, it was also an existential formation, the source of certain mental habits, above all that of clarity. A chemist who cannot express himself clearly is a bad chemist. The job of a chemist in a small paint factory (just like Italo Svevo)[5] was fundamental for me as a source of prime material, a capital of stories to tell. But writing was strictly limited to the evenings, after 6 p.m.

Notes

1   Giulio Bollati (1924–96) was a key figure in the Einaudi publishing house, before leaving to found his own firm Bollati Boringhieri.

2   All the names Levi gives are of Italian writers of his generation. He knew personally Italo Calvino (1923–85) and Natalia Ginzburg (1916–91). He also knew Mario Rigoni Stern (1921–), author of war and nature novels. Stefano D'Arrigo (1919–92) was the author of the immense novel *Horcynus Orca* (Milan: Mondadoris 1975). Both he and Rigoni Stern are included in *La ricerca delle radici*. Elsa Morante (1912–85) was the author of several fantasy novels as well as *La Storia* (Turin: Einaudi, 1974; *History*, London: Allen Lane, 1978), a grand-scale and bestselling novel set in wartime Rome.

3   Isaak Babel (1894–?1941) was a Russian Jewish writer, author of *Red Cavalry* (1926; London: Alfred Knopf, 1979), stories of the horrors of war, written from first-hand experience, and other stories about Russian life in Odessa, his birthplace. He died at some unknown date inside a Soviet prison.

4   On Porta, see the interview discussing *The Wrench* on pp. 96–7. Shalom Aleichem (1859–1916) was a popular Yiddish writer, creator of 'Tevye the Milkman' (source of *Fiddler on the Roof*), among others.

5   Italo Svevo (pseud. Ettore Schmitz, 1861–1928), Jewish author of *The Confessions of Zeno* (1923; Harmondsworth: Penguin, 1964) and friend of James Joyce (he was a model for Leopold Bloom), worked for a paint company as Levi did.

If Not Now, When? (1982)

Rosellina Balbi

Some years ago, writing about *If This is a Man*, Primo Levi said: 'The need to tell our story was so strong in us that I began to write the book right there, in that German laboratory, frozen, heavy with war and with spying eyes. I knew that I had no way of preserving those scribbled notes because, if they had found them on me, they would have cost me my life. But I wrote the book as soon as I returned, in a few short months, the memory burning within me.'

At the start of *If Not Now, When?*, which has just been published by Einaudi, there used to be a sort of distich which was later removed from the final version: 'The actors are ready, or almost. Their profiles are still veiled, they have not yet emerged from the indistinct, from the universe of things that do not yet exist, but want to exist. They stir weakly, grey on a grey background; they speak in muted tones or perhaps they do not speak at all, but rather murmur and moan, like new-born pups. They are waiting, in hope and fear, to make their entrance.'

I say to Primo Levi: it strikes me that for the first time since If This is a Man *you felt the urgent need, an overwhelming, irresistible impulse to write. And you have set the events of* If Not Now, When? *in more or less the same period as that of* If This is a Man *and then of* The Truce. *Why this return? I mean, is it because of certain attitudes that are once more in the air today? Because of the more or less creeping wave of anti-*

From 'Mendel, il consolatore', *La Repubblica*, 14 April 1982.

*Semitism? Only a few days ago we had the news of two German univer-
sities refusing to name themselves after Heine and Einstein...*

Levi listens attentively. (Later he tells me I am the only person, until
now, who has read his book in its entirety – 'at Einaudi they actually
printed it without reading it' – and so he was extremely curious to
know what I was going to ask him.) He thinks for a moment, and then
shakes his head. 'No, I wouldn't say so. Or at least, if there was that
motivation, I wasn't aware of it. What I did feel very deeply was the
desire to show how unfounded the accusation is – made by Jews as
much as by anyone else – that the Jews stood still, were passive, let
themselves be led to the slaughter like sheep.

'Ten years ago I was much struck by a story I was told by my friend
Emilio Vita Finzi. In 1945, Vita Finzi worked as a seventeen-year-old
in the Assistance Office in via Unione, Milan. There one day he
found the group of strange figures who became the protagonists of
my book. You will ask why I waited ten years after hearing the story to
write it. The fact is, I was too busy with other things: I was still
working as a chemist. So at that time I just wrote out a page or so of
notes. And when I came later on to clear out my 'storehouse of
dormant ideas', I found the page and decided to make a novel out
of it. But Vita Finzi no longer remembered exactly how the story
went... So I had to undertake a series of readings and research and
between finding the page of notes and finishing the book, almost a
year went by.

'What was the research for? To find out the nature of the Jewish
resistance movement, to confirm that it was indeed much more
important – in scale and in moral significance – than is commonly
thought. And more than just bands of Jews alone: there were also
Soviet groups led by Jewish officers or soldiers. There is substantial
Soviet documentation to prove it. Not that they specify who was
Jewish and who was not, but certain names are unmistakable.'

In this latest book, Levi narrates, as he says, the story of a group of
Jews who choose to resist (in a landscape so very different from our
Resistance in the mountains of the north, whose partisans had their
homes close at hand: here we are moving amongst forests, swamps
and icy landscapes, with no hinterland, in an endless solitude). The
group moves around, sometimes joining in with other bands, sometimes rejected by them too, and after many adventures ends up
reaching Italy. Reading the book, I thought of one of Levi's earlier
works, *La ricerca delle radici*, in which the writer proposes a series of
'reading itineraries' which all start from the Book of Job – the just
man oppressed by injustice – and move towards a form of salvation

by way of certain stops (each one represented by various authors): irony, knowledge, awareness of what it means to be human. In some way, I felt that the itinerary taken by the characters of this novel was not dissimilar to that intellectual itinerary suggested by Levi: here, too, we move from oppression and injustice and through a more or less limpid coming to consciousness, to reach salvation. (The refrain of the song sung by the band led by Gedaleh, from which the book takes its title, comes from a collection of rabbinic sayings of the second century AD: Rabbi Hillel says, 'If I am not for myself, who will be for me? And if I think only of myself, who am I? And if not now, when?')

I ask: do you, Primo Levi, identify with any of your characters? Mendel especially seems close to you...

'Quite. Deep down, I did identify with Mendel. I mean that he does what I would have done, or rather what I should have done if I had been able.'

Mendel is a watchmaker from Strelka, who had a wife who ended up 'in the ditch' like all the other Jews of the village. He fought the war with the Red Army and finally, in July 1942, lost touch with the army like so many others. 'They count the living and the dead; the missing are neither alive nor dead and they can't be counted. They're like ghosts.' The name Mendel 'is short for Menachem, which means "consoler", but I've never consoled anybody'. Perhaps not before, but throughout the novel, Mendel is a strong, knowing – and thus consoling – presence. Not that he harbours any illusions; on the contrary. He does what he does not because he covets this or that hope or because he has any dream of a future utopia. He is not even sure he has ever had or ever will have any free choice in the matter. Towards the end of the book, when he and his companions find themselves in a wealthy Milanese house, Mendel '[feels] disoriented: in a living room filled with beautiful things and polite people, and he felt also like a pawn in a gigantic, cruel game. Perhaps he had always been a pawn, the eternal pawn, since he had been a missing person, since he had met Leonid. You think you are making a decision and instead you are following a destiny that has already been written.' Shortly after, he will say to Gedaleh, 'Let's go, Gedaleh. Let's say goodbye. This is not a place for us.'

That Milanese drawing room...

'Indeed, that drawing room represents in some sense the collision between the shreds of Ashkenazi Jewry and Italian bourgeois Jewry, the one so different from the other... In any case, we too felt when we came back from the camps that we were in a different world from those people. They hadn't understood anything.'

Perhaps it's the same situation described by Edoardo De Filippo in Napoli milionaria *[1945]: the man who returns home after an horrific experience who wants to recount that experience, to share it with someone so as to free himself of it, but everyone tells him 'just leave it be, it's water under the bridge, now eat, drink and think no more about it'. And they move on to something else.*

Levi nods. 'It's curious you should say that. Just the other day, a friend and fellow deportee was quoting *Napoli milionaria*... And you will perhaps remember – I wrote about it in *If This is a Man* – that the most common dream of all the deportees in the camps was a dream of 'telling their story and not being listened to'. ('There is my sister here, with some unidentifiable friends and many others people [...]. It is an intense pleasure, physical, inexpressible, to be at home, among friendly people and to have so many things to recount: but I cannot help noticing that my listeners do not follow me. In fact, they are completely indifferent: they speak confusedly of other things among themselves, as if I were not there...')

You tell me that with this book you wanted to re-establish an historical truth: that the Jews did fight. But this capacity to rebel, to take up the struggle, did they show it everywhere across Europe?

'I can only say that here in Italy, we were not prepared. And I am not only talking about Jews. All my peers reached that moment of truth disarmed, literally and metaphorically. As for the Jews specifically, it should be said that the seeds of Jewish resistance were Zionist more than communist... Now in Italy, Zionism had had relatively scarce support: those rituals, the collective dancing, the acting together, had all appealed little to us.'

None of the characters in Levi's book is a Zionist: or almost none of them. Many of them will end up – we assume, although it is not certain as the book ends – in Palestine; but not because they are following some ancient dream, rather because they have no homes to go back to, they have no loved ones to search out, they have no identity to reclaim. Perhaps the only sign of hope, for Mendel, is the baby born on the very last page of the novel. The young girl Line says to Mendel as they wait for Rokhele to give birth: we too have just been born; Russia conceived us, nourished us, helped us grow in the dark inside her, like in a womb. She went into labour, she had her pains and contractions and she forced us out, and now here we are, naked and new, like babies. And Mendel thinks about the problem of beginning again. From where? And then he thinks of the woman giving birth and he says, they were right, they closed their eyes and forgot and now the seed has not gone to waste . . .

As if he has guessed what I am thinking, Levi says: 'I want to add something. When I began writing this book I was fascinated by the fact that, for the first time, I was testing myself as a novelist, a new profession for me. I had to make up the action from scratch, I had to invent all the characters in complete freedom. And I made up a whole troupe of them, characters capable of trickery, of dancing and shooting, of fear and courage. Only Polina, the girl-pilot, is a real person. Thus, especially during the first draft, I felt the paranoid sensation of having given birth to children. But then, once the children had been born, they took me by the hand, they rebelled, they – how can I put it? – started up a union and protested, they demanded their right to choose. And indeed they decided: above all, when it came to the women. I had an outline that I completely forgot later on. I had wanted to make Racinian heroes of them all, and they just wanted to have common, average parts to play, made up more of toil than of memorable gestures . . .'

A bit like Pirandello's six characters[1] . . .

'Quite. I think I have only now fully understood Pirandello . . . And the story of Pygmalion too, a great story.'

After a short pause, Levi picks up again: 'The character of a novel really is a strange creature. Made of paper, drawn in black and white, living inside a page. And yet we fall in love with them, we hate them, we are emotionally drawn into their lives. It happens even with characters created by others, so when you yourself gives life to one of these characters, you forge with them – or at least this is what happened to me – a special bond or reciprocity, of collaboration . . .'

So you do not rule out the possibility that your characters might put pressure on you, might persuade you, even force you to bring them back on stage?

'No, I can't rule it out. Well, I don't know. For sure, they are still buzzing around me...I think it will all depend on their desire for life.'

If not now, when?

Note

1   Luigi Pirandello (1867–1936) was the author of the play *Six Characters in Search of an Author* to which the interviewer is referring here. See L. Pirandello, *Collected Plays*, vol. 2. (London: John Calder, 1988).

The Drowned and the Saved (1986)

Giorgio Calcagno

On the highest shelf in Primo Levi's study there are ten big dark-green boxes.

They contain the letters Levi has received from all over the world in the last ten years. For the most part, they are about *If This is a Man*. But in a corner lower down, right behind the desk, there is an eleventh box, dedicated to 1986, that is filling up rapidly. The new letters are about *The Drowned and the Saved*, Levi's book that has just appeared, published by Einaudi. Forty years on, the writer has gone back to Auschwitz; he has gone back down in his memory through the circles of that old hell, not this time as a witness but instead as an interrogator. And the reaction of his readers has been immediate.

The Drowned and the Saved should have been, as Levi intended it, the title of his first book, and indeed it is there, hidden away as a chapter title. He had found the term in a bit of Dante, at the beginning of the fourth 'bolgia' of the *Inferno*: 'Di nuova pena me convien far versi / e dar matera al ventesimo canto / della prima canzon, ch'è de' sommersi'.[1] But Franco Antonicelli, his first publisher in 1947, had been struck by the phrase 'If This is a Man', tucked away in the verse epigraph to the book, and he had suggested the change of title. So the original title had to wait thirty-nine years to make its way onto the cover. And not, as with *If This is a Man*, against an image of deportees in their grim *Lager* uniform, but instead against the desperate, imploring faces of Memling's *Last Judgement*.[2] From chronicle to history, and beyond.

From 'Primo Levi: capire non è perdonare', *La Stampa*, 29 July 1986.

*Why did Primo Levi, after so many other experiences, literary and other-
wise, want to go back to this theme? From a need for truth, he replies at
once. To go against rhetoric.*

We ex-deportees are compared to ex-partisans and that is right and
proper. But there is a substantial difference between the victorious
struggle of the latter and the passive and degrading experience of
imprisonment of the former. I wanted to re-establish these points of
difference. I am ready to accept a certain amount of rhetoric, we need
it to live. We need monuments, celebrations: and monument, etymologically, means warning. But we also need a counterpoint, a prose
commentary on the flights of rhetoric. I have tried to provide this
whilst knowing that I might offend some sensibilities. These themes
are still rather taboo.

*And there is a second reason behind the origins of this book, a reason that
goes to the heart of our history.*

I feel the passage of the years, of my years too. And as they pass, I can
feel a slippage in the way these memories are understood in the
world.

Levi often meets young people, in schools.

In them I find strong, even violent emotional participation, but not
historical understanding. When I go into a classroom, I feel a flash of
amazement when they see the author of the book they've been reading, that I'm still alive and that I speak Italian, not Latin or Greek.

*The Italian-speaking writer feels a growing detachment from many readers
from the younger generations.*

And I wanted to show that these events belong to a past which is very
near, not only geographically. The seeds of Auschwitz must not be
allowed to sprout again; and yet violence is nearby, all around us, and
there is a violence that has been born of violence. There are subterranean links between the two world wars and the violence we have
seen in Algeria, Russia, the Chinese Cultural Revolution, Vietnam.
Our society, with its information media (which are so necessary in

many ways), disseminates violence. It deploys mechanisms that amplify it.

And indeed in this new book, the memory of the Lager *casts its shadow forward onto our world; here and there it seems to find disturbing points of contact. In the chapter – the fundamental chapter – on the 'Grey Zone', there is a careful analysis of the power that man, even the victim, tries to acquire over his fellow men, whoever is more victim that he. Is* The Drowned and the Saved *a book that addresses the historical specificity of that experience or the fear that it is still a problem for us today?*

One of my wishes was indeed to bring the problem up to date. The key question for me is: will we go back to it or not? I am no prophet. I don't think we will go back in this direction in Europe, at least in the foreseeable future. But that the threat still exists should be obvious. What little we know about Cambodia reminds us terrifyingly of what happened in Germany. A third of the population has been sacrificed for a fanatical ideal. They manage to make us swallow anything, to use those media I was referring to earlier to make people believe anything.

Two verbs recur insistently in The Drowned and the Saved: *to understand and to forgive, at times used negatively. Are these the book's two key terms?*

To understand, yes. I have spent forty years going around trying to understand the Germans. To understand how it could have happened is the aim of my life. But in a wider sense also, because there is another level of understanding that interests me: as a chemist, I want to understand the world around me.

And to forgive?

To forgive is not my verb. It has been inflicted on me. All the letters I receive, especially from young and Catholic readers, return to this theme. They ask me if I have forgiven. I think of myself as, in my own way, a just man. I can forgive a man, but not all men; I only feel able to judge case by case. If I had had Eichmann before me, I would have condemned him to death. I do not accept, as some ask me to, a wholesale pardon. Who are the Germans? I am not a believer, the phrase 'I absolve thee' has no precise meaning for me. I don't believe that anyone, not even a priest, has the power to bind and release others. Whoever commits a crime must pay for it, unless he repents. But this does not mean in words only. A verbal repentance is not enough. I am prepared to release whoever can show through his actions that he is no longer the person he was. And he must not wait too long to do so.

The chapter on the intellectual in Auschwitz underscores the disadvantages suffered by the cultured compared to the uneducated in the camps. And yet the chapter entitled 'Communication' demonstrates the need above all else to understand messages in order to survive. If language saves us, how is it that intelligence should lead to perdition?

I am speaking about everyday, familiar communication, not intellectual exchange. We are all thinking beings. But in Auschwitz we were deprived even of that everyday language, Italians above all. Of course, to understand was an advantage there. But it was counterbalanced by serious disadvantages, right from the moment of arrival. Whoever announced they were lawyers, teachers or philosophers was beaten up straight away. The cobbler or the electrician were better off.

And yet the intellectuals have been best able to analyse Auschwitz and bear witness to it.

Afterwards. Afterwards, of course, being an intellectual helps; to give shape to the experience. Auschwitz, after the form of school education I received, turned me into an intellectual. I have become one precisely as a result of the camp experience. Lidia Rolfi, a teacher in Mondoví, comes to mind: sent to Ravensbrück at the age of seventeen for having hidden a partisan, she survived through her will to understand and to fit in, just like me. On her return, she realized that the camp had been her university.'[3]

And how have these forty years changed the man who survived the drowning? Primo Levi is embarrassed to reply.

They have been forty years of life, work and above all of racking my brains to understand.

He picks up the first page of the book with the four lines by Coleridge: 'Since then, at an uncertain hour / that agony returns...'.[4] *He comments on the first verse:*

At an uncertain hour, that is, every now and again...It is not as though I live my life inside that world. Otherwise I would never have written *The Wrench*, I would never have had a family, I would never do many other things that give me pleasure. But it is true, at an uncertain hour, those memories return. I'm a recidivist.

The mark of Auschwitz cannot be erased: in the life of a man, in the history of the world.

Notes

1   'I must make verses of new punishments / and give matter now for Canto Twenty/ of this first canticle – of the drowned', *Inferno*, 20, ll.1–3, adapted from Allen Mandelbaum's translation (Berkeley, London: University of California Press, 1980).
2   Hans Memling (*c*.1435–94), born in Germany, was a religious painter of the Flemish school. Part of his *Last Judgement* (?1467) was used for the cover of the first edition of *The Drowned and the Saved*.
3   Lidia Beccaria Rolfi (1925–96) was the co-author with Anna Maria Bruzzone of *Le donne di Ravensbrück* ('The Women of Ravensbrück') (Turin: Einaudi, 1978) and *L'esile filo della memoria* ('The Thin Thread of Memory') (Turin: Einaudi, 1996).
4   From Coleridge's *Rime of the Ancient Mariner* (1798) which Levi frequently quoted and used in his books as an image for the returning survivor.

Part IV
Literature and Writing

A Mysterious Necessity
(1972)

Piero Bianucci

By profession a chemist, Primo Levi made his name as a writer with two books of autobiographical memoirs of his terrible experience in the Nazi camps: *If This is a Man* and *The Truce*. The first was also adapted into a successful stage version, confirming the importance of Levi's work of testimony. But alongside the Levi that we might call 'civically committed', there is also an equally important 'fantastic' Levi, who draws not on memory but on the imagination. Last year Einaudi published a book of stories under the title *Vizio di forma* which was a rewarding illustration of this other Levi. A writer, then, who is interesting for many different reasons, both because he writes literature as an amateur rather than a 'professional writer', treating it almost as a hobby, and also because his work offers us two such seemingly different directions to follow. So we have come to ask Primo Levi a few questions about the current literary scene as he sees it from his rather unusual perspective.

Setting aside your personal tastes, how would you judge in general the literary criticism you find in newspapers in our country today?

In my opinion, the ideal journalist-critic is someone who can get across his view of a work of literature without inundating you with

From Levi's written reply to questions by Piero Bianucci in 'E' una misteriosa necessità, di tutti i popoli del mondo', *Il nostro tempo*, 20 February 1972.

the waves of his own authority, describing the work itself in as simple and objective a way possible, so that you can think for yourself whether or not it is for you, whether you should overcome your natural inertia and get hold of a copy. To that end, he should obviously try to be impartial, that is, free from any bond of this or that church or camp, but also he should not abandon (and how could he anyway?) his own cultural and political position.

And what does academic criticism offer the cultural debate?

Today in Italy, it seems to me that this debate risks cutting itself off in its high, rarefied atmosphere. As a rule, I don't think it's desirable to separate the academic critic from the journalist-critic. The former has a duty to institute and maintain a dialogue with readers of newspapers and when he does so he must have the humility to set aside his illustrious gown and enter into debate on a level playing field, as it were. There might then be a gap between his views and those of the public, but he shouldn't be shocked by this. He should work at clarifying for himself and for his interlocutors the reasons for the gap and the nature of it, and maybe he should even be prepared to shift his own position.

There has been talk for decades now of a crisis in the novel, of the decline of the novel as literary form. What is your view on this issue?

The novel is valid: and it can still be valid today, besieged as it is by the rising tide of rapid information, written or otherwise (the novel also contains information, of course, but often in subtle and imperceptible forms, unknown to the reader). Each one of us still harbours deep within ourselves an infantile desire to be told stories. Each one of us, in the course of our lives, has periods of holidays or breaks (childhood, illness, retirement), brief gaps, I mean, that a good novel can fill. It doesn't matter if it's a classic or an experimental work, as long as the experiment isn't so extreme as to harm communication, the transmission of facts and images.

Often, when people talk of the crisis in the novel, they refer to the possibility that essays will come to replace narrative as a better form of 'written discourse' for our time and our needs. And there is indeed a boom in factual or essayistic writing these days. How do you judge this phenomenon?

Non-fiction reflects a different need, the need for precise and direct information, whether for utilitarian reasons or simply for a disinterested thirst for culture. Since the world around us is becoming ever more complicated, the level of ideas that a citizen in an industrial civilization requires is growing. This need is satisfied or should be satisfied by the enormous number of books on sale now from humble technical manuals to high-powered specialist tracts.

Many have also predicted a radical crisis in literate culture, which risks being overtaken and almost wholly substituted by a so-called 'culture of the image'. Do you agree that we have reached this historic cultural crossroads?

That there is a rivalry, or better, a convergence between the book and audio-visual media is easy to observe. Our children read less than us, and yet they often know a great deal more than we knew at their age. The phenomenon doesn't worry me unduly, except in one particular aspect. Today in Italy, the publishing business is relatively free, whereas radio and television are state-controlled, offering little in the way of choice. They are prone to becoming (indeed, they often have become) instruments of one side or another.[1] Apart from this specific question, I don't see why we should frown and fret over these news tools, which are often allies, not enemies of the printed word. We all know about the renewed success (even in sales) of half-forgotten books, after the transmission of film or TV adaptations.

Is poetry still a relevant way today for a writer to enter into dialogue with the public?

I don't have any statistics to hand, but it doesn't seem to me that poetry (in print, because poetry is less adaptable to the audio-visual media) is less favoured today than it was in the past. Despite the loss of many traditional links, I note that Quasimodo, Ungaretti and Montale[2] are understood and loved even by young readers, such as primary school students. Nor should this surprise us: poetry has been a mysterious necessity of all epochs and all human civilizations; it is a pregnant language that is both natural and artificial, whose origins are older than those of prose.

Notes

1　In the 1970s, RAI was under close government control, in particular that of the dominant governing party, the Christian Democrats.
2　Salvatore Quasimodo (1901–68), Giuseppe Ungaretti (1888–1970) and Eugenio Montale (1896–1981) are probably the three greatest poets of twentieth-century Italy. Quasimodo and Montale won the Nobel Prize for Literature in 1959 and 1975 respectively.

A Conversation with Primo Levi (1979)

Giuseppe Grassano

For the general public your name is linked to two exemplary texts, If This is a Man *and* The Truce. *How do you react to this labelling? Does it feel reductive today?*

A little, yes. It is no coincidence that in my most recent book, *The Wrench,* I have completely thrown off my role as a witness and ex-deportee. I am not denying anything. I haven't stopped being an ex-deportee or a witness, I still feel that also, and deeply so. But I have no wish to be only that, to be pigeon-holed in some way, cloistered. I see myself as free to write on any theme, just as I don't rule out a return to the theme of the *Lager.* Indeed, I have just such an idea in mind.

In a reality like today's, with its renewed impulse towards destructive violence and the rejection of reason and tolerance,[1] how do you live your experience as a survivor of Auschwitz?

I am sure that today's violence and the other form I experienced have nothing in common. That was state violence and I don't give much credence to the idea that today's violence is state-sponsored. I believe what we are seeing today has many other roots. It is a secondary, even biological product of overcrowding, unrootedness,

Interview published in G. Grassano, *Primo Levi*, Florence: La Nuova Italia, 1979, pp. 3–17.

poor government. I don't believe in a precise plan of violence on the part of our state today. For sure, the state is badly governed, but an intent to foment violence, no. On the other hand, the violence of Auschwitz was planned, by the state. Nevertheless, I think it is healthy for us and especially for the young, to think about that violence. We should all ponder very carefully that when tolerance is missing, and thus reason too, since tolerance and reason coincide, you are on the road to Auschwitz. This seems to me a lesson easily absorbed by the young and one which should be taught to them all.

More than once, critics have identified a thread linking all your books in their defence of the dignity and respect of the human as well as their autobiographical inspiration. After The Periodic Table *and* The Wrench *the underlying nature of the thread seems to me clearer still: it centres on the redemption of work, from the punitive and destructive work of the camps ('Arbeit Macht Frei') to the alienating and despised work of the factory to the vocation of work in the two recent books as a sign of ability and love.*

I would cut the reference you make to 'Arbeit Macht Frei', since that really was not work. It was pure suffering. And not even the biblical suffering of 'by the sweat of your brow you will eat bread'. There it was bread earned for others. The link between cause and effect was completely absent, as was the idea that work sustains you. It was not work, it was like being whipped.

But work can save us: for you in the camp, your work as a chemist became your salvation.

For entirely external reasons. It was a trick to save my skin, just as I could have, I don't know, forged a document or something like that. I didn't experience that as work either. And I ought to clarify one thing here. All of us survivors are, by definition, exceptions, because in the *Lager* you were destined to die. If you did not die it was through some miraculous stroke of luck: you were an exception, a singularity, not generic, totally specific. That stands as a broad generalization. As a chemist I worked in a chemistry lab, I was saved really by the skin of my teeth, through an unpredictable fate. The fate of the majority was quite different, it was to die; and it was to die working. So my work experience cannot carry great weight. My work in the lab, which I did not experience as work, which I tried to sabotage whenever I could . . . although there was no need, since the Russians were at the gates, so in effect I achieved nothing. Even those who reached such positions in the *Lager* system earlier on, the very few who managed to become plumbers, say, or cooks, did not see it as liberating work, or more precisely it was liberating externally but not in any internal sense. It was a form of work with which you did not identify. So I would exclude work in the *Lager*.

That aside, it is true that in my last two books, especially the most recent [*The Wrench*], there is a polemical charge against those who deny what you might call the redeeming power of work. My prime source for this notion of work are the writings of Conrad, who is in fact quoted at the end of *The Wrench*. I've always felt a certain affinity between the career that I ended up in and the apparently very different work of a sea captain: both allow you an immense margin of error. Any form of work that never entails error is beyond the human condition. Repetitive, mechanical work is a case in point, and of course, many are forced into it. But I wanted to talk about something else. Some have asked me, 'why didn't you write a book about a worker on a production line?' But that is not the book I wanted to write. I wanted to describe another human condition: not someone stuck in a repetitive job, as so many are in today's world, but someone who follows an ancient, timeless destiny, who measures himself against the world through his own work, who takes the risk of getting it wrong, who will try and try again an infinity of times until at last he gets it right, finds the answer, hits the target. Mine is precisely an idea of work as destiny, work as the human condition.

This latest book [The Wrench *] has caused some to express reservations: you have been accused of offering an out-of-date morality, or at least of swimming against the tide. But it seems to me you were lucky to publish at the right time, just when certain interpretative schemas of work and other things were being called into question.*

That wasn't luck: I knew exactly what I was doing. I was annoyed, like many others, by the crass position that says 'work is to be rejected!'. If work is rejected, if everyone rejects it, basically we all die of hunger. We need to discuss this. My position does not in any way exclude battles over work. In *The Wrench*, I didn't give Faussone any union background, but I easily could have. And in any case, I worked in a factory and I know that often the best specialists are also good union activists. Often but not always. The one does not exclude the other. I know communist and also Catholic unionists who were fairly hard-nosed in relations with their bosses but who were extremely serious when it came to work.[2] They were like Faussone, living by the rule that if you do a job you do it well.

Let's discuss your work with language. In The Wrench *you experiment in a very original way with language; but if in that book it is a large-scale operation, wouldn't you say that all your earlier books have shown on a smaller scale the same determination to vary the linguistic register, to fit it to character or situation? I am thinking not only of certain parts of* The Truce *or* The Periodic Table *but also of many of the stories of* Storie naturali *and* Vizio di forma, *where you draw on technical, scientific language.*

Several of those stories were written as parodies of scientific papers. But this is no discovery of mine: anyone who tries their hand at writing knows that if all characters spoke the same language they would appear as flat as cardboard cut-outs. You perhaps noticed that in *The Truce* Cesare has a language of his own, but also that I begin to speak his language when I am speaking of him. Wherever there is some indirect discourse referring to Cesare, the language slips towards his. Such a step is essential to keep up a certain concreteness in the writing. When you introduce a character, he must be whole, he must have his own life and also his own language. As you know, a writer of Italian has great difficulty in using direct speech since Italian is not a much spoken language and thus spoken Italian is rather poor as a language. Often dialects of Italian or slang are richer. For this reason, it was quite natural for me to have Faussone speak as he does. It's not an invented form of speech; you find it spoken in the workplace, at least in Piedmont. In the workshops of Lombardy or Campania, they might speak differently, but that's how it is here. It came quite spontaneously to give him that syntactically quite poor but technically extremely precise voice: he talks about what he knows, things whose names he knows. His technical competence is also linguistic.

On several occasions you have declared your commitment to clear writing, linked to your identity as a chemist who writes and who is thus used to scientific clarity, to weighing up and checking results even on the page. Do you agree that in our present world, this position has a certain political value as a rejection of woolly ambiguity, as a defence of the 'civically committed' role of the writer who wants to be understood by others?

Recently I was invited to Milan to the Festival dell'Unità[3] and I took part in a public debate. The public was distracted, it was thinking about the sausages on show more than us. My interlocutor was Paolo Volponi[4] and we discussed this very subject. He disagreed with me. He said that a writer must be like a locomotive for the reader, not running level with him, but a bit ahead. He must tow the reader forward, informing and also forming him. And therefore he can or he must speak a free language, as it comes to him. If he wants and feels the need to speak in an intricate, even abstruse language, he can, indeed he must do so. And the reader must work his way towards the writer. Now, I am against any prescription on writing. My way is my own and I would never dare force it on Volponi, or anyone else. If you write you have to write as you want to write. For myself, I have chosen a path not for any didactic or pedagogical reasons, but for my own internal clarity. I believe that when an idea is clear, it automatically finds expression in clear language. The confusion of styles, used by many of my colleagues as a reflection of confusion of the mind, seems to me off-beam. Many tell me, 'I want to capture the confusion of today's world and so I write confusedly'. I cannot see that that resolves anything, it leaves everything as it is. We know the world is confused and it adds nothing to describe it in a confusing way.

Having said all that, I have to confess that I am a great devotee of some obscure writers. I like Joyce, for example, and it would be complicated to explain why. I think his obscurity is only apparent. With a certain amount of effort I can penetrate it and then it gives me pleasure. Other writers whose style I cannot penetrate remain definitively obscure to me and I run up the white flag. In visual arts too, alongside many honest painters and sculptors, there are some who dishonestly smuggle in empty work under the guise of 'informal' art. The same happens with writers: there are those who, beneath the din of their unhinged, uneven language, are hiding nothing at all. As I was saying earlier, I don't like to lay down laws: you must all do this, you must all write with subject, verb and object. Do as you wish. It just seems to me more civil to write so that the reader, maybe with some effort, can follow you.

The reader.... Which reader? Here another polemic, another big debate, rears its head. Unfortunately there are readers who follow nothing, who don't read or who read only comics. Fine, it is part of the job of a writer to get through to and capture, to win over even these readers. And I can tell you that one of the aims, so to speak, of the bet I made with myself with *The Wrench* was precisely that. A bet I won, because I found out that all forty-six riggers from a Turin factory read it, and what is more, they all read it because it was passed on from one to the next. That gave me a great sense of joy, not because I've saved any souls or anything like that, but because I introduced to the world of the written book people who had never been there before.

Another question: looking over the path your œuvre has taken, apart from noting your double identity as a writer-chemist, there is the issue of the links between literature and science-technology-industry, which has been the subject of heated debates and polemics. What is your position?

Let me repeat once again: I have no wish to lay down laws for anyone. I am perfectly happy to acknowledge that a writer can know absolutely nothing about science and technology and still be highly respectable and important. It can happen and indeed it does happen. Montale, for example, has lived beyond the world of science and technology as far as I know. But I think it would be a good thing if a writer didn't live in an ivory tower, or better in a furrow or length of piping that starts off at Dante and goes as far as 'L'infinito', which he travels along without ever looking out to see the world beyond.[5] If we live in a world suffused with technology and science, it is best not to ignore it, if only because Science with a capital S and Technology with a capital T are formidable sources of inspiration. Apart from the fact of their existence and thus the need to respond to them in some way in writing, in my opinion or at least for me, they are quite formidable stimuli. Anyone today who knows nothing about, say, what astrophysicists are up to, their instruments or even more remarkably their artificial satellites (*Explorer* and the like), is making themselves out of date. Even Kant, to mention a name, had studied astronomy before he began writing. It strikes me as a sort of self-inflicted blindness. It means losing the measure of the universe we live in ... The fact that there are two cultures is harmful from the outset. There should be one single culture: Galileo had one culture, so did Spallanzani and Magalotti.[6] They had no sense or perception of a split. Galileo was a very great writer precisely because he was not a writer at all. He simply wanted to expound what he had seen.

In some of your works, such as The Periodic Table *and* The Wrench, *there is a clear sense of your intent to communicate to a broad public the significance and fascination of science and technology. But there have also been attempts at more complex interpretations, at existential evaluations of this work. To stick with* The Periodic Table, *the reference there to the Great Curve, to 'Hyle',[7] unruly matter that man attempts to tame, seems to suggest that science is simply another form of man's struggle to dominate himself and reality, as in every field of endeavour.*

You put it very well and I can only agree. In a book by Russell, *The Conquest of Happiness,*[8] there is a phrase of that kind, where he says that happiness never comes without effort. For biological reasons, because we are hunters. If we lived in a land of plenty, in which we stayed in bed and food fell from on high, we would probably die or fall sick, at least mentally we would become atrophied and stupid. Practice, measuring oneself against others and against the material world, however tiring and painful it might be, is indispensable. A life without such a measure, and thus without defeat, is unthinkable.

Let's come back to the Conradian concept of life. And bearing in mind your frequent references to authors seen as exemplars in some way – Conrad, but also Dante, Thomas Mann, Rabelais – I would like to ask you which writers and which works are your favourites, which have influenced your writing: readings that have left their mark, in short?

Those you refer to first of all. And then a myriad of others too. I am an eccentric reader. I am reading Proust now, for example, which is rather late. Also I have read a great deal of work-related books which have been just as useful to me as those great writers you cite. To write *The Wrench,* for example, I read a lovely book on bridges which was almost as fundamental as *The Divine Comedy.* But I'm going off the point perhaps, these are more factual documents than books of the sort you're interested in. In general, their authors pay little attention to style and much more to what they are writing, although this does no harm, doesn't worry me at all. On the contrary, I'd say that often you find an extremely lively and concrete style comes out of this need to get things across. Recently I read a book by Spallanzani which I liked very much indeed. He relates how he managed to put slings on toads to help him observe their fertilization. I mentioned Magalotti, too, a moment ago, because I am reading his *Relazione sulla Cina* [Account of China]. It is a short book of around a hundred pages, but it is very beautiful. As is Marco Polo's *Milione.*[9]

Let's talk a little about your relation with critics. Beppe Fenoglio[10] confessed that he was surprised at what critics managed to uncover in his work, but that he was equally surprised at what they managed to miss. Do you share his impression?

I agree. Fenoglio put it marvellously. It's true that, at times, they have often helped me clarify to myself, things about myself, and often they have found things I had no idea I had put in, or rather, that I hadn't put in. A typical case is the polemic that has pursued me for my whole career, the relationship between my first two books and my two books of stories, *Storie naturali* and *Vizio di forma*. The issue is clearer to my readers than to myself. I see relatively little in the latter of the *Lager* revisited, of an attempt to reproduce or to review the world of the *Lager* in the world of today. I don't wholly agree with those who make these links, that alienation in today's world is no different from the alienation of the camps. Try spending some time in a concentration camp . . . I feel the same when I see graffiti on walls saying 'PS=SS'. The Pubblica Sicurezza [Police] may not be pleasant, but the SS were something quite different. Recently I was sent some poems by Sante Notarnicola,[11] and they are rather good poems, but he put in an inscription that rather disturbed me. His dedication read, 'As you can see, the camps are coming back today'. I wrote back saying his poems were good, but that in Auschwitz 10,000 people died every day, whereas today if a single prisoner, political or criminal, dies in state custody, there is a great scandal. And quite rightly so: there should be no such deaths. But only one. That makes a difference. And in Auschwitz no one published books of poems. On the other hand, readers can probably find in my stories contours of the figure of the camp-prisoner that I did not know I had put there. It's probable and in some cases, quite apparent. In 'Versamina' and 'Angelic Butterfly' [*The Sixth Day*], for example, I deliberately set up links with my earlier experiences. In other stories, there may well be such links but that does not mean I intended them. Of course, the experience of the concentration camp was traumatic and trauma stays with you and jumps out even imperceptibly in what you write.

To come closer to more recent works, I wanted to pick up on the polemic over The Wrench *from those who scolded you for having written about work-ing-class experience without being working class yourself?*

In *Lotta continua*[12] I saw a fiercely hostile letter which said 'how dare you talk about the working class condition if you are not a worker? Leave it to us.' That means sealing all our mouths shut.

All in all, do you think the critics have dealt with your work fairly?

Most often, yes. There are good and bad critics, inattentive critics who haven't read all they should have, who have summed up the books and little more. But coming back to the issue we talked about earlier, that is, the two cultures that should be one, I think there has been a failure to pick up on that from most critics, almost all of whom have a humanities background. Someone who did pick up on it with perspicacity was Roberto Vacca, who is an engineer.[13] I liked his review of *The Wrench* more than most others, and I also liked the review by Bruschi, a union man, in [the union magazine] *Battaglie di lavoro* [Work Battles]. That made me happiest of all: it was in the form of a dialogue between a union man and an independent worker. It hit the nail on the head.

Many have underlined – in fact you have done so yourself in black and white in The Periodic Table *and* The Wrench *– your taste for or pleasure in storytelling. My next question is: how are your books born?*

For the most part, they are born as oral stories. Faussone's stories are almost all either adventures that others have narrated to me or adventures that I have attributed to Faussone, to a Faussone. So they are born first in a spoken form. The same goes for *If This is a Man*. I came back from the camp with a narrative impulse that was pathological. I remember very clearly certain train journeys in 1945, just after my return, travelling around Italy to salvage, to put back together, my work prospects. I was looking for a job. And on the train I remember telling my stories to whoever I found myself with. I've quoted Coleridge's 'Ancient Mariner' to describe this, who tells his tale to wedding guests as they arrive and they don't want anything to do with him. Well, I was exactly the same. If you ask me why I wanted to tell the stories, I couldn't answer. Probably it was part of an understandable instinct: I wanted to free myself from them. But often I have thought of Ulysses when he arrives at the Phaeacian court. Tired as he is, he spends the night telling the story of his adventures. All veterans want to narrate what they have done. You know Tibullus: I have always remembered by heart his phrase '*ut mihi potanti possit sua dicere facta miles et in mensa pingere castra mero*' ('so that he can tell me his war exploits, as I am drinking, and draw the encampments on the table in wine').[14] That is what it was like for me. There was no asking why, it was profoundly obvious, evident that I had to do so. I would have suffered if I had been deprived of the pleasure of *'pingere castra mero'*.

That goes for your first two books . . .

But to a lesser extent for the others also. I'd say I am built that way: I like to tell people my stories. And indeed I do tell them, mostly stories that have really happened to me or ones that have been told to me by others. Telling them and retelling them I feel as though I am in line with a millennial dynasty that goes back all the way to the popular storytellers of Africa and Asia. If you ask me why, I'll suggest you talk to a psychoanalyst, because I am not very expert in the roots of being human. I'm not alone: the pleasure of telling stories is shared by many, even if not all. Anyone with the gift of words loves to exercise their gift. No, not quite anyone, I know people who don't tell stories at all, who live differently, who don't know the liberating joy of telling a story.

This pleasure of storytelling goes together, I would say, with a feeling of equilibrium, of optimism. Antonicelli[15] noticed this even in If This is a Man, *a diary of dreadful events, but one that manages to transmit a desire for life.*

It's true. In part, that's just down to my nature – I was born an optimist – but in part, it is a deliberate choice. I think it would do a disservice to the reader or humanity or the totality of those who read a book to inject doses of pessimism. To be a pessimist essentially means to throw up your hands and say, let's just let everything fall into ruin. Since there is a very real risk of ruin, the only remedy is to roll up our sleeves. And if we are going to do something, to defend ourselves from some enemy, we need to be optimists, otherwise we wouldn't take up arms in the first place. And there is a battle to be fought. You cannot go to war convinced that you're going to lose, and this is a case of going to war. This attitude of mine comes from my roots and isn't thought out or deliberated: it's a constitutional optimism. But I have also rationalized it, I believe there is a collective advantage in putting across a message that is not defeatist. Of course it isn't always easy to be an optimist. You need a great deal of care and judgement, but wherever possible, I think there is a duty to be so.

What about future projects? We are used to sudden changes of direction from you, to your 'skidding off' in different directions, as you put it . . .

It's true that I've skidded this way and that and I'll carry on doing so precisely because I'm something of a centaur. I am a 'liceo' student with a humanistic education, but also a chemist and an ex-deportee. So I have at least three different sources for my writing. If we put my studies and literature on one side together, then there's the experience of Auschwitz. Lidia Rolfi says that the camps were her university and I picked up this comment of hers. For me too, Auschwitz was a second university. And lastly, there's my career, a very concrete career as a factory chemist. I have no desire to abandon any one of these three experiences. Now there's a fourth experience to be added to them, if you like, the experience of being a writer, of having managed to transmit ideas, information, news, accounts of events, by way of the written word. This is a fourth experience that comes on top of and is a summation of all the other three and that in its turn could be the source of some other thing. Some trace of this desire to tell stories, some theorizing on how things get narrated has made its way into *The Wrench*.

But now what will come next? Giovanni Raboni spoke of the experimentalism of The Wrench. *Where will that go now?*

I don't know. I don't think I'll write a second *The Wrench*. Rather I am thinking . . ., I'm thinking . . .: well, I feel in my stomach, in my guts, something that I haven't quite digested, connected to the theme of the *Lager* seen again from thirty-five years' distance. After all the polemic about the identification between victim and oppressor, the theme of guilt, the extreme ambiguity of that place, the grey band that separated the oppressed from the oppressors. I've published a number of short stories in *La Stampa* and all of them have these themes in mind. I don't know yet if I'll go back to these stories and rework them, or if I'll write essays or whatever.[16] I'd like to talk about a theme which is already there in *If This is a Man* and in *The Truce* and which I've found also in Manzoni, when Renzo Tramaglino threatens don Abbondio with a knife.[17] Manzoni observes that the oppressor, don Rodrigo, is also responsible for the minor acts of oppression carried out by his victims. It's a theme I recognize all too well. It is a stupid mistake to see all the demons on one side and all the saints on the other. It wasn't like that at all. The saints, the oppressed, were

more or less forced into compromises, sometimes very grave compromises, which it is very hard indeed to judge. I am no jurist and I
think these things are extremely difficult to decide on. But they
should be judged, and above all we should be aware of them and
not ignorant. To divide into black and white means not to know
human nature. It's a mistake, it is useful only for celebrations. Take
German political prisoners, for example: how can we judge people
who spent ten years in the camps? Inevitably, some of them ended up
making tacit compromises with the Nazis. Some were truly strong
and held out until the end, but they were extremely few in number.
Many acted otherwise: they accepted jobs, for example, they beat up
those beneath them. Difficult to judge even that, since beatings of
certain kinds, some slaps and punches, were at heart a sort of language: there was no other available. What else could you do to force
someone in your command into a certain action, maybe even an
action beneficial to that person? I had to beat him, otherwise he
wouldn't understand. We are dealing with extremes . . .

You referred earlier to short stories in La Stampa. *Some derive from your
camp experiences but others are light-hearted, fantastic, surreal stories. Are
the latter just 'breaks' for you?*

They are 'breaks'. If I think of a story that seems fun or good or useful
in some way, but even if it isn't useful, it could just be like going for a
ride, why shouldn't I write it? I'm not so severe with myself as to write
always and only improving pieces.

And the poems that sometimes appear in La Stampa, *what value, what
significance do they have?*

In my view, their value is minimal. My natural state is that of not
writing poetry, but every now and then I get this curious infection,
like an exanthematic illness that gives you a *rash*.[18] I'd never write
poetry methodically. I have on occasion written five or six in the space
of two or three days, such as those at the start of *L'osteria di Brema*
[The Inn at Brema].[19] It is happening now for I don't know what
reason, perhaps because I have more free time, but it is quite out of
my control. At some point you discover the kernel of a poem within
you, the first line or one line, then the rest follows. Sometimes it
works, other times I throw them away, but it's a phenomenon I don't
understand, that I don't know about or know how to think about,

whose mechanics I reject. It's not part of my world. My world is one of thinking about something, developing it almost...like a rigger, yes, building it up bit by bit. The other method of producing by way of flashes of inspiration amazes me. And indeed, I've written maybe thirty poems in forty years.

Are you someone who finds it easy to write, who moves forward smoothly once you've found your direction?

As a rule, yes. Writing *If This is a Man* came extremely easily to me. I've said as much: I wrote it on the train, in trams, in the lab. The same for *The Truce*, although that proceeded with great regularity, one chapter a month. But always after dinner, because I had my job at the factory. Even my short stories came with some facility. As for my latest book, *The Wrench*, I found that very easy to write too. I still have the manuscript: typed straight out with hardly a correction. It seemed very easy to write it that way, as if I was getting rid of all the constraints of being a literary writer. It really felt as though I was recording with a tape recorder what someone else was telling me out loud.

And yet of all your books this is the one that most openly resorts to the fiction of writing, that makes up stories. You've turned into a 'counterfeiter' as you yourself have put it.

This problem of being a counterfeiter, of feeling false, worries me. Often I ask myself questions. For example, this subject that I want to deal with, revisiting the *Lager*, I would have to talk about events seen thirty-five years ago. But am I sure they all happened and am I obliged to tell them exactly as they were? Couldn't I, for example, change them a little to serve my purpose, or even invent them from scratch? There's a clear difference between telling stories you claim are true, demanding to be believed to the letter, and telling stories like Boccaccio, for another purpose, not to record facts but for pleasure or edification, if you like? These are questions I haven't resolved yet. I'm still thinking about them.

Notes

1   The interviewer's specific reference here is probably to the wave of political violence and terrorism, the so-called 'years of lead', that dogged Italy throughout the 1970s.
2   The three main union organizations in Italy – CGIL, CISL and UIL – have traditionally been linked with political forces, respectively the communists, the Catholic Christian Democrats and others.
3   The Festival or Feste dell'Unità were cultural fairs sponsored by the Italian Communist Party (PCI) and its newspaper, *L'Unità*, in cities throughout Italy.
4   Paolo Volponi (1924–94) was an important writer and intellectual, particularly associated with novels about modern industrial society.
5   'L'infinito' is the most famous lyric poem by the most important Italian poet of the early nineteenth century, Giacomo Leopardi (1798–1837).
6   Lorenzo Magalotti (1637–1712) was a writer of both scientific and travel literature; Lazzaro Spallanzani (1729–99) was one of the founders of modern biology and wrote travel literature also. Galileo Galilei (1564–1642) 'was not only the founder of modern science, but also a remarkably talented man of letters' (*Cambridge Companion to Italian Literature*, Cambridge: Cambridge University Press, 1996, p. 316).
7   The 'Great Curve' is a reference to a mysterious allegorical figure in Ibsen's *Peer Gynt* (1867), also known as the Great Boyg, who is typically taken to represent all that has been in the world. 'Hyle' is the Greek term for matter. Levi refers to both in *The Periodic Table*, in the chapter 'Chromium'.
8   Bertrand Russell, *The Conquest of Happiness* (London: Allen and Unwin, 1930). Levi included an extract from Russell's book in *La ricerca delle radici*.
9   Marco Polo (1254–1324) wrote his account of his oriental travels in 1298 from prison in Genoa. They are commonly known as the *Milione*. An extract is in *La ricerca delle radici*.
10   Beppe Fenoglio (1922–63) was an important postwar Italian writer, especially renowned for narrative about the anti-Fascist Resistance in 1943–5 in which he took part. He was Piedmontese, like Levi.
11   Sante Notarnicola was a criminal who became active in prisoners' revolts and the movement for prisoners' rights in the 1970s.
12   *Lotta continua* [continual struggle] was both an extreme-left group of this period and also the daily newspaper of that movement.
13   Robert Vacca is a scientific writer and speculator on the future whom Levi cites frequently and obviously admired.
14   From Tibullus's elegy 1.10, 'Quis fuit horrendos', ll.31–2. See Tibullus *Poems* (Harmondsworth: Penguin, 1972).

15 Franco Antonicelli was responsible for the original publication (and title) of *If This is a Man* in 1947, through his small publishing house, De Silva.

16 Here Levi is beginning to plan the writing of *The Drowned and the Saved*.

17 Alessandro Manzoni (1785–1873) was the author of the most important novel in Italian, *I promessi sposi* (*The Betrothed*, 1840–42; London: J. M. Dent, 1997). At the outset, the hero, Renzo Tramaglino, is prevented from marrying his fiancée when the lustful local baron, don Rodrigo, threatens the cowardly priest don Abbondio who is to marry them.

18 In English in the original.

19 *L'osteria di Brema* (Milan: Scheiwiller, 1975) was Levi's first, small book of poems. Its poems were later included in the larger collection *Ad ora incerta* (At An Uncertain Hour) (Milan: Garzanti, 1984).

Interview for a Dissertation (1981)

Paola Valabrega

Why does geographical denotation play such a dominant role in your work?

I'm not sure I accept the premise of the question. In my first two books [*If This is a Man* and *The Truce*] it is fundamental because they are both factual. Indeed, I drove Einaudi mad over the map in the school edition of *The Truce*. It's true, I could have left it out, but it reflected a schema in my mind. When I read a book I like to have as much data as possible about Time and Space. If dates or places are missing, I feel frustrated and so, in revenge, I put in as many and as precise details as I could (it felt crucial to me, after all those two books are testimonies and a testimony that has no 'where' and 'when' is not worth much) and I asked the publisher to put the map in to show how absurd the journey was: without the map it wouldn't have seemed absurd.

In the two books of short stories, geography plays a less prominent role, or it is there as a fictional determinant, for that same personal impulse of mine. In *The Wrench*, the geography returns, but here too it seemed essential for the book to define the main character and to show how he inhabits the five continents of the world and moves between them with great ease.

From an Interview with Paola Valabrega in February 1981, carried out as part of her MA degree dissertation, later published as 'Conversazione con Paola Valabrega' in Marco Belpoliti (ed.), *Primo Levi* (Riga 13 / Marcos y Marcos: Milan, 1997), pp. 74–82.

And what about the fantastic, mythical, legendary geography, for example in the stories 'Lead' and 'Mercury' [The Periodic Table] and others?

The answer would be the same, these too come out of my mental schema, my sense that any story without a place is truncated, handicapped. It's a need of mine when I read, so I try to satisfy it when I write.

Your preferred landscapes seem to be mountains, forests, woods... how important are other sites – the sea, water in general?

The reason is simple: I've been in the mountains a good deal and only rarely to the sea. I hardly know the sea at all. When I want to include maritime details I have to look them up in books, rather than draw on my own experience, which is almost nil in this case. On the other hand, as a free citizen I've seen many mountains, both as a climber and a tourist, and then my great journey as a prisoner crossed through vast forests, a shocking sight for an Italian. As to whether there are some deeper meanings to these landscapes I wouldn't know.

Water does recur often in your work: there's a story called 'Ottima è l'acqua' ['Excellent is The Water', The Sixth Day].

Yes, but that is a very special water, it's chemical water, contaminated water. It could well be that there's some Freudian business here too: I've never been in analysis myself.

Turin: how is the city reflected in your work and what other cities are important?

Here, too, it's a question of fact. I've always lived in Turin, with the exception of a year spent in Milan during the war. The third city on my list would be Katowice, where I stayed before setting out on the journey of *The Truce*, so, strangely, that horrendous mining city would have to come third in terms of length of stay.

So Turin comes quite naturally to me as a point of reference. In any case, I have nothing to compare it to, not having lived for any time anywhere else. I find it hard to describe urban settings other than Turin, out of pure ignorance, out of lack of input.

Moving on from questions of Space to Time, what is your conception of time? Contemplative or end-focused?

Not contemplative. End-focused, like any writer, I'd say. But as well as this, there's a biological question of time that concerns me considerably, which I often come back to: time as subjective perception, as 'inner' time. I've written somewhere, more than once, that subjective time works like an accordion, that is, it has no precise mode of measurement. Often, at the age of twenty, time seems much longer because you can do so many things and think of so many ideas, whereas later time seems to shrink ever more, the days seem shorter and shorter.

Perhaps the most fundamental experience of this notion is in *If This is a Man*, one shared by many prison companions I know, and also by normal prison inmates not in the *Lager*. Looking back on that time, absurd as it may appear now, the days seemed very long but the years extremely short. It was an eternity to reach the end of a day but as soon as it was over, the memory began to fade or shrink because very little actually happened, every day was the same as the last, it was hard to distinguish in your memory one day from the next. I'd say this is the aspect of time that I've written about with most precision.

I've noticed a certain haste, a certain anxiety in the characters in your short stories (in Vizio di forma *and* Storie naturali, *stories such as 'Il Versific-atore' ['The Versifier', not included in* The Sixth Day] *and 'I procacciat-ori di affari' ['The Hard-Sellers']). What does this haste represent?*

You're right. But I don't know the reason. Let me suggest a possible explanation. I wrote all those stories whilst I was working in a factory and I was in a hurry. I was in a hurry because factory life – in a serious factory like mine – consists in always having too many things to do. And on top of this there was my own private hurry, because I was writing these pieces not in work hours but in my own time. So maybe it reflects a haste of my own, which was a constant factor.

Do you think that the weather reflects the state of mind of your characters?

I can tell you that I've never made any effort in that direction. I have never knowingly distorted the weather to *match*,[1] to fit the state of mind of my characters. If I've ever done it unknowingly, well, you can't talk about what is unknown. Writing is not an activity that takes place in broad daylight. In the preface to my 'personal anthology' that is about to come out I've written something about this: that the journey from mind to paper goes not only via the hand but via long detours through who knows which other organs.

Let's move on to characters. It strikes me that in your physical descriptions certain details have great weight, for example hands; and that physique, the myth of classical beauty, is neither deformed nor perfectly formed but rather ironized. Why?

Again, I can try and suggest a tentative explanation. I have never been handsome and as a child I fretted about this (someone had told me I was ugly). From the age of eight to twelve I was really rather tormented by it. Perhaps some of the *Storie naturali* reflect this ('La misura della bellezza' ['The Measure of Beauty'] for example), since everything there is ironized, including the beauty myth: it's all a quiet debunking. I'm sure my childhood worries about beauty had some influence.

As for hands, it isn't always intentional when the manual and the practical are to the fore; but with Faussone, for example, it was deliberate.

The same motif recurs in The Truce *and in* The Periodic Table, *for example in the 'calloused' hands of Sandro Delmastro or the 'able' hands of Henek in* The Truce . . .

I don't think they're of primary importance. I do remember that when I read Sherlock Holmes as a boy, I was struck by how much Holmes could glean from characters' hands. In some sense, we answer for our own hands: they tell us more than a face. And the rest of the body is unseen: only our face and hands are visible.

Hands speak more, it's nothing to do with the subconscious, it's rational. You don't need to be Sherlock Holmes to learn a lot about a character from their hands – how manicured they are, how treated, the difference between left and right, the state of the nails. So it's useful to describe people's hands, on quite an open level, as a guide for the reader.

How do you explain the predominance of animal reality, and in particular your preference for insects, in your work?

This certainly is out in the open. I have a sort of unrequited love for biology and zoology. I've been a chemist but I have always read popular books on animals. But is there some reason for these things, is it decipherable?

I know I have often used animals as terms of reference, that is, describing a character by comparing him to one or more animals: I remember, for example, comparing the Greek (in *The Truce*) to a preying fish or a night bird. It comes quite naturally to me, but there's also a cultural influence here, one I've written about, even theorized about, in *La Stampa* in an article called 'The Writer and Animals'. As far back as the 1940s, I read an essay by Huxley, Aldous Huxley, a writer born into a dynasty of zoologists and biologists (his brother, grandfather and great-grandfather were all famous physiologists and biologists).[2] The essay, which I liked a lot, begins something like this: a boy came to me and said I want to be a writer, where should I begin? Huxley answers the boy: buy yourself a couple of cats and watch them. Then Huxley gives an amusing description of what the female cat does when the male returns from a foray on the roofs, and he concludes that the cats are useful examples because they are like us but with no lid, they have no inhibitions. The female, when she sees the male come back all bruised and tired, dirty, scratches at him from head to tail, rather than making a scene. Then Huxley described a cat playing with her kittens and I was especially struck by this, I even brazenly borrowed it myself. I don't keep cats, but it's as if I did. I take great pleasure in finding cross-references between human and animal behaviour. I've read Lorenz[3] and I've found his work worthy in this and many other respects. It relates to an extremely important issue that concerns me: how much of the animal is there in us, how much of the animal was there in the Nazis? I still think that one of the roots of Nazism was zoological. Lorenz describes what happens to a rat of one tribe who is introduced into another tribe's territory and it makes your blood run cold: it is the gas chambers in embryonic form.

Turning now to human relationships (friendship, family relations, love, professional relationships): when you write about families, I've noticed that you concentrate more on the father–son than on the mother–son relationship. What is the reason for this?

The reason is very simple. My mother is still alive, you can hear her walking around, and you don't write about the living.

As for friendship, it is clearly a very important bond for you.

Yes, it is.

Almost more important than sentimental bonds, or relations between a man and a woman?

For this, too, the explanation is one of discretion: I prefer to keep private my sentimental relations for reasons of decency, discretion and reserve. Friendship is less delicate.

You often ironize love or described it 'scientifically': is this for the same reason?

Yes, I'd say so.

The motif of work as a skill, a 'travail bien fait' recurs in your writing. What role does this play?

In part it's based on my own experience, because I had a job I liked, as a chemist and another job I liked as a writer. So I did both well, despite a common and violently theorized notion that abounded in 1968 and after, that work must be unpleasant by definition, a punishment. *The Wrench* has its origins in this, in essence, in my disagreement with the extremist thesis that work is the great enemy. It does not have to be, at times it is, of course, but it is not inevitable. You can do a lot to stop work being punitive: not everything is society's fault.

Do you see manual work as a contrast to bookish, scholastic abstraction?

Yes, I do. This also reflects an unease I felt and described in *The Periodic Table*, the unease with *liceo* or *ginnasio* [pre-*liceo*] culture (even if at the *ginnasio* it's still embryonic). At the 'liceo' I was sensitive to the lack of practical work, as were my friends at the time (who are still my friends today – I'm loyal in my friendships). We suffered from its absence. Then and indeed still now, there was no serious manual labour, no one even thought of it. The chapter 'Hydrogen' in *The Periodic Table* is fairly representative of this attitude, that is, we had to go off and find for ourselves manual, practical labour, the challenge of the physical world. Otherwise we only came across it in incomprehensible Greek terms in our philosophy lessons, as *hyle*. It left me hungry for more, feeling completely empty. Together with that group of friends – some of whom are still together, others have drifted away – I felt a quite specific and continual need to experience with my own senses the sheer presence of matter.

On the problem of communication, I see two levels at work, one which is universal, natural and instinctive and another which is human and social and which creates incommunicability, the tower of Babel, the confusion of tongues. Do you agree?

Yes, but the two levels are complementary. One of the central experiences of the *Lager* for me was the failure of communication and I have been surprised not to find it in other accounts (I read a lot on the camps). I have found everything I described myself (the hunger, the cold, the blows, the fear, the death, the illness, etc) except for this topos of the failure of communication. I think there are two reasons for this: the first is my own personal nature as one who needs to communicate constantly, who suffers if he cannot communicate. I need to speak and to write, to have two-way communication if possible, but also one-way as when you write, and there, in the camps, I had neither. The second reason was the particularly difficult conditions of Italian prisoners in the camps. All the others had better linguistic tools than us. The Italian prisoners almost all died at once, for lack of communication. It's a lacerating fact that I haven't seen in other accounts, but it was clear to see: not understanding and not being understood meant an early death. It was a frightful handicap that I felt and that other Italians felt with me, and it was specific to us, only the Greeks were equally disarmed (but by the time I arrived there were very few Greeks left, and those that were left were those who knew how to get by). When I arrived in Auschwitz, the Italians were the laughing stock of the camp, they called them 'two-left-hands', they were intellectuals and they spoke neither German nor Yiddish nor Polish and so they were clumsy, 'intellectuals', although in inverted commas, because what sort of intellectual cannot even make himself understood? The other prisoners, and not only the SS and the Kapos, mocked the Italians because they were all lawyers and doctors, unable to handle a shovel and also unable to talk. They were bugbears, scarecrows.

    This is one of the themes of *If This is a Man* that perhaps I should have dwelt on more. I've often felt I wanted to talk more of it, in another arena, about the wasteful use people make nowadays of the term 'incommunicability', when you think of what true lack of communication is. If you go abroad today, for tourism, work or whatever else, you are ready, you know you'll find partners who perhaps don't speak Italian, French or English, but who are willing, and some common linguistic terrain emerges. In the camps, it was total deprivation. I studied German in the *Lager* to survive: I paid for lessons with bread, from that same Pikolo of the 'Canto of Ulysses' chapter.

In the stories in Storie naturali *and* Vizio di forma, *the Rousseauesque link between nature and civilization seems important.*

I see this as largely ironic too. Of course, it's one of today's great questions. I'm no puritan ecologist, I don't think I give that impression or at most only as a metaphor.

I noticed, for example, in the stories 'Versamina' and 'Verso occidente' [*'Westward', both in* The Sixth Day], *a reversal of natural instinct, an unnaturalness derived, in my view, from that same opposition between nature and civilization.*

I'm not sure. As far as I am aware, I am at home in nature, I'd like to live like my friend Mario Rigoni Stern.[4] I envy him when I see him, but I don't dislike living in the city, I'm an urban animal, domesticated. The theme may well emerge, perhaps not quite spontaneously, don't imagine it comes from deep within. Perhaps it's a sop to current debates on the return to nature, on urban contamination.

Another problem that recurs frequently in your narrative is that of hunger. Should we see it as a symbol of a degenerate human condition deriving from the Lager *experience (for example in 'Procacciatori d'affari'* ['The Hard-Sellers'] *and 'La nutrice'* ['The Nurse'])?

It's certainly an allusion, part of my own retrospective vision. But not exclusively so: besides my own experience of hunger, you only have to read the newspapers to know that a third of the world's population is undernourished. I don't think you have to have been in Auschwitz to be aware of the problem of hunger, so I don't see it as something particular to me. Perhaps I give it a certain extra weight, but not much.

Moving on now to the theme of death: in If This is a Man, *death is always violent, whereas in* Storie naturali *it can be an existential and philosophical choice. What are your thoughts on this?*

Many years divide the two books. Although neither contains a mystical or religious conception of death. I'm not very expert on these things, I've never been religious, let alone a mystic. Not even in Auschwitz. I'm perfectly happy to admit that I'm a 'deserter': every alert person should ponder these problems, but I prefer to worry about other things. To put it in somewhat polemical terms, let's say I'm not interested in the theme of death, I prefer to think of matters of life.

What do you mean by the term 'destiny', which occurs frequently in your books?

Destiny is an ambiguous term. You could read it deterministically, as what is written, prescribed, marked out in advance; or non-deterministically, as the unexpected that awaits, the unwritten that you will encounter. I don't see one of these two meanings as right and the other as wrong, but I don't have much faith in written destiny and in this I think I'm passively in line with modern thinking. Today, determinists are few and far between. We have something of the determinist in our blood, however, especially chemists and physicists who are used to being able to predict phenomena and who are rather shocked and annoyed when they cannot predict their own actions or those of their lab colleagues. And yet it happens, it happens all the time that we cannot predict what Germany, Japan or the Soviet Union will do in five years' time, nor even what your sister, your brother, your wife will do in five minutes' times, and this really is shocking. But that's how it is. There is an inevitable gap between our ability to predict physical phenomena and to exploit or tame them, and our inability to predict human behaviour, both individual and collective.

What is your attitude to religion in general and to Judaism in particular?

My attitude is one of respect for believers but of substantial indifference at a personal level. I would never even think of signing up to any religion, it's not a need I feel. Not that I am always happy with what I do or have done, but I remember very clearly the moment during the October selection, described in *If This is a Man*, when it came to my turn and I felt the impulse to pray. Then, I thought to myself, the prayer would be blasphemous, to turn to God only when I needed him, and I desisted. I censored myself.

Another important theme is memory. What is the value of memory for you? Is it always ethical or can it also be aesthetic?

You're right that it's a subject close to my heart. I see memory as a gift but also as a duty. We ought to cultivate our memories, we should not let them go to ruin.

Now, I am sixty-two years old and at sixty-two your memory deteriorates quite noticeably, just as you lose the strength in your muscles and your eyesight. The third age begins with memory. It could be that in my most recent writing this fact comes through, this concern not to let one's own memories fade, not to lose the ability to store away new memories.

And then there is also, as you say, an aesthetic value to memory. The pleasure of recall is real, and like many other pleasures, it too diminishes with age, you have to make an effort not to let it wilt too much.

There is something approaching a myth of the Primo Levi who indignantly refuses to hate the Nazis. To what extent can hatred be rationalized?

You're right, there really is a myth. It's a question that obsesses me. I don't know if you've seen the school edition of *If This is a Man*. At times, I am almost ashamed not to feel hatred, it seems compulsory, that it's monstrous not to be able to mobilize in the service of hatred. But that is the way things are with me, it's true, it's a failing of mine, a psychological lacuna, if you like. It was already part of me (perhaps this will help you) when I was at school: I was already legendary as Primo Levi, the one who never loses his temper. My Christian friends at school, at the time of the Race Laws, had spotted this and would gently reproach me for it. I could be indignant, but I had no access to more noisy reactions. I hardly ever lose control. Hatred *per se*, as I've written and as I ask again here, what end does it serve? It gets confused with a desire for justice, but they are two different things. On its own it is ungovernable, it can cause great harm. I said that paradoxically I am sometimes ashamed not to be able to hate, but in fact I'm quite happy not to.

On the issue of cultural influences on your work, I've found a few references to cinema, very few indeed to painting, and none at all to classical music. On the other hand, there is extensive reference to and quotation from literary texts.

Let me reply by reading you an extract from my next book, *Personal Anthology*:[5] 'Thirty authors dug up from thirty centuries of literary works, just a drop in the ocean. Many omissions are down to limits of space, to my own excessive specialization, to the clear conviction that some of my preferences are pathological, mere whims, a craze perhaps and wholly unjustifiable, untransmittable. Other omissions are more serious, but they are a product of my own deafness or lack of sensibility or some emotional block that I'm well aware of and cannot hide. Enmities are as inexplicable as friendships and I confess that I read Balzac and Dostoevsky out of duty, late in life, with some struggle and little profit. Other texts, especially poetry, I have omitted for the opposite reason. I did not feel it right to include foreign writers I hold dear who write in languages I know – such as Bellow, Lewis Carroll and Heine – because the existing translations seemed reductive to me, and I was not up to providing my own. And for those in languages I do not know, such as the Greek poets, I was too aware of the deceptions that translations can hide. In other cases, there must also have been a threshold point, a question of my overcoming an obstacle or a barrier at the level of language and style after which the terrain would have been easier. I failed to take that step out of laziness, prejudice or lack of time. If I had made the effort, I would perhaps have made a new friend, have added a new province to my territory and a wondrous one at that, since every unexplored land is by definition wondrous. I must confess my guilt: I prefer to stick to the tried and tested, to make a hole and then nibble away at it, perhaps for an entire lifetime, like woodworms when they find a piece of wood to their taste. Finally, of course, there are the gaps, some of them quite large, bottomless pits, voids in my self-taught, imbalanced, partisan, Sunday-afternoon culture, with violent flaws: no music, no visual arts, little or nothing of the sentimental. Well, I cannot pretend to be someone I am not.'

There, that seems to answer your question. I studied at a difficult time when the choices of today were simply not available. Reading an American book, for example, was quite rare, there were some but only a very few.

On painting, I confess that still today I am a terrible 'looker': no one taught me how to and it does not come naturally.

Music I did once understand quite well, but then I let it rust because of pressure of time. I'd like to go back to it now, but I must say, I feel I'm wasting time whenever I put a record on.

In the area of science-fiction writing have you been influenced by any particular authors?

Not particularly. I haven't read that much and I am not really a science-fiction fanatic. I don't see myself as a fan either as writer or reader. On the whole I think it's second-division literature, with some exceptions in the first division. But nowadays it's lost much of its quality.

Notes

1   In English in the original.
2   Levi is referring to his article 'Romanzi dettati dai grilli' ('Novels Dictated by Crickets'), *La Stampa*, 16 November 1979, later in *L'altrui mestiere* (*Other People's Trades*, 1985). Aldous Huxley's brother was the biologist Julian Huxley (1887–1975), his grandfather T. H. Huxley (1825–90), the natural scientist, public thinker and friend of Darwin. His best-known great-grandfather was not a scientist, but the educationalist headmaster of rugby school, Dr Thomas Arnold (1795–1842), himself father of the writer Matthew Arnold (1822–88). Levi might have had in mind, as the third scientist of the family, Aldous's half-brother, the Nobel-prizewinning physiologist, Andrew Huxley.
3   Konrad Lorenz (1903–89) was an Austrian zoologist and founder of the field of ethology. He won the 1973 Nobel Prize for Physiology or Medicine.
4   Mario Rigoni Stern (1921–) was a soldier on the Russian front in the 1940s and author of war and nature novels.
5   Levi is clearly reading from the preface to *La ricerca delle radici*, before the book acquired its final form and title.

Encounter with Primo Levi (1981)

Graziella Granà

In an amicable setting, at the end of a bright afternoon, Primo Levi arrives on time, shakes my hand, smiles and waits. We don't waste time on courtesies. I ask him not for an interview but for a long, friendly conversation. He's happy to agree.

Are your characters always completely true, or have they been reshaped by your inner vision?

I don't think any character is either wholly true or wholly invented. However much a writer struggles to be objective – even a writer of history or historical novels – he always leaves his own mark and every character is distorted in some way as a result. Conversely, if you set out to invent a character from scratch, to make a montage, you cannot help but draw on your own experiences, your own previous human contacts and so in both cases the character is a hybrid.

As for me, I've written two declaredly autobiographical books, with a large number of figures whom I tried to portray as they were, but I have no doubt that I reshaped them, even unconsciously. Indeed, the people themselves who have survived and read my books sometimes protest, usually very courteously, that they are not as I have described them, that they never said what I claimed they had said or don't have the character I gave them: they could be right...

From 'Incontro con Primo Levi', *Controcampo*, June 1981. The final part of the interview, where the conversation moves on to non-literary issues, is omitted.

Or they think they don't have...

In any case, the question is a Pirandellian one.[1] What is character? Is it how you see yourself or how others see you? Alteration, distortion are inevitable, part of human nature.

The muted sound of the traffic filters up from the street. As we talk, a grandfather clock accompanies us. Of course we are always the usual trio: who we are, who we think we are and who others see.

In my latest book, *The Wrench*, for example, I took it upon myself to invent the protagonist. In practice, I ended up stitching together fragments of people I had met. In intention he was my own creation – although the name isn't so relevant, I think, ... even if I've been told that I called him Faussone because he is false, I don't think... [*he laughs*].

At a subconscious level, where anything can happen, it may be...but I don't think so. I tried to build him up from scratch and in the end I took Tom's baldness, Dick's turn of phrase and Harry's adventures and a character as complex as any other was born.

So the aunts on via Lagrange [in The Wrench*]...?*

They really don't exist, but they, too, are an amalgam of other aunts. I confess that in this instance I consciously tried to cheat my reader, that is, not only to invent a character but also to paint it in *trompe-l'œil*, to trick the reader. And for the most part it worked.

It worked completely, I'd say. The Piedmontese Italian of Faussone, a language you don't hear any more, is extraordinary.

That's true in Turin, but if you go to Lanzo [outside Turin] you'll still find it.

I was laughing out loud at some of the phrases I had forgotten.

I'm grateful for that, because that's exactly what I wanted, to make people laugh.

At the end of The Truce, *you write that when you had his permission, you would say more about the 'character' Cesare and indeed you recently published an article about him in* La Stampa.[2] *Is Cesare really as you describe him in the book and the article?*

Yes, that article for *La Stampa* has its own little story behind it. Before writing it, I went to Rome to talk to Cesare and to compare his memories with my own. Or rather his story and my memory of his earlier story – of thirty years ago. They were both rather faded, blurred at the edges. So Cesare and I agreed as best we could and I reconstructed it. Afterwards I sent him a copy of the article. Cesare hasn't replied, but I don't think he's upset because he never replies. He is cut off from these things, he's made another personality for himself – which is understandable, no one can live an entire life as Cesare (which isn't his real name, anyway). He returned to Rome, gave up his roving, picaresque life of smuggling and cheating on the weight and cost of what he was selling. He found himself a normal job, got married, had children. So I have disrupted his new life a little, I know. That's why I chose not to use his real name. If I go to Rome, I'll find out what he feels about it, but I'm fairly sure that he won't be wholly pleased. It's understandable. A person who becomes a character – positive or negative, makes no difference – always suffers a little.

Because he sees himself, perhaps.

Because he sees himself and because he sees how others see him.

What effect does it have to meet people who were first of all acquaintances and friends and then became your and our 'characters'?

As I was saying, I usually find in them a certain sense of unease; and the unease is transmitted to me, because I begin to feel pangs of guilt at having used them. Some, not all, are quite sensitive about this minor violation, I see it in them. I should say that there aren't very many of my characters who put me in this position: only very few of them survived, of course, many are unrecognizable (I changed names, places of birth, even nationality), so the violation is no longer there. But even when I've tried to build up around a real figure a character who is more positive, fuller, better, more beautiful, even then at times I've felt some resistance. For example, perhaps you remember the chapter 'Iron' in *The Periodic Table*, which is about my school-friend and later Resistance fighter Sandro Delmastro. I tried to express my thoughts about him, that he was a truly exceptional man, in his courage, his consistency, his self-belief, his role as a catalyst for the growth of others. I described him in these terms and many approved, but not his nephews – born a few years before his death – who called me up to take me to task quite fiercely.

Do you think that writing autobiographically represents a constraint for an author?

It's almost impossible not to be autobiographical, even if in subterranean ways, unbeknownst to yourself. How can you get away from your own perceptions?

Can you write all your life in an autobiographical key?

Yes. If your life is very rich, very full. And even the life of a housewife can be full. You have to know how to live life to the full, otherwise you risk becoming repetitive, repeating other people's lives.

Or you risk having nothing new to say, having nothing to risk.

Then you stop writing. As you know, there are illustrious examples of people who have written exclusively about themselves from birth to death (or literary death at least).

Has it been or is it difficult for you to overcome your reserve or modesty to envisage that what you write today about yourself will be printed, will become public knowledge tomorrow?

No, I must say it isn't, I don't suffer from that sort of modesty...so, no, I don't feel laid bare, so to speak. I'll say one thing, though: I'm about to publish an anthology of the books and texts that mean most to me [*La ricerca delle radici*]. In the preface I write that I felt more exposed in putting together this anthology – in declaring, confessing my favourite books – than in any of my first-person writings. I don't recall ever having felt shame, modesty, a sense of exposure when writing *If This is a Man* or *The Truce*, perhaps because they weren't only my stories, they were everyone's. They weren't intimate stories, or were only minimally so, whereas with the anthology I felt strangely open or unveiled.

Was the choice of texts a difficult one?

No, because I keep all these books together – though they are extremely varied – I keep them near to hand because they are the books that struck me most, whether as a boy or only five years ago or yesterday. They are all worth rereading, whatever their official or intrinsic value. Some are canonical books, of course, like *The Odyssey*, but there are also books that no one will know, a chemistry tract, for example. The latter is there for a very precise reason, because in this tract there is concrete good advice on how to protect yourself, what to do to avoid disasters. I realized that, from when I learned to read, this is the only book I know that told me these things, that took on the role of the father and told you 'son, do this and try not to do that', even if in the form of laboratory procedure. Those four pages of rules on how to avoid accidents were certainly of great value to me in my thirty years as a chemist – and not only in the field of chemistry – because they inculcate in their reader the mental habits of caution, prudence, realism. Habits not found in other books, at least I've never found them.

You wrote one of your books, Storie naturali, *under the pseudonym Damiano Malabaila. Why?*

There is a reason. As I was writing *If This is a Man* and *The Truce*, I wrote some short stories, some of which were published in *Il Mondo* and others in the newspaper *Il Giorno*, and I wanted to collect them together as a book. But I felt a certain hesitancy. Those first two books had their own identity and they had their own readership, not only in Italy. For them, especially for the ex-deportees and their families, I felt it was improper to publish a volume of stories that were so different, lighter, more insubstantial in nature. Many years had passed, of course (they came out in 1966) but I still felt I would be letting them down, upsetting that audience, so I suggested to the publisher a pseudonym. The publisher thought it was an excellent idea, but it was a mistake, because by then the public knew Primo Levi. Later they were reprinted with my real name.

Why Malabaila?

The name has become legendary. [*He laughs.*] At the time I was working at Settimo [outside Turin] and I was driving there and back twice a day. On the way I passed by a car mechanic's called Malabaila. I liked the name a lot, I envied it, because . . . Levi, four letters, who wasn't called Levi? Malabaila was a wonderful name so I stole it. Later, psychoanalyst friends argued that the choice wasn't accidental, that the mechanic was a pretext, that I wanted to call myself bad (*male*) wet-nurse (*balia*) . . .

In some reviews you have been defined as a 'writer-chemist'. Despite my complete ignorance of all things chemical, you managed in The Periodic Table *to smuggle through to me some of your learning, so I found myself drawn to and pleasantly intrigued by the descriptions of all your experiments.*

Thank you. That's the effect I was after: to show that it isn't a sterile, arid profession, without poetry. On the contrary, it is where man today can have his adventures when the older forms are gone: I mean the adventures of the explorers, or of Robinson Crusoe, pirates, sailors and artists. The latter are ever less common nowadays, for those of us who live modern urban lives, but they can be replaced, they are replaced by equivalent experiences such as those my profession has given me. Essentially – to use a quotation by Pavese[3] that I repeat *ad nauseam* – the only two experiences of adulthood are success and failure. I have always felt the need to do something – chemistry, physics, medicine, physiology – that I could later work on and transmit to others, because telling stories to others, in person or in writing, is extremely important to me: I cannot live without it.
[. . .]

Notes

1   The novelist and playwright Luigi Pirandello (1867–1936) built much of his *œuvre* around the problem of the relativity or multiplicity of personal identity, whether in fictional or real characters.
2   'L'impresa piú ardita di un reduce scaltro', *La Stampa*, 7 September 1980, later as 'Il ritorno di Cesare' in *Lilít* ('Cesare's Last Adventure', *Moments of Reprieve*).

3   Cesare Pavese (1908–50) was a novelist and poet, a key figure in postwar Italian literature, for his own work and his influence on others, both before and after his suicide. Like Levi, he was from Turin. As a key figure in the Einaudi publishing company, he was probably partly responsible for turning down Levi's *If This is a Man* in 1947.

An Assault Called Franz Kafka (1983)

Federico De Melis

In your bookshops now, just out, is a sober volume that smacks of older times. Bluish cover, smaller than a paperback. It is the first book in a new Einaudi series 'Writers Translated by Writers'. The series starts off with Franz Kafka's *The Trial*. The translator is Primo Levi. We met the author of *If This is a Man* in Turin, his native city.

Can you tell us a bit about this publishing project?

Einaudi's idea was to relaunch some classics with new translations by contemporary writers. Mine is the first in the series, the second will be *Madame Bovary* by Gustave Flaubert, translated by Natalia Ginzburg. The idea is an intelligent, original and provocative one. Clearly, each of these books will be discussed in their own right and could become the subject of interesting and amusing analysis. Each work is, in a sense, spurious, because each has two authors. You can tell even from the covers: the title and the translator are in white and the author is in black. Like all cross-breeding, it is a fertile operation. That is the idea. I ended up living this idea in full because I must confess that I was constantly at war with myself, split between my philological conscience that said I must respect Kafka and my personal reflexes, my own personal habits as a writer – what is called style – which are by now quite firmly fixed in me. My style is something that I am not much aware of, that my reader knows better than I do, like

From 'Un'aggressione di nome Franz Kafka', *Il manifesto*, 5 May 1983.

one's own portrait in profile. We hardly know or ever see ourselves in profile.

Why bring together Franz Kafka and Primo Levi?

It was not my choice: the publishers made the choice, proposed it to me and I accepted. To tell the truth I was rather hasty, I never thought it would involve me so deeply. I have to admit that Kafka has never been one of my favourite authors, and I'll tell you why: it isn't necessarily the case that you prefer authors you feel closest to, often the exact opposite occurs. I think my feelings for Kafka were born less of disinterest or boredom than of a certain defensiveness, and I noticed this as soon as I began to translate *The Trial*. I felt assaulted by this book and I had to defend myself. Precisely because it is a marvellous book that runs you through like a spear, like an arrow. Every one of us feels on trial. Furthermore, it is one thing to read the book sitting in your armchair, rapidly, without dwelling on it, and quite another to plough through it word by word, piece by piece, as you do when you are translating. Translating *The Trial*, I have understood the reason for my hostility towards Kafka. It is a form of defence born of fear. Perhaps for the very particular reason that Kafka was a Jew and I am a Jew. *The Trial* opens with a surprise and unjustified arrest and my career, too, opened with a surprise and unjustified arrest. Kafka is an author I admire – I do not love him, I admire him, I fear him, like a great machine that crashes in on you, like the prophet who tells you the day you will die.

What choices did you make, what ingredients did you use, in your transla-tion laboratory?

I tried not to weigh the reader down with the syntactic density of the German language. German has a syntactic complexity that the Italian reader is not used to. Giorgio Zampa, in his 1973 translation of *The Trial*, respected the original syntax, always. I diverged at times. Con-fronted with certain harsh, rough moments, I pared them down, I cut up some of the sentences. I had no hesitation in this, as long as the meaning remained. Kafka has no compunction in using repetition, in the course of ten lines he repeats the same word three or four times. I tried to avoid this, since it is not found in conventional Italian. It may be that this was an arbitrary decision on my part, that in Italian, too, repetition can work to produce a certain effect. But I took pity on the Italian reader, I tried to give him something that didn't smack too much of being a translation.

There are two opposite poles of translation. At one extreme, there is Vincenzo Monti who translates *The Iliad*.[1] He goes back to retell the old stories in a language that has nothing to do with the original, but which is modelled instead on contemporary taste. At the other extreme is line for line translation, scholastic, word-for-word translation that tries to render as best it can the meaning of the text. The first mode gives the reader something that he is used to, the second gives the impression of reading a translated text from the outset. Zampa chose to do this with *The Trial* and his is a highly respectable and thoughtful choice. So, I tried to find a middle course between these two extremes, also because I did not want to distort myself too much as a writer. Above all in the dialogue, it felt artificial to create an Italian made to measure by aping the modes of a German that is itself somewhat outdated and distant in time and space, from Prague of the 1920s. Thus, my characters, starting with Josef K., speak present-day Italian.

In your note to The Trial *you write of a lack of affinity with Kafka...*

The lack of affinity that I was referring to is, I think, due to this: Kafka is a visionary writer, he endlessly writes about his hallucinations which are amazing, admirable. He never diverts from this furrow, he never holds out a hand to explain to you what is behind them, what they mean. He leaves to the reader this immense burden of interpretation, and indeed interpretations of Kafka are legion; of this one book, *The Trial*, there are at least twenty different readings. For myself, conscious of the qualitative abyss that divides me from Kafka, I have always taken a different route in my books. I began writing about the camps and I carried on writing about things that happened to me, but always trying to explain, to resolve problems. I have been reproached for this tendency towards the didactic. Half of *If This is a Man* is dedicated to trying to explain to myself, and thus to the reader, the reasons for that apparent anomaly that the German camps represented. Similarly in *The Periodic Table* I tried to explain my equivocal and ambiguous position between chemistry and literature. I have never chosen Kafka's way (or almost never – in one or two stories I have tried my hand at it), that is, giving free rein to what is located 'down below', in the subconscious mind.

Kafka is considered a writer who smothers life, who sings of the absence of and nostalgia for life and love. His ascetic atmosphere is the distillate of a life that has been lost. In Primo Levi there is nothing of this, and especially when he relates his experiences in the Lager . . .

We had very different fates. Kafka grew up in very serious conflict with his father; he was the product of three intermingled cultures, Jewish, German and the culture of Prague. He was unhappy in his emotional life, frustrated in his work, and in the end seriously ill. He died young. I, on the other hand, despite the episode of the *Lager* which marked me deeply, have had a different life, a less unhappy life. My own personal happy ending, that fact of having survived the camps, made me stupidly optimistic. Today, I am less of an optimist. At that time I was more so. At that time I committed an illogical transfer of my own personal happy ending – which enriched me, by making me a writer – on to all human tragedies.

If This is a Man, although it deals with terrifying things, has very little in common with Kafka. It has been noted by many that it is an optimistic and calm book in which you breathe the air rising up from the depths, especially in the last chapter. It seemed absurd to think that from those depths, from the ditch, from the *Lager* there might not be a better world to come. Today, my thoughts are quite different. I think that only another *Lager* can be born from the fact of the *Lager*, that only bad can come of this experience. After having witnessed how a modern, organized, technicized, bureaucratized state could give birth to Auschwitz, one cannot but think in terror of the possibility that it might happen again. That experience can recur, it does not have to recur, but it certainly can, and I see this and I fear it.

You have borne witness to the barbarity of the Nazi camps. Kafka prefigured them: do you agree?

We have to concede that Kafka had some gift that went beyond everyday reason. He certainly had an almost animalesque sensitivity, like snakes that know when earthquakes are coming. Writing in the first few decades of this century, either side of the First World War, he foresaw many things. In the midst of so many other confused signals, in the midst of a cross-breeding of ideologies, he was able to clarify and identify the signals of what would become the fate of Europe twenty years later, twenty years after his death.

In *The Trial* there is a precocious intuition that violence comes from bureaucracy, this growing, irresistible power that is the fruit of our century. Kafka's sisters all died in the camps, victims of that corrupt and abject machine that he had foretold. I should add that this is perhaps a very personal interpretation of *The Trial*. I know there are many others. One key to understanding the book is that it is not a bureaucratic court putting Josef K on trial, but rather the sickness that is the punishment, the sickness within Kafka himself. Or again, there is a theological key, that the court is an unknown god, the god that we can never know.

Kafka's books, and especially *The Trial*, appear contradictory; Josef K feels by turn guilty and innocent. But there is no contradiction. Man is not always equal to himself. Kafka is not equal to himself. We can feel successively and simultaneously both innocent and guilty. To go in search of a rationality behind a text such as *The Trial* is to distort it, deny it, destroy it.

Degradation condemns the executioner as well as the victim, it disperses difference and distance. Perhaps this is the central theme of If This is a Man *and it is a Kafkaesque theme.*

At the beginning of that book there is a Hungarian doctor who has studied in Italy and who speaks a little Italian, although with a strong accent. He is the camp dentist. He is a criminal, he says so himself. He is a 'privileged' *Häftling* [prisoner], a victim turned jailer. He is also mad, he seems mad to us and perhaps he is mad since he describes the details of camp life with minute accuracy, snapping us out of our crushed state. He tells us, for example, that anyone who can box has a chance of becoming a chef. This strikes us as absurd, crazy. But later we will understand that he is quite right, because a cook must be able to defend his product by delivering knockout punches. There is certainly a hint of Kafka in this. This distortion of the world is Kafkaesque. In the camps you constantly came up against something unexpected, and that moment of opening a door and finding not what you were looking for, but something different, quite different, is quite typical of Kafka.

Who is your version of The Trial *for?*

I have to say that whilst translating the book I went through a whole series of contrasting feelings: interest, even enthusiasm, joy at problems solved, knots untied; but also fear, deep sadness. So whilst I have always in the past spread the word about my books with great enthusiasm to all and sundry, I am not so willing to pass *The Trial* on to everyone. I wonder if it is a good idea to give a book like this to a fifteen-year-old. I wouldn't bother. It seems to me a book heavily burdened with foreboding. 'Altro dirti non vo'; ma la tua festa/ ch'anco tardi a venir non ti sia grave' [I shall not tell you more; but do not fret if your own festival seems slow in coming'].[2] *The Trial* makes us more aware. Think of the end of the book, the final scene: the blue sky and that form of execution at the hands of two men, in essence two automata who hardly ever speak, who swap crass insults and are wholly indifferent. They are quite expert in the rules of execution and they want to do everything just so, according to their orders. But this is a death penalty, they twist the knife in his heart. Now this ending is so cruel, so unexpectedly cruel, that if I had a young child I would spare him. I fear it would disturb him, make him suffer, although of course it is the truth. We will die, each of us will die, more or less like that.

Notes

1   Vincenzo Monti (1754–1828) was a neo-classical poet whose blank verse translation or version of *The Iliad* appeared in 1810.
2   Levi is quoting Giacomo Leopardi's poem 'Il sabato del villaggio', ll. 51–2 (from his *Canti*, 1835).

Primo Levi (1984)

Rita Caccamo De Luca and Manuela Olagnero

There is always a more or less hidden impulse behind writing, no matter whether it is carried out as part of a literary career or alongside other professional activities. In your case, what made you write and continues to make you do so?

Mine is something of an anomalous case. I did not choose to be a writer. I was turned into one. By education and profession I am a chemist; by family history, too, since my father and grandfather were engineers and my home was full of my father's books, maths text-books, physics, geology...

If there is an impulse behind my writing it is linked to my deportation, to the suffering of others. I was deported at the age of twenty-four, in February 1944. I came back at the age of twenty-six. Many people have asked me if I would have been a writer in any case. I don't know: how can we predict a future that never happened? Hidden in a corner of *If This is a Man* there's a passage where I relate how, when I was working in the laboratory inside the camp, the urge to tell the story of what I had seen was so strong that I wrote some notes, even though I knew I would have to destroy them at once. When I returned home in October 1945 I began writing and telling these things to anyone, immediately, obsessively. In *The Rime of the*

From 'Primo Levi', *Mondoperaio*, March 1984. A biographical introduction and the final part where Levi goes on to discuss the camps more directly have been omitted.

Ancient Mariner, Coleridge tells the story of a man of the sea and his long and strange adventures on the South Seas. He is cursed because he killed an albatross. And when he comes home, he grasps on to guests as they are arriving at a wedding, stops them and has such a will and a power that he holds them and tells them the strange story of his curse. After my return from the camps, I felt all too similar to the Ancient Mariner. It was a need, a physiological need to break free from that experience by telling the story. A few months later, in December 1945, I had already written the later chapters of *If This is a Man*: I wrote each chapter all in one go, with no plan, no idea even that I was writing a book. What mattered was to get it written down, to record not so much the facts as the impressions linked to the facts. My memory was my only source, I had no other weapons. Of the journey home, I had, literally, a sort of train timetable, a journey plan: that day I was in this or that place. I found it again almost fifteen years later and it became the framework for *The Truce*. For *If This is a Man*, though, I had no framework. I just wrote, wherever and whenever I could, without suffering over it. I felt time and space expanding as I wrote. I even wrote on the train between Turin and Avigliana where I was working in a factory. I wrote at night or during my lunchbreak. Almost the entire chapter 'The Canto of Ulysses' was written in half an hour between 12.30 and 1 p.m. one day. I was in a sort of trance.

Then when I had finished writing, I shut up shop. I thought I had settled my account. I felt personally liberated and I felt I had fulfilled my civic duty to bear witness, and so for twelve or fifteen years, I stopped writing. A phase of my life was over. Also for concrete practical reasons, because that first edition of *If This is a Man* was almost stillborn: they printed 2500 copies and sold about 1500. The others were all flooded in Florence in 1966[1] . . . Given the poor sales I had to give up any idea I might have had of becoming a writer. It was an unattainable utopia. I rushed headlong into my career as a chemist.

After that long period of silence, what brought you back to writing, and what had changed in terms of content and style in the meantime?

In 1958 I got the book republished, by Einaudi. It was translated into several languages within a few years. So the idea that I could travel a second road – that of writing – surfaced once again. I wanted to tell the stories not of the camps but of my journey home and so I began to write *The Truce*. This time I was much more methodical, I knew I was writing a book. Beginning from the beginning, I decided to write a chapter a month, and that's how it went. There is a profound difference between the first book and all the rest. *If This is a Man* was written without even a hint of literary worries: if there is literature there, it is unwanted, an intrusion. I certainly never considered problems of style. With the others, I did, from *The Truce* onwards. I wouldn't be able to define my style. Some have tried to pigeon-hole me with the neo-realists,[2] but I don't really see it. But I am sure – as I've often said – that my work as a practising scientist has influenced my way of writing, has been a stimulus towards concision and precision. I think that has been a constant in my work.

You describe yourself as an anomaly as a writer who had to engage in writing alongside a career as a chemist. Have you felt split between these two worlds, or have you viewed them and lived them as resources to draw on, as different 'weapons'?

For many years, my life has been split not into two but into three parts, three parallel lives: my factory work, my family and my writing. And there was little communication between the three. It might seem odd, but for the most part I have created my books at work, in scraps of time here and there. I didn't want to take anything away from nor harm my professional work; after all, it was providing me with a living. And what is more, I thought it a good thing – a stimulant – that ideas came to me when I was in the factory or during the boring journey from home to work. Then I would write them out in the evenings or on Sundays. Even today, now that I have retired, I still feel the echoes of my factory routine: I can never write before six in the evening. There was a time when my three lives interacted happily: 1946–7, for example, were years of happiness when I felt full of energy and strength; I was returning to life after a long period consumed with suffering. In the chapter 'Chromium' in *The Periodic Table*, I tell the story of the three successes that came all at once at that time: I met the woman who would soon be my wife; I came through and was cured of the nightmare of the *Lager*, as reflected in the complex, intense and new pleasure I felt in writing; and I discovered ways of 'winning out' with my abilities as a chemist over the stubborn resistance of matter (at the time I discovered a chemical compound that worked against rust). I must say that, after that time, things faded somewhat, the future was not as clear and brilliant as it seemed then.

Every literary undertaking goes through alternate stages of creative tension and feelings of emptiness and paucity. Have you felt this alternation in your work?

The productivity of writing varies widely from zero to very high figures indeed. And there are desperate days when you cannot write a single word. It happened to me at the end of 1981, after I had finished my most recent book, *If Not Now, When?*. Nineteen eighty-one had been a good year. I had tried something new: for the first time I had done research, looking up texts, checking historical, geographical, linguistic data. And when it had come to the writing, I had gone at it constantly, even if not quite from morning to evening which would be impossible. When the party was over, however, after the book came out and all the interviews, reviews, prizes and so on were done, I felt totally numb, as if I had given it my all. I had the acute and painful sense that I had shut up shop. For some months I felt only painful anxiety when I looked at what I'd written, because I was sure I could never reach that level again, I even felt *that it had been written by someone else*, someone different, more alive, more intelligent, with a better memory and a finer sensibility.

Apart from the inner, creative side of things, there is also a need for an external point of comparison to uphold one's image as an intellectual. Often others, even in a limited, unpredictable way, can unblock a communicative mechanism that has got snarled up. It must have happened to you also. Can you remember anything of this kind?

Yes, I remember when my first book passed almost unnoticed when it was published, in a slightly shorter version, in 1947. In 1955 – to mark the tenth anniversary of the liberation of the camps – they organized a photographic exhibition on the deportations, in Turin and elsewhere. Until then I had felt a fearful panic about speaking in public. During the war and the Race Laws, I was part of a very small group of Jewish youths in Turin who had set themselves the task of showing how the Bible and Fascism were incompatible, so that a Jew could only be anti-Fascist. Our tendentious or at least rather rough-hewn project was this, to search out in the Torah, the Pentateuch, all those episodes that proved that justice and liberty were fundamental aspects of Jewish culture. Many non-Jewish friends came along to have a look, to see what on earth we were up to. Anti-Fascism at the time was so bland that even weak voices such as ours served some purpose. Since any form of associationism was forbidden, unless licensed by the police, there was a local policeman at all the meetings: poor thing, he sat in a corner, not understanding a word, smoking his pipe, reading the newspaper or sleeping.

When I had to get up and speak I was terrified. I ineptly read my piece on anti-Semitism . . . I was nineteen and I swore to myself that I would never speak in public again, that I was not up to it. And I stuck to my promise until 1955 when I went to that exhibition to explain the meaning of those photographs. And I found an audience of young people who were so enthusiastic, warm and nice that I was overwhelmed: I saw that my book, even though it had sold so poorly, had spread around, had left a mark, had touched people. This, too, drove me towards writing *The Truce*.

When you write, you never really know who you are writing for. Sometimes, a possibility emerges of a coincidence between the inner motivations of the writer and the demands of the reader: in this case, the demand to know and to understand events suppressed in the collective memory.

Who my readers are, I don't know. My impression is that *If This is a Man*, for example, spread by word of mouth, horizontally, one reader following the suggestion of another. And when they made a school edition, something very curious began to happen: the book began to be passed from children to their parents. A whole new demand was born from below, from among schoolchildren.

My rapport with German readers has been very particular. I received many letters from them. One girl wrote to me continuously for months, trying to explain what had happened in Germany, why parents never spoke of these things to their children. The children – from eighteen to twenty-five to thirty years old – would write to me as if to say sorry, saying 'it's scandalous that, as a German, I found these things out from a foreigner'. I've kept all these letters. I made a proposal to publish them, but nothing has ever come of it.[3]
[. . .]

Notes

1   The great flood of 1966 in Florence was particularly disastrous for the low-lying area around the Biblioteca nazionale (National Library) where the remaining copies of Levi's book were probably stored.

2   Neo-realism was the label applied to a loose cluster of books and films of the 1940s in Italy, which tended to deal in a direct, unelaborate way with

contemporary subjects, in particular the recent war and the anti-Fascist Resistance.

3   Some of these letters made their way into a chapter of *The Drowned and the Saved*, 'Letters from Germans'.

The Essential and the Superfluous (1987)

Roberto Di Caro

'Oh no: I can't tell you everything. Either I tell you about the place or I tell you what happened, but if I were you I'd choose what happened because it's a good one. Then, if you want to tell it yourself, you can work on it, straighten it out, sand it down, get rid of the smears, give it a bit of a finish and you'll have yourself a story'.

The Wrench opens with this montage of words that the writer Primo Levi gives to his protagonist Faussone, a world-hopping rigger of cranes, mechanical structures, petrochemical plants and suspension bridges. Not that the narrator thinks so differently from his character on the question of the job of the writer. After thirty years spent 'stitching together long molecules which would hopefully be of use to my fellows', at the age of fifty-five (twelve years ago now) Levi chose 'with nostalgia but no regrets' the road of the storyteller, the stitcher of words and ideas. So after *If This is a Man* and *The Truce* were born books such as *Storie naturali*, *Vizio di forma*, *The Periodic Table*, *The Wrench*, *La ricerca delle radici*, *Ad ora incerta* and others, up to *The Drowned and the Saved*, published by Einaudi towards the end of last year [1986].

Writing as a work of montage, straightening, sanding, finishing: for yourself as much as for Faussone. Is that how it is?

There isn't a great deal of difference between putting together a lab apparatus and putting together a good story. It needs symmetry, it

From 'Il necessario e il superfluo', *Piemonte vivo*, I, 1, 1987.

has to fit the purpose, it has to have nothing superfluous, but not to miss out anything essential. And it has to work.

Is writing, too, a technical problem?

For me, yes. Anyway I have always dealt with technical problems: planning, production, sales. For twenty years, even when I was already in management, I spent time in the laboratory, the brains of the factory. I made certain assemblies with my own hands, on a scale of decimetres and metres, of course. I miss that work with its precision, its finely focused aim and its results that you could see on the same day or a few days later, not having to wait five or six years as with the big projects.

Is writing less to do with precision?

On the contrary, for me it is high precision work.

Faussone again: 'When no one was watching, I went at it with the hammer too, because the hammer fixes everything. At Lancia they called it "the engineer".' Does 'the hammer' work in writing also?

God, I'll have to think about that for a moment... There are twisted sentences, gone wrong, that you need to get rid of and replace. Just after you've written it, a text is illegible, it makes no sense, it's like looking in the mirror and always seeing the same face. You need to leave it to rest a little, a few days or weeks, and then go back to it. Then a bit of hammering works fine. Or better, the clippers. The Macintosh is a wonderful tool for this, for pitiless cutting that doesn't leave a trace.

Is there much difference between writing on a computer and typing?

More than between writing by hand and by computer. Using a pen, it's easy to cut and paste, insert and modify, to change the text. And with a computer it's even easier, it's all done on screen. With a typewriter, the negligible difficulty of taking the page out or using whitener to remove errors often makes you give up, through inertia or laziness, and not put a sentence or a passage right. But I don't think a philologist could tell whether a text has been written by pen, type-writer or computer.

You miss the end-projected nature of your former job as a chemist. When you make a machine or a lab instrument, the aim is that it should work, should do what it is made for. What about when you write a book?

It has to satisfy the reader. I don't write for myself, or if I do, I tear it up, I destroy what I've written. I think it's wrong to write for oneself. Of course, everyone is free to do as they please, it doesn't harm anyone, but it feels like time wasted to me. In general, my books have been written for an audience, indeed, for an Italian audience, at the level of an Italian reader. And I respect and feel for that reader. The letters I receive confirm as much.

Do you remember any in particular?

There are so many... Yes, I remember one, unsigned. A lady who had read *The Truce* and she told me that doing so had solved some serious problems, although she didn't say what they were. I like the idea that my books might help people. That helps me. I wish they could help me as much.

And they don't?

On occasion. Before, writing was... I don't know...

A pleasure?

A need, that came over me every evening. I wrote at least three books whilst working as a chemist: *If This is a Man, The Truce, Storie naturali* and part of *The Periodic Table*. I can't understand now where I found the time to do both. Today I have all the time in the world and I write less than I did then, and with less intensity. Although there's a difference between being thirty and being almost seventy. Time moves at a different pace. Every now and then, I have the impression that the cupboard is bare, that I have nothing more to say, no more stories to tell.

Do you already know what you will write next?

Yes, I'm already writing it. But reluctantly. And I'd prefer not to talk about it. The truth is I am living a neurotic life, with draining gaps between one book and the next; such as now, after *The Drowned and the Saved*.

Pauses for thought?

No. Irritating pauses for PR. Books have to be presented, talked about on tours, in society, and I dislike all that. It's like when I worked in customer services (I've done that too; there's a story about it in *The Periodic Table*), and I had to go and visit clients, convince them or placate them. I always did it reluctantly.

And now they ask you to do the same for your books?

Sometimes, yes. For example, I'm under great pressure from America. They want me at Brandeis University, to give me an honorary degree, but I don't think I'll go. Travelling isn't easy for me, for family reasons and also because I've internalized all the obstacles and I now find myself resistant to the idea of setting out on the road. Ten years ago it would have been different, I had much more strength and the desire to follow many more things. Now I'm tired. And I wonder, 'what's the point?' Once, when the translation of a book of mine arrived at my home, it was cause for celebration, now it has no effect. Even revising translations in languages I know – English, French and German; I had a clause put into every contract – has turned into nothing other than boring extra work. You grow immune. Anyway, what can you do, cultural organization is highly random, it works by chance. The great success my books have had abroad in the last year or so was down to the fact that *The Periodic Table* was picked up by an Italian scholar who translated it and passed it on to Saul Bellow. That was all it took to set off an explosion of interest, to spur Summit Books, a subsidiary of Simon and Schuster, to buy up all my books including those as yet unwritten. The English and then the Germans followed on behind, although they kept to work already written.

Let's go back to the techniques of writing. Can you try to go into the procedures of narration, composition, fabulation?

Let's try. First we should make a distinction between poetry and prose. I'm only an occasional poet: when all's said and done I've written just over one poem a year, even if there are periods when it comes quite naturally to me to write in verse. But it's an activity which has nothing to do with any other mental activity I know of. It is completely different: it's like a mushroom sprouting in a single night; you wake up one morning with a poem in your head or at least the kernel of it. Then it's a matter of lengthy variants and continuous corrections. And a computer is the perfect instrument for this sort of work, to the humiliation of all future scholars who will have no manuscripts of successive drafts. It shows 'how the punishment fits the crime': many years ago, in *Storie naturali*, I wrote a story about a poet who buys a mechanical, automatic versifier ['Il Versificatore']: all he had to do was choose the theme, the period, the metre, the length and the subject and the machine gave birth all on its own to the desired product.

The secret dream of many an aspiring poet?

I wouldn't know. My versifier was a commercial composer, paid by commission. So they would request, for instance, an ode to Milan's victory over Juventus... Of course, there's a complicated work of assembly behind even the *Orlando furioso*,[1] but I don't worry about that since my poems all come in under one hand-span.

And prose?

The decisive element for narrative procedure is a careful balance between the essential and the superfluous. I read a bit of everything, but I prefer writers who don't indulge too much in excess. Oh, but I'm a great fan of Sterne's *Tristam Shandy*, with all of its digressions, and the uncontainable *Horcynus Orca* by Stefano D'Arrigo. But I could never write like that. My books, I think I can fairly boast, have nothing inessential. It comes spontaneously and naturally to me to abstain from embellishment, from extras added in just to make the writing look good.

This is a typically Piedmontese trait, isn't it?

Probably, yes: an object is an object, there's no need for fancy flourishes. Of course, we had our baroque in Piedmont too, but in reality it was imported from outside, and in any case, later they pruned away all the affectations and elaborations. The fact is that, whereas the rhythm of poetry make it closely related to music, the literary text is in a sense closer to manual labour. You make a plan, at least mentally, an outline, a design, and then you try to make the product as close as possible to the plan. Naturally, as I had Faussone say, it is much less dangerous to write a book than to build a bridge: if a bridge collapses it can do a lot of harm, to people also. If a book collapses, the only damage done is to the author.

So writing is a low-risk profession?

There is only one risk, of writing badly.

And uselessly?

They are the same. For me, at least, although there are also badly written but useful books, such as some manuals or memoirs written without a second thought by unknowns. Sometimes I am sent out of the blue manuscripts which are not to be scorned, by people who have something to say but do not know how to write. You wish you could take them and rewrite them.

Have you ever done that?

No. Although many have asked me, have offered up their lives to me, 'mon coeur mis à nu',[2] and we would have split the royalties. Writing as a sort of work by proxy, I suppose. I don't deny, though, that if I came across the right story, a life worthy of the telling, I could accept a contract of that kind, why not?

So it is possible to write by proxy?

Papillon[3] is a case in point, I think, but you wouldn't know it just by reading the book.

This is the second or third time you've talked about the inscrutability of the written text. Do you have a problem with scholars and critics or are you keen to preserve the aura of mystery surrounding literary work?

No, I don't believe there is any mystery in the written text; except in the cases of authors lost in the mist of time whom we know next to nothing about. As for the immense toil undertaken by some scholars in recent years in mechanized philology, counting up the frequency of words to try and prove or disprove attributions of certain texts to certain authors, it all seems very marginal to me, in the end, useless.

Do you suffer a lot when you write?

Oh, sometimes, yes.

For what you are writing about or for the writing itself?

No, not for what I'm writing about. I sometimes feel the inadequacy of the medium. Ineffability, it's called, and it's a beautiful word. Our language is human, born to describe things at a human level. It collapses, falls apart, cannot cope (this goes for all languages, always) when it has to talk about, say, a supernova, as I tried to show once in a short story, 'Una stella tranquilla' ['A Quiet Star'].

How much of you goes into what you write?

There are writers who have put themselves in their books just as they were, without any cosmetic alteration. Henri Frédéric Amiel,[4] for example. But these are fairly rare cases. For the most part, authors choose one part of themselves, the better part. At times I have portrayed myself in my books as brave, at others as cowardly, prophetic or naive, but always, I think, as a balanced individual.

And aren't you a balanced individual?

I'm not very balanced at all. I go through long periods of imbalance, no doubt linked to my concentration-camp experience. I find it very hard to cope with problems. This side of myself I've never written about.

And you never will?

Perhaps one of these days I will. I get many letters which express admiration for the strength I showed in bearing up to my year of imprisonment. But that was a passive strength, the strength of a rock bearing up to the impact of the floodwater. I am not a strong man. Not at all.

But you need strength to recount those experiences also.

On the contrary. Recounting them was a need, you would need strength not to write or talk about them. In my books, in the first but also in my most recent, *The Drowned and the Saved*, I see, if anything, an immense need to put things in order, to put order back into a world of chaos, to explain to myself and to others. On a day-to-day basis, however, my life is very different, unfortunately it is much less methodical and systematic. Writing is a way of creating order. It's the best way I know, even if I don't know many.

So there's a split, a schism, between the author in flesh and blood and the author we reconstruct through the pages of his books. The reader imagines you quite differently from the way you feel yourself to be . . .

Quite differently, judging by the letters I receive. They think of me as a sort of guru. Perhaps there is a sort of wisdom that seeps through from my books which I don't feel within myself. For me, it is just a case of good measure, not running before you can walk; a Piedmontese virtue, perhaps. As I wrote in the preface to the collection of my stories and articles for *La Stampa* that came out a couple of months ago,[5] 'I ask the reader not to go in search of messages. It's a word I detest because it puts me in an impossible position, in clothes which aren't my own, which belong to a type I distrust: the prophet, the oracle, the seer.' They are the curse of our time, prophets. Or perhaps the curse of all times.

Why shouldn't we enquire into the future?

Because it is almost impossible to distinguish a true prophet from a false one. They sound exactly the same.

So it is their language that deceives us, that has something essentially mystificatory in it?

I'm sorry, but are you a philosopher?

No. Your tone suggests that you distrust philosophers too. Is that right?

Well, yes. Perhaps because of ignorance. Listen, I've always made paints, I'm used to a concrete life, in which you either solve a problem or throw it away. Philosophical problems, by contrast, haven't changed since the Pre-Socratics, they keep going around and around them, working them over and over... And also, all philosophers share the vice of wanting to invent their own private language which you need to struggle your way through before you can understand what they mean. No, it's not for me ...

Notes

1 *Orlando furioso* (final version 1532) is the great romantic epic poem by Ludovico Ariosto (1474–1535).
2 *Mon coeur mis à nu* was the title Baudelaire gave to his late autobiographical project which was never finished: it became the title of part of his posthumously gathered *Journaux intimes* (1887).
3 Henri Antoine Charrière, *Papillon* (Paris: Robert Laffont, 1969; translated with the same title, London: Hart-Davis, 1970) is the ghosted 'oral history' of a criminal.
4 Henri Frédéric Amiel (1821–81) was a Swiss writer and essayist, best known for his massive, posthumously published *Journal intime*.
5 *Racconti e saggi* (1986).

Part V
Auschwitz and Survival

Round Table: The Jewish Question (1961)

QUESTIONNAIRE

1 Have there been in the course of history any other attempts at the radical and programmatic destruction of a people comparable to that perpetrated by the Nazi 'Final Solution' on the Jews?

2 What concrete historical reasons – political, economic, social – led Germany to enact such an insane project?

3 Is there such a thing – and if so, to what degree? – as a 'collective responsibility' of the German people for the genocide?

4 What are the deep reasons for anti-Semitism as felt and practised more or less virulently by various peoples in the course of history? And which of the many interpretations of this aberrant phenomenon – from religious to psychoanalytical – can be taken as the most plausible and convincing?

5 Before Nazism and its own ideologues, such as Rosenberg,[1] can we identify the 'prophets of anti-Semitism' who share part of the moral and intellectual responsibility for the Nazi persecution of the Jews?

Levi was one of four 'round-table' respondents to a questionnaire on 'La questione ebraica', published in *Storia illustrata*, June 1961.[2]

6   Is there still a danger of a return to anti-Semitism and racial persecution as practised by the Nazi system in the world today?

7   Can events such as the Eichmann trial or historical documentation of Nazi crimes have educational, exemplary value, especially for the younger generations? Are they useful in the struggle against every form of racial hatred and every ideology that smacks of Nazism or Fascism?

1   Human history is full of massacres: the Aztecs slaughtered by the Spanish, the Armenians by the Turks, 'coloured' people in general by colonizers. And yet, despite moments of stasis and lapses, thirty years ago it seemed legitimate to think that mankind had progressed, that the destruction of entire peoples, like slavery, like unrestrained warfare, might belong to civilization's barbaric infancy. It has been the sad privilege of our generation to witness the resurgence of these monsters. Perhaps there have been, in distant times, other massacres of peoples, but none so ferocious, so total in both intention and effect, as that willed by Hitler's Germans in the heart of Europe, a Europe which proclaims itself the world's teacher in matters of civilization.

2   No reason that could be called concrete: and it is precisely the uselessness, the gratuitousness that emerges from the public speeches of the great Nazi leaders, from Hitler's private conversations, to the convulsive writings of Streicher[3] and Rosenberg, that is most worrying.

It means that the man of yesterday – and so also the man of today – can act against all reason, with impunity. He can state obvious errors as fact, and be believed and applauded. He can order senseless massacres and be obeyed.

I have never had much faith in the moral instinct of humanity, in mankind as 'naturally' good. But I did believe that history could be interpreted in a utilitarian key, as progress. But if you look at recent history, you cannot but feel confusion in the face of slaughter for its own sake, with no private or collective purpose, triggered only by a form of zoological or biological hatred and, what is more, a hatred acclaimed, inculcated and praised as such.

3   The very expression 'collective guilt' is a contradiction in terms, and it is a Nazi invention. Every person is singly responsible for their actions. Every German (and non-German) who took part in the murdering is fully guilty; their accomplices are partially guilty, and we should include amongst the latter the eminent signatories of the Race Manifesto in Italy;[4] less guilty but still contemptible are the many who did nothing in the full knowledge of what was happening, and the mass who found ways of not knowing because of their hypocrisy or poverty of spirit.

In this way, we can build up a picture which belies the heroic inventions of Nazi propaganda: not collective guilt, but collective cowardice, a collective failure of intellectual courage, a collective foolishness and abandonment of civilization.

4 Anti-Semitism has ancient and multiple roots: at times it has been religious in character, at others ethnic or economic. But in Germany, in its most virulent form, it was an irrational impulse, intimately biological in its make-up, even when dressed up in low-grade Romantic philosophy. The '*rassenbiologisch*' quality of Nazi anti-Semitism was openly declared by Hitler's ideologues.

Indeed, in the text of the Nuremberg Laws it is easy to discern touches of the sacred or mystical which are the end-point of a certain twisted and corrupted Romanticism. The Jew is not the non-believer, the foreigner nor even the usurer; instead the Jew is a Platonic idea, a transcendent source of infection, the eternal enemy. For Hitler, the great enemies of humanity are St Paul and Karl Marx, both Jews, and in turn the destroyers of Rome and Germany. It is there in the *Tischreden* collected by Martin Bormann.[5]

5 There are many who might rightfully claim the title 'prophet of anti-Semitism', and not all of them are German. One of particular importance was a Christian-Social group in the Reichstag of 1870 which had an openly anti-Semitic programme.

But it does not seem that unarmed prophets, whether good or evil, have had much influence on the history of recent centuries; I share the suspicion that they represent more the pointer on the scales than the propellant charge. In any case, in the face of the deeds of their bloody disciples, it strikes me that the responsibility of a Gobineau or a Chamberlain pales somewhat.[6]

6 Anti-Semitism has not disappeared and mass racial persecution can return. Nasser[7] in Egypt has openly proclaimed that the elimination of Jews (and Christians) is an essential part of his 'ideology'. The trials of Jewish doctors perpetrated by Stalin and Beria[8] was an alarming symptom.

No less alarming are the actions of senseless youths all over the world. They may be occasional acts of gratuitous violence, against almost randomly chosen victims, but their relation to Fascist squads and to Nazism is self-evident and often welcomed. A new Hitler, in whichever country he came to power, with the terrifying arms of modern technology and propaganda at his disposal, would find followers with almost derisory ease. Now, experience teaches us that in these instances, scapegoats, objects of violence, are searched out amongst minorities. Up till now, in Europe, the typical, model minority has been the Jews.

7   The Eichmann trial and historical documentation of Nazi crimes certainly have educational value, but they alone are not enough. Their effectiveness, the extent of their impact, will not be great for as long as there remains, in Germany but also in Italy, the ambiguous climate of moral vacancy that was instigated under Fascism and has survived it, in part through inertia, in part through foolish calculation.

The moral restoration that we need can only come from schools. That Eichmann is guilty is easily shown; but every citizen, from schooldays onwards, needs to learn the meaning of truth and lies, that they are not exchangeable; that from the moment you abdicate your own conscience, as soon as you replace it with a cult of the leader 'who is always right', you risk becoming guilty of the gravest crimes.

Notes

1   Alfred Rosenberg (1893–1946) was a Nazi leader and author of *The Myth of the Twentieth Century*, a racist tract inspired by the theories of Gobineau and Chamberlain (see note 6). He was executed at the Nuremberg war tribunal.

2   The other three participants were the philosopher Remo Cantoni, the psychoanalyst Cesare Musatti and the jurist Francesco Carnelutti.

3   Julius Streicher (1885–1946) was a Nazi from the early days of the movement, a journalist, pornographer and politician. He founded and edited the viciously anti-Semitic *Der Stürmer* from 1923 to 1945. He was hanged at the Nuremberg trials.

4   The *Manifesto degli scienziati razzisti* ('Manifesto of the Racial Scientists'), the peak of the public anti-Semitic campaign leading up to the Race Laws of late 1938, was published on 14 July 1938, declaring among other things that 'there exists a pure Italian race . . . Jews do not belong to the Italian race'.

5   Levi is here referring to Hitler's wartime conversations recorded by Martin Bormann, in the so-called *Bormann-Vermeke* ['Bormann Notes'], published in part in German as *Hitlers Tischgespräche* (Bonn: Athenaum Berlag, 1951) and in full in English as *Hitler's Table-Talk*, edited by Hugh Trevor-Roper (London: Weidenfeld and Nicolson, 1953).

6   Joseph Arthur, comte de Gobineau (1816-82) was a French diplomat and man of letters and the chief nineteenth-century French proponent of the theory of Nordic supremacy. His major work was *Essai sur l'inégalité des races humaines* (1853–55; *The Inequality of Human Races*, London: Heinemann, 1915). Houston Stewart Chamberlain (1855–1927) was born in England but moved to Germany (where he became Wagner's son-in-law). His most famous work on race and German superiority was *Foundations of the Nineteenth Century* (1899 in German; 1911 in English). Both were profoundly anti-Semitic.

7   Gamal Abdel Nasser (1918–70) took part in a military coup in Egypt in 1952 and became leader of the country from 1954 to 1970.

8   Lavrenti Pavlovich Beria (1899–1953) was a Soviet secret police chief and minister under Stalin and briefly part of the ruling group after Stalin's death, before being executed in 1953.

A Self-Interview: Afterword to *If This is a Man* (1976)

Someone a long time ago wrote that books, too, like human beings, have their destiny: unpredictable, different from what is desired and expected. This book, too, has had a strange destiny. Its birth certificate is distant: it can be found where one reads that 'I write what I would never dare tell anyone.' My need to tell the story was so strong in the Camp that I had begun describing my experiences there, on the spot, in that German laboratory laden with freezing cold, the war, and vigilant eyes; and yet I knew that I would not be able under any circumstances, to hold on to those haphazardly scribbled notes, and that I must throw them away immediately because if they were found they would be considered an act of espionage and would cost me my life.

For the 1976 schools edition of *Se questo è un uomo* Levi wrote this 'Appendice' ('Afterword') in which he asks himself, and answers, eight of the most frequently asked questions from his encounters with students. The translation given is by Ruth Feldman, reproduced from the 1986 English edition of *If This is a Man*, for which Levi himself made a number of small changes. A five-page passage of the original at the start of the answer to question 7 that was omitted from the English edition has been translated and reinserted here.

Nevertheless, those memories burned so intensely inside me that I felt compelled to write as soon as I returned to Italy, and within a few months I wrote *If This is a Man*. The manuscript was turned down by a number of important publishers; it was accepted in 1947 by a small publisher who printed only 2,500 copies and then folded. So, this first book of mine fell into oblivion for many years: perhaps also because in all of Europe those were difficult times of mourning and reconstruction and the public did not want to return in memory to the painful years of the war that had just ended. It achieved a new life only in 1958, when it was republished by Einaudi, and from then on the interest of the public has never flagged. In Italy the book has sold more than 500,000 copies; it has been translated into eight languages and adapted for radio and theatre. This belated success encouraged me to write *The Truce*, the natural continuation of its older brother which, unlike it, immediately met with an excellent reception from the public and critics.

In the course of the years, I have been asked to comment on the two books hundreds of times, before the most diverse audiences: young and adult, uneducated and cultivated, in Italy and abroad. On the occasion of these encounters, I have had to answer many questions: naive, acute, highly emotional, superficial, at times provocative. I soon realized that some of these questions recurred constantly; indeed, never failed to be asked: they must therefore spring from a thoughtful curiosity, to which in some way the text of the book did not give a satisfactory reply, I propose to reply to these questions here.

1   In these books there are no expressions of hate for the Germans, no desire for revenge. Have you forgiven them?

My personal temperament is not inclined to hatred. I regard it as bestial, crude, and prefer on the contrary that my actions and thoughts, as far as possible, should be the product of reason; therefore I have never cultivated within myself hatred as a desire for revenge, or as a desire to inflict suffering on my real or presumed enemy, or as a private vendetta. Even less do I accept hatred as directed collectively at an ethnic group, for example, all the Germans; if I accepted it, I would feel that I was following the precepts of Nazism, which was founded precisely on national and racial hatred.

I must admit that if I had in front of me one of our persecutors of those days, certain known faces, certain old lies, I would be tempted to hate, and with violence too; but exactly because I am not a Fascist or a Nazi, I refuse to give way to this temptation. I believe in reason and in discussion as supreme instruments of progress, and therefore I repress hatred even within myself: I prefer justice. Precisely for this reason, when describing the tragic world of Auschwitz, I have deliberately assumed the calm, sober language of the witness, neither the lamenting tones of the victim nor the irate voice of someone who seeks revenge. I thought that my account would be all the more credible and useful the more it appeared objective and the less it sounded overly emotional; only in this way does a witness in matters of justice perform his task, which is that of preparing the ground for the judge. The judges are my readers.

All the same I would not want my abstaining from explicit judgement to be confused with an indiscriminate pardon. No, I have not forgiven any of the culprits, nor am I willing to forgive a single one of them, unless he has shown (with deeds, not words, and not too long afterwards) that he has become conscious of the crimes and errors of Italian and foreign Fascism and is determined to condemn them, uproot them, from his conscience and from that of others. Only in this case am I, a non-Christian, prepared to follow the Jewish and Christian precept of forgiving my enemy, because an enemy who sees the error of his ways ceases to be an enemy.

2   *Did the Germans know what was happening?*

How is it possible that the extermination of millions of human beings could have been carried out in the heart of Europe without anyone's knowledge?

The world in which we Westerners live has grave faults and dangers, but when compared to the countries in which democracy is smothered, and to the times during which it has been smothered, our world has a tremendous advantage: everyone can know everything about everything. Information today is the 'fourth estate': at least in theory, the reporter, the journalist and the news photographer have free access everywhere; nobody has the right to stop them or send them away. Everything is easy: if, you wish you can receive radio or television broadcasts from your own country or from any other country. You can go the news-stand and choose the newspaper you prefer, national or foreign, of any political tendency – even that of a country with which your country is at odds. You can buy and read any books you want and usually do not risk being incriminated for 'anti-national, activity' or bring down on your house a search by the political police. Certainly it is not easy to avoid all biases, but at least you can pick the bias you prefer.

In an authoritarian state it is not like this. There is only one Truth, proclaimed from above; the newspapers are all alike, they all repeat the same one Truth. So do the radio stations, and you cannot listen to those of other countries. In the first place, since this is a crime, you risk ending up in prison. In the second place, the radio stations in your country send out jamming signals, on the appropriate wavelengths, that superimpose themselves on the foreign messages and prevent your hearing them. As for books, only those that please the state are published and translated. You must seek any others on the outside and introduce them into your country at your own risk because they are considered more dangerous than drugs and explosives, and if they are found in your possession at the border, they are confiscated and you are punished. Books not in favour, or no longer in favour, are burned in public bonfires in town squares. This went on in Italy between 1924 and 1945; it went on in National Socialist Germany; it is going on right now in many countries, among which it is sad to have to number the Soviet Union, which fought heroically against Fascism. In an authoritarian state it is considered permissible to alter the truth; to rewrite history retrospectively; to distort the news, suppress the true, add the false. Propaganda is substituted for information. In fact, in such a country you are not a citizen possessor of rights but a subject, and as such you owe to the state (and to the dictator who represents it) fanatical loyalty and supine obedience.

It is clear that under these conditions it becomes possible (though not always easy; it is never easy to deeply violate human nature) to erase great chunks of reality. In Fascist Italy the undertaking to assassinate the Socialist deputy Matteotti was quite successful, and after a few months it was locked in silence. Hitler and his Minister of Propaganda, Joseph Goebbels, showed themselves to be far superior to Mussolini at this work of controlling and masking truth.

However, it was not possible to hide the existence of the enormous concentration camp apparatus from the German people. What's more, it was not (from the Nazi point of view) even desirable. Creating and maintaining an atmosphere of undefined terror in the country was part of the aims of Nazism. It was just as well for the people to know that opposing Hitler was extremely dangerous. In fact, hundreds of thousands of Germans were confined in the camps from the very first months of Nazism: Communists, Social Democrats, Liberals, Jews, Protestants, Catholics; the whole country knew it and knew that in the camps people were suffering and dying.

Nevertheless, it is true that the great mass of Germans remained unaware of the most atrocious details of what happened later on in the camps: the methodical industrialized extermination on a scale of millions, the gas chambers, the cremation furnaces, the vile despoiling of corpses, all this was not supposed to be known, and in effect few did know it up to the end of the war. Among other precautions, in order to keep the secret, in official language only cautious and cynical euphemisms were employed: one did not write 'extermination' but 'final solution', not 'deportation' but 'transfer', not 'killing by gas' but 'special treatment', and so on. Not without reason, Hitler feared that this horrendous news, if it were divulged, would compromise the blind faith which the country had in him, as well as the morale of the fighting troops. Besides, it would have become known to the Allies and would have been exploited as propaganda material. This actually did happen but because of their very enormity, the horrors of the camps, described many times by the Allied radio, were not generally believed.

The most convincing summing-up of the German situation at that time that I have found is in the book *Der SS Staat* (*The Theory and Practice of Hell*) by Eugen Kogon, a former Buchenwald prisoner, later Professor of Political Science at the University of Munich:

What did the Germans know about the concentration camps? Outside the concrete fact of their existence, almost nothing. Even today they know little. Indubitably, the method of rigorously keeping the details of the terrorist system secret, thereby making the anguish undefined, and hence that much more profound, proved very efficacious.

As I have said elsewhere, even many Gestapo functionaries did not know what was happening in the camps to which they were sending prisoners. The greater majority of the prisoners themselves had a very imprecise idea of how their camps functioned and of the methods employed there. How could the German people have known? Anyone who entered the camps found himself confronted by an unfathomable universe, totally new to him. This is the best demonstration of the power and efficacy of secrecy.

And yet . . . and yet, there wasn't even one German who did not know of the camps' existence or who believed they were sanatoriums. There were very few Germans who did not have a relative or an acquaintance in a camp, or who did not know, at least, that such a one or such another had been sent to a camp. All the Germans had been witnesses to the multiform anti-Semitic barbarity. Millions of them had been present – with indifference or with curiosity, with contempt or with downright malign joy – at the burning of synagogues or humiliation of Jews and Jewesses forced to kneel in the street mud. Many Germans knew from the foreign radio broadcasts, and a number had contact with prisoners who worked outside the camps. A good many Germans had had the experience of encountering miserable lines of prisoners in the streets or at the railroad stations. In a circular dated 9 November 1941, and addressed by the head of the Police and the Security Services to all . . . Police officials and camp commandants, one reads: 'In particular, it must be noted that during the transfers on foot, for example from the station to the camp, a considerable number of prisoners collapse along the way, fainting or dying from exhaustion . . . It is impossible to keep the population from knowing about such happenings.'

Not a single German could have been unaware of the fact that the prisons were full to overflowing, and that executions were taking place continually all over the country. Thousands of magistrates and police functionaries, lawyers, priests and social workers knew generically that the situation was very grave. Many businessmen who dealt with the camp SS men as suppliers, the industrialists who asked the administrative and economic offices of the SS for slave-labourers, the clerks in those offices, all knew perfectly well that many of the big firms were exploiting slave labour. Quite a few workers performed their tasks near concentration camps or actually inside them. Various university professors collaborated with the medical research centres instituted by Himmler, and various state doctors and doctors connected with private institutes collaborated with the professional murderers. A good many members of military aviation had been transferred to SS jurisdiction and must have known what went on there. Many high-ranking army officers knew about the mass murders of the Russian prisoners of war in the camps, and even more soldiers and members of the Military Police must have known exactly what terrifying horrors were being perpetrated in the camps, the ghettos, the cities, and the countrysides of the occupied Eastern territories. Can you say that even one of these statements is false?[1]

In my opinion, none of these statements is false, but one other must be added to complete the picture: in spite of the varied possibilities for information, most Germans didn't know because they didn't want to know. Because, indeed, they wanted *not* to know. It is certainly true that state terrorism is a very strong weapon, very difficult to resist. But it is also true that the German people, as a whole, did not even try to resist. In Hitler's Germany, a particular code was widespread: those who knew did not talk; those who did not know did not ask questions; those who did ask questions received no answers. In this way, the typical German citizen won and defended his ignorance, which seemed to him sufficient justification of his adherence to Nazism. Shutting his mouth, his eyes and his ears, he built for himself the illusion of not knowing, hence not being an accomplice to the things taking place in front of his very door.

Knowing and making things known was one way (basically then not all that dangerous) of keeping one's distance from Nazism. I think the German people, on the whole, did not seek this recourse, and I hold them fully culpable of this deliberate omission.

3   Were there prisoners who escaped from the camps? How is it that there were no large-scale revolts?

These are among the questions most frequently put to me by young readers. They must, therefore, spring from some particularly import-ant curiosity or need. My interpretation is optimistic: today's young people feel that freedom is a privilege that one cannot do without, no matter what. Consequently, for them, the idea of prison is immedi-ately linked to the idea of escape or revolt. Besides, it is true that, according to the military codes of many countries, the prisoner of war is required to attempt escape, in any way possible, in order to resume his place as a combatant, and that according to The Hague Conven-tion, such an attempt would not be punished. The concept of escape as a moral obligation is constantly reinforced by romantic literature (remember the Count of Montecristo?), by popular literature, and by the cinema, in which the hero, unjustly (or even justly) imprisoned, always tries to escape, even in the least likely circumstances, the attempt being invariably crowned with success.

Perhaps it is good that the prisoner's condition, not-liberty, is felt to be something improper, abnormal – like an illness, in short – that has to be cured by escape or rebellion. Unfortunately, however, this picture hardly resembles the true one of the concentration camps.

For instance, only a few hundred prisoners tried to escape from Auschwitz, and of those perhaps a few score succeeded. Escape was difficult and extremely dangerous. The prisoners were debilitated, in addition to being demoralized, by hunger and ill-treatment. Their heads were shaved, their striped clothing was immediately recogniz-able, and their wooden clogs made silent and rapid walking impos-sible. They had no money and, in general, did not speak Polish, which was the local language, nor did they have contacts in the area, whose geography they did not know, either. On top of all that, fierce reprisals were employed to discourage escape attempts. Any-one caught trying to escape was publicly hanged – often after cruel torture – in the square where the roll calls took place. When an escape was discovered, the friends of the fugitive were considered accom-plices and were starved to death in cells; all the other prisoners were forced to remain standing for twenty-four hours, and sometimes the parents of the 'guilty' one were arrested and deported to camps.

The SS guards who killed a prisoner in the course of an escape attempt were granted special leaves. As a result, it often happened that an SS guard fired at a prisoner who had no intention of trying to escape, solely in order to qualify for leave. This fact artificially swells the official number of escape attempts recorded in the statistics. As I have indicated, the actual number was very small, made up almost exclusively of a few Aryan (that is, non-Jewish, to use the terminology of that time) Polish prisoners who lived not far from the camp and had, consequently, a goal towards which to proceed and the assurance that they would be protected by the population. In the other camps, things occurred in a similar way.

As for the lack of rebellion, the story is somewhat different. First of all, it is necessary to remember that uprisings did actually take place in certain camps: Treblinka, Sobibor, even Birkenau, one of the Auschwitz dependencies. They did not have much numerical weight; like the analogous Warsaw Ghetto uprising they represented, rather, examples of extraordinary moral force. In every instance they were planned and led by prisoners who were privileged in some way and, consequently, in better physical and spiritual condition than the average camp prisoner. This is not all that surprising: only at first glance does it seem paradoxical that people who rebel are those who suffer the least. Even outside the camps, struggles are rarely waged by *Lumpenproletariat*. People in rags do not revolt.

In the camps for political prisoners, or where political prisoners were in the majority, the conspiratory experience of these people proved valuable and often resulted in quite effective defensive activities, rather than in open revolt. Depending upon the camps and the times, prisoners succeeded, for example, in blackmailing or corrupting the SS, curbing their indiscriminate power; in sabotaging the work for the German war industries; in organizing escapes; in communicating via the radio with the Allies, furnishing them with accounts of the horrendous conditions in the camps; in improving the treatment of the sick, substituting prisoner doctors for the SS ones; in 'guiding' the selections, sending spies and traitors to death and saving prisoners whose survival had, for one reason or another, some special importance; preparing, even in military ways, to resist in case the Nazis decided, with the Front coming closer (as in fact, they often did decide), to liquidate the camps entirely.

In camps with a majority of Jews, like those in the Auschwitz area, an active or passive defence was particularly difficult. Here the prisoners were, for the most part, devoid of any kind of organizational or military experience. They came from every country in Europe, spoke different languages and, as a result, could not understand one another. They were more starved, weaker and more exhausted than the others because their living conditions were harsher and because they often had a long history of hunger, persecution and humiliation in the ghettos. The final consequences of this were that the length of their stays in the camps was tragically brief. They were, in short, a fluctuating population, continually decimated by death and renewed by the never-ending arrivals of new convoys. It is understandable that the seed of revolt did not easily take root in a human fabric that was in such a state of deterioration and so unstable.

You may wonder why the prisoners who had just got off the trains did not revolt, waiting as they did for hours (sometimes for days!) to enter the gas chambers. In addition to what I have already said, I must add here that the Germans had perfected a diabolically clever and versatile system of collective death. In most cases the new arrivals did not know what awaited them. They were received with cold efficiency but without brutality, invited to undress 'for the showers'. Sometimes they were handed soap and towels and were promised hot coffee after their showers. The gas chambers were, in fact, camouflaged as shower rooms, with pipes, faucets, dressing rooms, clothes hooks, benches and so forth. When, instead, prisoners showed the smallest sign of knowing or suspecting their imminent fate, the SS and their collaborators used surprise tactics, intervening with extreme brutality, with shouts, threats, kicks, shots, loosing their dogs, which were trained to tear prisoners to pieces, against people who were confused, desperate, weakened by five or ten days of travelling in sealed railroad cars.

Such being the case, the statement that has sometimes been formulated – that the Jews didn't revolt out of cowardice – appears absurd and insulting. No one rebelled. Let it suffice to remember that the gas chambers at Auschwitz were tested on a group of 300 Russian prisoners of war, young, army-trained, politically indoctrinated, and not hampered by the presence of women and children, and even they did not revolt.

I would like to add one final thought. The deeply rooted consciousness that one must not consent to oppression but resist it instead was not widespread in Fascist Europe, and it was particularly weak in Italy. It was the patrimony of a narrow circle of political activists, but Fascism and Nazism had isolated, expelled, terrorized or destroyed them outright. You must not forget that the first victims of the German camps, by the hundreds of thousands, were, in fact, the cadres of the anti-Nazi political parties. Without their contribution, the popular will to resist, to organize for the purpose of resisting, sprang up again much later, thanks, above all, to the contribution of the European Communist parties that hurled themselves into the struggle against Nazism after Germany, in 1941, had unexpectedly attacked the Soviet Union, breaking the Ribbentrop – Molotov pact of September 1939. To conclude, reproaching the prisoners for, not rebelling represents, above all, an error in historical perspective, expecting from them a political consciousness which is today an almost common heritage but which belonged at that time only to an elite.

4   Did you return to Auschwitz after the liberation?

I returned to Auschwitz in 1965.[2] As I have indicated in my books, the concentration camp empire of Auschwitz did not consist of only one camp but rather of some forty camps. Auschwitz central was constructed on the outskirts of the town of the same name (Oswiecim, in Polish). It had a capacity of about 20,000 prisoners and was, so to speak, the administrative capital of the complex. Then there was the camp (or, to be more precise, the group of camps – from three to five, depending on the period) of Birkenau, which grew to contain about 60,000 prisoners, of which about 40,000 were women, and in which the gas chambers and cremation furnaces functioned. In addition, there was a constantly varying number of work camps, as far away as hundreds of kilometres from the 'capital'. My camp, called Monowitz, was the largest of these, containing, finally, about 12,000 prisoners. It was situated about seven kilometres to the east of Auschwitz. The whole area is now Polish territory.

I didn't feel anything much when I visited the central camp. The Polish government has transformed it into a kind of national monument. The huts have been cleaned and painted, trees have been planted and flower-beds laid out. There is a museum in which pitiful relics are displayed: tons of human hair, hundreds of thousands of eyeglasses, combs, shaving brushes, dolls, baby shoes, but it remains just a museum – something static, rearranged, contrived. To me, the entire camp seemed a museum. As for my own camp, it no longer exists. The rubber factory to which it was annexed, now in Polish hands, has grown so that it occupies the whole area.

I did, however, experience a feeling of violent anguish when I entered Birkenau Camp, which I had never seen as a prisoner. Here nothing has changed. There was mud, and there is still mud, or suffocating summer dust. The blocks of huts (those that weren't burned when the Front reached and passed this area) have remained as they were, low, dirty, with draughty wooden sides and beaten earth floors. There are no bunks but bare planks, all the way to the ceiling. Here nothing has been prettied up. With me was a woman friend of mine, Giuliana Tedeschi, a survivor of Birkenau.[3] She pointed out to me that on every plank, 1.8 by 2 metres, up to nine women slept. She showed me that from the tiny window you could see the ruins of the cremation furnace. In her day, you could see the flames issuing from the chimney. She had asked the older women 'What is that fire?' And they had replied: 'It is we who are burning.'

Face to face with the sad evocative power of those places, each of us survivors behaves in a different manner, but it is possible to describe two typical categories. Those who refuse to go back, or even to discuss the matter, belong to the first category, as do those who would like to forget but do not succeed in doing so and are tormented by nightmares; and the second group who have, instead, forgotten, have dismissed everything, and have begun again to live, starting from zero. I have noticed that the first group are individuals who ended up in the camps through bad luck, not because of a political commitment. For them the suffering was traumatic but devoid of meaning, like a misfortune or an illness. For them the memory is extraneous, a painful object which intruded into their lives and which they have sought – or still seek – to eliminate. The second category is composed, instead, of ex-political prisoners, or those who possessed at least a measure of political preparation, or religious conviction, or a strong moral consciousness. For these survivors, remembering is a duty. They do not want to forget, and above all they do not want the world to forget, because they understand that their experiences were not meaningless, that the camps were not an accident, an unforeseen historical happening.

The Nazi camps were the apex, the culmination of Fascism in Europe, its most monstrous manifestation, but Fascism existed before Hitler and Mussolini, and it survived, in open or masked forms, up to the defeat of the Second World War. In every part of the world, wherever you begin by denying the fundamental liberties of mankind, and equality among people, you move towards the concentration camp system, and it is a road on which it is difficult to halt. I know many ex-prisoners who understand very well what a terrible lesson their experience contains and who return every year to, 'their' camp, guiding pilgrimages of young people. I would do it myself, gladly, if time permitted, and if I did not know that I reached the same goal by writing books and by agreeing to talk about them to my readers.

5   Why do you speak only about German camps and not the Russian ones as well?

As I have already written in my reply to the first question, I prefer the role of witness to that of judge. I can bear witness only to the things which I myself endured and saw. My books are not history books. In writing them I have limited myself strictly to reporting facts of which I had direct experience, excluding those I learned later from books or newspapers. For example, you will note that I have not quoted the number of those massacred at Auschwitz, nor have I described details of the gas chambers and crematoria. This is because I did not, in fact, know these data when I was in the camp. I only learned them afterwards, when the whole world learned them.

For the same reason I do not generally speak about the Russian camps. Fortunately I was never in them, and I could repeat only the things I have read, which would be the same things known to everyone interested in the subject. Clearly, however, I do not want to, nor can I, evade the duty which every man has, that of making a judgement and formulating an opinion. Besides the obvious similarities, I think I can perceive substantial differences.

The principal difference lies in the finality. The German camps constitute something unique in the history of humanity, bloody as it is. To the ancient aim of eliminating or terrifying political adversaries, they set a monstrous modern goal, that of erasing entire peoples and cultures from the world. Starting roughly in 1941, they became gigantic death-machines. Gas chambers and crematoria were deliberately planned to destroy lives and human bodies on a scale of millions. The horrendous record belongs to Auschwitz, with 24,000 dead in a single day, in August 1944. Certainly the Soviet camps were not and are not pleasant places to be, but in them the death of prisoners was not expressly sought – even in the darkest years of Stalinism. It was a very frequent occurrence, tolerated with brutal indifference, but basically not intended. Death was a by-product of hunger, cold, infections, hard labour. In this lugubrious comparison between two models of hell, I must also add the fact that one entered the German camps, in general never to emerge. Death was the only foreseen outcome. In the Soviet camps, however, a possible limit to incarceration has always existed. In Stalin's day the 'guilty' were sometimes given terribly long sentences (as much as fifteen or twenty years) with frightening disregard, but a hope – however faint – of eventual freedom remained.

From this fundamental difference, the others arise. The relationships between guards and prisoners are less inhuman in the Soviet

Union. They all belong to the same nation, speak the same language, are not labelled, 'Supermen' and 'Non-men' as they were under Nazism. The sick are treated, though all too inadequately. Confronted with overly hard work, an individual or collective protest is not unthinkable. Corporal punishment is rare and not too cruel. It is possible to receive letters and packages with foodstuffs. Human personality, in short, is not denied and, is not totally lost. As a general consequence, the mortality figures are very different under the two systems. In the Soviet Union, it seems that in the harshest periods mortality hovered around 30 per cent of those who entered. This is certainly an intolerably high figure, but in the German camps, mortality mounted to between 90 and 98 per cent.

I find very serious the recent Soviet innovation, that of summarily declaring certain dissenting intellectuals insane, shutting them into psychiatric institutions, and subjecting them to treatments that not only cause cruel suffering but distort and weaken their mental functioning. This shows how greatly dissent is feared. It is no longer punished but there is an effort to destroy it with drugs (or with the threat of drugs). Perhaps this technique is not very widespread (it appears that in 1985 these political 'patients' do not exceed a hundred) but it is odious because it constitutes a despicable use of science and an unpardonable prostitution on the part of the doctors who lend themselves so slavishly to abetting the wishes of the authorities. It reveals extreme contempt for democratic confrontation and civil liberties.

On the other hand, and as far as the precisely quantitative aspect is concerned, one must note that in the Soviet Union the camp phenomenon appears to be on the decline, actually. It seems that around 1950, political prisoners were numbered in the millions. According to the data of Amnesty International they would number about 10,000 today.

To conclude, the Soviet camps remain anyway a deplorable manifestation of illegality and inhumanity. They have nothing to do with Socialism; indeed, they stand out as an ugly stain on Soviet Socialism. They should, rather, be regarded as a barbaric legacy from Tsarist absolutism from which the Soviet rulers have been unable or have not wished to liberate themselves. Anyone who reads *Memories of a Dead House*, written by Dostoevsky in 1862, will have no difficulty recognizing the same prison 'features' described by Solzhenitsyn a hundred years later. But it is possible, even easy, to picture a Socialism without prison camps. A Nazism without concentration camps is, instead, unimaginable.

6   *Which of the characters in* If This is a Man *and* The Truce *have you seen again since the liberation?*

Most of the people who appear in these pages must, unfortunately, be considered to have died during their days in the camp or in the course of the huge evacuation march mentioned in the last chapter of the book. Others died later from illnesses contracted during their imprisonment. I have been unable to find a trace of still others. Some few survive and I have been able to maintain or re-establish contact with them.

Jean, the 'Pikolo' of the 'Canto of Ulysses', is alive and well. His family had been wiped out, but he married after his return and now has two children and leads a very peaceful life as a pharmacist in a small town in the French provinces. We get together occasionally in Italy, where he vacations. At other times I have gone to join him. Strange as it may seem, he has forgotten much of his year in Monowitz. The atrocious memories of the evacuation march loom larger for him. In the course of it, he saw all his friends (Alberto among them) die of exhaustion.

I also quite often see the person I called Piero Sonnino, the man who appears as Cesare in *The Truce*. He, too, after a difficult period of 're-entry', found work and built a family. He lives in Rome. He recounts willingly and with great liveliness the vicissitudes he lived through in camp and during the long journey home, but in his narratives, which often become almost theatrical monologues, he tends to emphasize the adventurous happenings of which he was the protagonist rather than those tragic ones at which he was passively present.

I have also seen Charles again.[4] He had been taken prisoner only in November 1944 in the hills of the Vosges near his house, where he was a partisan, and he had been in the camp for only a month. But that month of suffering, and the terrible things which he witnessed, marked him deeply, robbing him of the joy of living and the desire to build a future. Repatriated after a journey much like the one I described in *The Truce*, he resumed his profession of elementary school teacher in the tiny school in his village, where he also taught the children how to raise bees and how to cultivate a nursery for firs and pine trees. He retired quite a few years ago and recently married a no-longer-young colleague. Together they built a new house, small but comfortable and charming. I have gone to visit him twice, in 1951 and 1974. On this last occasion he told me about Arthur, who lives in a village not far from him. Arthur is old and ill, and does not wish to receive visits that might reawaken old anguish.

Dramatic, unforeseen, and full of joy for both of us was rediscovering Mendi, the 'modernist rabbi' mentioned briefly. He recognized himself in 1965 while casually reading the German translation of *If This is a Man*, remembered me, and wrote me a long letter, addressing it in care of the Jewish Community of Turin. We subsequently wrote to each other at length, each informing the other about the fates of our common friends. In 1967 I went to see him in Dortmund, in the German Republic, where he was rabbi at the time. He has remained as he was, 'steadfast, courageous, and keen', and extraordinarily cultivated besides. He married an Auschwitz survivor and has three children, now grown up. The whole family intends to move to Israel.

I never saw Dr Pannwitz again. He was the chemist who subjected me to a chilling 'state examination'. But I heard about him from that Dr Müller to whom I dedicated the chapter 'Vanadium' in my book *The Periodic Table*. When the arrival of the Red Army at the Buna factory was imminent, he conducted himself like a bully and a coward. He ordered his civilian collaborators to resist to the bitter end, forbade them to climb aboard the train leaving for the zones behind the Front, but jumped on himself at the last moment, profiting from the confusion. He died in 1946 of a brain tumour.

I have lost contact with almost all the characters in *The Truce*, with the exception of Cesare (of whom I have spoken before) and Leonardo. Dr Leonardo De Benedetti, a native of Turin like myself, had lost his dearly beloved wife at Auschwitz. After returning to our city, he resumed his profession with courage and commitment and was a precious friend, wise and serene, for many years. Besides his patients, innumerable others turned to him for help and advice and were never disappointed. He died in 1983 at the age of eighty-five, without suffering.

7 *How can the Nazis' fanatical hatred of the Jews be explained?*

Hatred of the Jews, wrongly termed anti-Semitism, is a special case of a wider phenomenon, that is, hatred for whoever is different from us. Its origins are undoubtedly zoological: different groups of animals belonging to the same species show evidence of intolerance of each other. It happens with domestic animals too: it is well known that a hen from one hen-house, when introduced into another, is pecked at and rejected for several days. The same thing happens with mice and bees and generally with all social animals. Now, man is for sure a social animal (as Aristotle has told us): but woe betide us if all the zoological impulses that survive in man were to be tolerated! Human laws serve just this purpose: to rein in our animal instincts.

Anti-Semitism is a typical phenomenon of intolerance. For intolerance to arise, there must be a perceptible difference between two groups in contact with each other: it could be a physical difference (black or white, dark-haired or blond), but our complicated civilization has made us sensitive to more subtle differences also, such as language or dialect or even accent (as southern Italians forced to migrate to the North know all too well); religion, with all its external trappings and its profound influence on ways of life; dress or gestures; public and private habits. The tormented history of the Jewish people has meant that in almost all places and times, the Jews have displayed at least one of these differentiating features.

In the extremely complex tangle of peoples and nations in conflict with each other, the history of this particular people shows certain special characteristics. It was (and in part still is) the heir to a very strong internal bond, coming from both religion and tradition; thus, despite its numerical and military inferiority, it opposed with desperate bravery the conquest of the Romans which led to deportation and dispersal, but the bond nevertheless survived. The Jewish colonies that built up, first, all around the coasts of the Mediterranean and then in the Middle East, Spain, the Rhineland, Southern Russia, Poland, Bohemia and elsewhere, stayed firmly loyal to that bond which had in the meantime been consolidated in an immense body of written laws and traditions, minutely codified religious practices and a visibly peculiar set of rituals which pervaded all their daily actions. The Jews, in a minority wherever they went, were therefore different, recognizably different and often (rightly or wrongly) proud of their difference. All this made them very vulnerable, and indeed they were fiercely persecuted in almost all lands and periods. In the face of persecution, a small number of Jews reacted by assimilating, that is, by fusing with the surrounding population. For the most part, however, they would emigrate once again to more hospitable countries, although this meant that their 'difference' was only made greater and they were exposed to new restrictions and persecutions.

If anti-Semitism is in its deepest essence an irrational form of intolerance, it has, in all Christian countries, from the time when Christianity began to establish itself as a state religion, had a predominantly religious or indeed theological aspect. According to St Augustine, the Jews were condemned to be dispersed by God himself, for two reasons: as punishment for their failure to recognize Christ as the Messiah and because the Catholic Church needs them in all countries so that their deserved unhappiness might be visible to the faithful everywhere. Therefore, the dispersal and separation of the Jews must never end: through their suffering, they must bear eternal witness to their error and thus to the truth of Christian faith. Since their presence is necessary, if follows that they must be persecuted but not killed.

And yet the Church has not always proved to be so moderate in its aims: from the earliest centuries of the Christian era a far harsher accusation was levelled at the Jews, that of being collectively and eternally responsible for the crucifixion of Christ, or 'deicide'. This formula, which in the distant past was part of the Easter liturgy and was only finally suppressed by the Second Vatican Council (1962–5), has been the source of various disastrous and continually renewed popular beliefs: that Jews poison wells to spread plague; that they habitually profane the consecrated host; that they kidnap Christian children at Passover and dip unleavened bread in their blood. These beliefs have offered pretexts for numerous bloody massacres and also the mass expulsion of the Jews, first from France and England and then (1492–8) from Spain and Portugal.

An uninterrupted sequence of massacres and migrations takes us all the way to the nineteenth century and the general rebirth of national consciousness and a recognition of the rights of minorities. With the exception of Tsarist Russia, legal restrictions on the lives of Jews which had been invoked by the Christian Church (in various forms, depending on time and place, from the order to reside in ghettos and special zones to wearing a distinguishing mark on their clothes to bans on joining certain professions, on mixed marriages etc.) are abolished throughout Europe. Anti-Semitism survives, however, especially in countries where a rough-hewn religion continues to point the finger at the Jews as Christ-killers (Poland and Russia) and in countries where nationalist claims had left behind them a residue of generic hostility towards neighbours and foreigners (Germany, but also France, where at the end of the nineteenth century clerics, nationalists and the military combine to unleash a violent wave of anti-Semitism following the false accusation of high treason against the Jewish army official Alfred Dreyfus).

In Germany in particular, throughout the last century, a string of philosophers and politicians insisted on perpetuating fanatical notions according to which the German people, too long divided and humiliated, had a natural right to supremacy in Europe and perhaps the world, and were the heirs to ancient and noble traditions and cultures and was made up of substantially homogeneous individuals in terms of blood and race. The Germanic peoples should have built themselves into a strong warrior state, ruling over Europe, decked in almost divine majesty.

This notion of a mission for the German nation survives the defeat of the First World War and indeed emerges all the stronger from the humiliation of the Peace Treaty of Versailles. It is taken over by one of the most sinister and dark characters in history, the political agitator, Adolf Hitler. The German middle classes and the industrialists lend their ear to his inflammatory pronouncements. Hitler looks promising, he will manage to divert onto the Jews the hostility of the German proletariat towards the class that led them to defeat and to economic catastrophe. In the space of only a few years, from 1933, he makes the most of the anger of a humiliated country and of the nationalistic pride stirred up by the prophets that preceded him (Luther, Fichte, Hegel, Wagner, Gobineau, Chamberlain, Nietzsche). His obsession is a dominant Germany, not in some far-off future, but now; not through some civilizing mission, but through the force of arms. All that is not German is inferior or better detestable, and the first enemies of Germany are the Jews, for a great many reasons that Hitler enumerates with dogmatic fury: because they are of 'different blood'; because they are related to other Jews, in England, Russia and America; because they have inherited a culture of reason and debate rather than obedience, which forbids the worship of idols, whereas he aspires to be venerated as an idol himself. He does not hesitate to declare that 'we must distrust intelligence and conscience and place all our faith in instinct'. Finally, many Jews are in key positions in the economy, in finances, in arts, science and literature: Hitler, a failed painter and a failed architect, turns all his resentment and frustrated envy against the Jews.

This seed of intolerance, falling on well-nurtured ground, takes root with incredible vigour but it grows in new forms. Fascist anti-Semitism, spread amongst the German people by the Word of Hitler, is more barbaric than all previous anti-Semitisms. Converging within it are artificially distorted biological doctrines which say that weak races must yield to the strong; absurd popular credences that common sense had buried for centuries; and incessant propaganda. Unheard-of extremes are reached. Judaism is not a religion that can be changed through baptism, nor is it a cultural tradition that can be abandoned for another: it is a human sub-species, a different race, inferior to all others. Jews are only apparently human beings: in reality they are something other, something abominable and indefinable, 'further removed from Germans than monkeys are from men'. They are guilty of everything from greedy American capitalism to Soviet Bolshevism; from the defeat of 1918 to the hyperinflation of

1923. Liberalism, democracy, socialism and communism are all Satanic Jewish inventions that threaten the monolithic solidarity of the Nazi state.

The passage from theoretical preaching to practical results was swift and brutal. In 1933, just two months after Hitler arrived in power, the first *Lager* is born at Dachau. In May of the same year works by Jewish authors and other enemies of Nazism burn in the first bonfire (but over a century earlier the Jewish-German poet Heine had written, 'if you burn books, sooner or later you will end up burning people'). In 1935, anti-Semitism is codified in the monumental and minutely detailed act of legislation, the Nuremberg Laws. In 1938, in a single night of disorder controlled from on high, 191 synagogues are burned down and thousands of Jewish-owned shops are destroyed. In 1939, the Jews of recently occupied Poland are enclosed in ghettos. In 1940, the camp of Auschwitz opens. In 1941–2, the extermination is in full flow: the number of victims will reach millions by 1944.

The hatred and contempt of Nazi propaganda are fulfilled in the everyday workings of the extermination camps. Not only death found its place there, but also a mass of maniacal and symbolic minutiae, all aimed at proving or confirming that the Jews and the gypsies and the Slavs are cattle, litter, detritus. Remember the tattooing at Auschwitz, which marked men like oxen; the journey in cattle-trucks, permanently closed so that deportees (men, women and children!) are forced to lie for days in their own filth; the registration number in place of a name; the refusal to hand out spoons (when the storerooms at Auschwitz, after liberation, were found to be full of them), so that prisoners would have to lick up their soup like dogs; the wicked exploitation of corpses, treated as just any source material to be mined for gold in the teeth, hair as a textile, ashes as a fertilizer; men and women reduced to guinea-pigs to try out drugs on before killing them off.

Even the very manner of the killing (chosen after careful experiment) was openly symbolic. The gas prescribed and used was the same used for disinfecting ships' holds and sites invaded by bugs or lice. More painful deaths have been devised over the course of the centuries, but none more pregnant with derision and contempt.

As is well known, the extermination project reached an advanced stage. The Nazis, although engaged in a terrible war which by now had become a war of defence, inexplicably rushed on with their task: the convoys of victims being taken to the gas chambers or transferred away from *Lagers* near the front line took precedence over military transports. Only Germany's defeat prevented it from reaching completion, but even Hitler's political will, dictated only hours before his suicide with the Russians only metres away, ended as follows: 'Above all else, I order the German government and people to uphold in full the racial laws and to fight to the last against the poisoner of all nations, international Judaism.'

It can be said, then, that anti-Semitism is one particular case of intolerance, that for centuries it had a prevailingly religious character; that in the Third Reich it was exacerbated by the nationalistic and military pre-disposition of the German people and by the 'differentness' of the Jewish people; that it was easily disseminated in all of Germany – and in a good part of Europe – thanks to the efficiency of the Fascist and Nazi propaganda which needed a scapegoat on which to load all guilts and all resentments; and that the phenomenon was heightened to paroxysm by Hitler, a maniacal dictator.

However, I must admit that these commonly accepted explanations do not satisfy me. They are reductive; not commensurate with, nor proportionate to, the facts that need explaining. In rereading the chronicles of Nazism, from its murky beginnings to its convulsed end, I cannot avoid the impression of a general atmosphere of uncontrolled madness that seems to me to be unique in history. This collective madness, this 'running off the rails', is usually explained by postulating the combination of many diverse factors, insufficient if considered singly, and the greatest of these factors is Hitler's personality itself and its profound interaction with the German people. It is certain that his personal obsessions, his capacity for hatred, his preaching of violence, found unbridled echoes in the frustration of the German people, and for this reason came back to him multiplied, confirming his delirious conviction that he himself was the Hero prophesied by Nietzsche, the Superman redeemer of Germany.

Much has been written about the origin of his hatred of the Jews. It is said that Hitler poured out upon the Jews his hatred of the entire human race; that he recognized in the Jews some of his own defects, and that in hating the Jews he was hating himself; that the violence of his aversion arose from the fear that he might have 'Jewish blood' in his veins.

Again, these explanations do not seem adequate to me. I do not find it permissible to explain a historical phenomenon by piling all the blame on a single individual (those who carry out horrendous orders are not innocent!). Besides, it is always difficult to interpret the deep-seated motivations of an individual. The hypotheses that have been proposed justify the facts only up to a point, explain the quality but not the quantity. I must admit that I prefer the humility with which some of the most serious historians (among them Bullock, Schramm, Bracher)[5] confess to *not understanding* the furious anti-Semitism of Hitler and of Germany behind him.

Perhaps one cannot, what is more one must not, understand what happened, because to understand is almost to justify. Let me explain: 'understanding' a proposal or human behaviour means to 'contain' it, contain its author, put oneself in his place, identify with him. Now, no normal human being will ever be able to identify with Hitler, Himmler, Goebbels, Eichmann, and endless others. This dismays us, and at the same time gives us a sense of relief, because perhaps it is desirable that their words (and also, unfortunately, their deeds) cannot be comprehensible to us. They are non-human words and deeds, really counter-human, without historic precedents, with difficulty comparable to the cruellest events of the biological struggle for existence. The war can be related to this struggle, but Auschwitz has nothing to do with war; it is neither an episode in it nor an extreme form of it. War is always a terrible fact, to be deprecated, but it is in us, it has its rationality, we 'understand' it.

But there is no rationality in the Nazi hatred: it is a hate that is not in us; it is outside man, it is a poison fruit sprung from the deadly trunk of Fascism, but it is outside and beyond Fascism itself. We cannot understand it, but we can and must understand from where it springs, and we must be on our guard. If understanding is impossible, knowing is imperative, because what happened could happen again. Conscience can be seduced and obscured again – even our consciences.

For this reason, it is everyone's duty to reflect on what happened. Everybody must know, or remember, that when Hitler and Mussolini spoke in public, they were believed, applauded, admired, adored like gods. They were 'charismatic leaders'; they possessed a secret power of seduction that did not proceed from the credibility or the soundness of the things they said but from the suggestive way in which they said them, from their eloquence, from their histrionic art, perhaps instinctive, perhaps patiently learned and practised. The ideas they proclaimed were not always the same and were, in general, aberrant or silly or cruel. And yet they were acclaimed with hosannahs and followed to the death by millions of the faithful. We must remember that these faithful followers, among them the diligent executors of inhuman orders, were not born torturers, were not (with a few exceptions) monsters: they were ordinary men. Monsters exist, but they are too few in number to be truly dangerous. More dangerous are the common men, the functionaries ready to believe and to act without asking questions, like Eichmann; like Höss, the commandant of Auschwitz;[6] like Stangl, commandant of Treblinka; like the French military of twenty years later, slaughterers in Algeria; like the Khmer Rouge of the late seventies, slaughterers in Cambodia.

It is, therefore, necessary to be suspicious of those who seek to convince us with means other than reason, and of charismatic leaders: we must be cautious about delegating to others our judgement and our will. Since it is difficult to distinguish true prophets from false, it is as well to regard all prophets with suspicion. It is better to renounce revealed truths, even if they exalt us by their splendour or if we find them convenient because we can acquire them gratis. It is better to content oneself with other more modest and less exciting truths, those one acquires painfully, little by little and without short cuts, with study, discussion, and reasoning, those that can be verified and demonstrated.

It is clear that this formula is too simple to suffice in every case. A new Fascism, with its trail of intolerance, of abuse, and of servitude, can be born outside our country and be imported into it, walking on tiptoe and calling itself by other names, or it can loose itself from within with such violence that it routs all defences. At that point, wise counsel no longer serves, and one must find the strength to resist. Even in this contingency, the memory of what happened in the heart of Europe, not very long ago, can serve as support and warning.

8   What would you be today if you had not been a prisoner in the camp? What do you feel, remembering that period? To what factors do you attribute your survival?

Strictly speaking, I do not and cannot know what I would be today if I had not been in the camp. No man knows his future, and this would be, precisely, a case of describing a future that never took place. Hazarding guesses (extremely rough ones, for that matter) about the behaviour of a population has some meaning. It is, however, almost impossible to foresee the behaviour of an individual, even on a day-to-day basis. In the same way, the physicist can prognosticate with great exactitude the time a gram of radium will need to halve its activity but is totally unable to say when a single atom of that same radium will disintegrate. If a man sets out towards a crossroad and does not take the left-hand path, it is obvious that he will take the one on the right, but almost never are our choices between only two alternatives. Then, every choice is followed by others, all multiple, and so on, *ad infinitum*. Last of all, our future depends heavily on external factors, wholly extraneous to our deliberate choices, and on internal factors as well, of which we are, however, not aware. For these well-known reasons, a person does not know his future or that of his neighbour. For the same reason no one can say what his past would have been like 'if'.

I can, however, formulate a certain assertion and it is this: if I had not lived the Auschwitz experience, I probably would never have written anything. I would not have had the motivation, the incentive, to write. I had been a mediocre student in Italian and had had bad grades in history. Physics and chemistry interested me most, and I had chosen a profession, that of chemist, which had nothing in common with the world of the written word. It was the experience of the camp and the long journey home that forced me to write. I did not have to struggle with laziness, problems of style seemed ridiculous to me, and miraculously I found the time to write without taking even one hour away from my daily professional work. It seemed as if those books were all there, ready in my head, and I had only to let them come out and pour on to paper.

Now many years have passed. The two books, above all the first, have had many adventures and have interposed themselves, in a curious way, like an artificial memory, but also like a defensive barrier, between my very normal present and the dramatic past. I say this with some hesitation, because I would not want to pass for a cynic: when I remember the camp today, I no longer feel any violent or dolorous emotions. On the contrary, on to my brief and tragic experience as a deportee has been overlaid that much longer and complex experience of writer-witness, and the sum total is clearly positive: in its totality, this past has made me richer and surer. A friend of mine, who was deported to the women's camp of Ravensbrück, says that the camp was her university. I think I can say the same thing, that is, by living and then writing about and pondering those events, I have learned many things about man and about the world.

I must hasten to say, however, that this positive outcome was a kind of good fortune granted to very few. Of the Italian deportees, for example, only about 5 per cent returned, and many of these lost families, friends, property, health, equilibrium, youth. The fact that I survived and returned unharmed is due, in my opinion, chiefly to good luck. Pre-existing factors played only a small part: for instance, my training as a mountaineer and my profession of chemist, which won me some privileges in the last months of imprisonment. Perhaps I was helped, too, by my interest, which has never flagged, in the human spirit and by the will not only to survive (which was common to many) but to survive with the precise purpose of recounting the things we had witnessed and endured. And, finally, I was also helped by the determination, which I stubbornly preserved, to recognize always, even in the darkest days, in my companions and in myself, men, not things, and thus to avoid that total humiliation and demoralization which led so many to spiritual shipwreck.

Notes

1   From Eugen Kogon, *The Theory and Practice of Hell: The German Concentration Camps and the System Behind Them* (London: Secker and Warburg, 1950).
2   Levi returned again in 1982. See the following interview, 'Return to Auschwitz'.
3   Giuliana Tedeschi is the author of important works of testimony, including *Questo povero corpo* ('This Poor Body', Milan: EdIt, 1946) and *C'è un punto della terra*... (Florence: Giuntina, 1988; published in English as *There is a place on earth*, London: Minerva, 1994), both about her time in Birkenau.
4   Charles and Arthur (mentioned below) were two French companions of Levi's very final days in the camp, described at the end of *If This is a Man* and at the start of *The Truce*.
5   All three are authors of important studies of Hitler, among other things: Alan Bullock, *Hitler, A Study in Tyranny* (London: Odham, 1952); P. E. Schramm, *Hitler* (1963, trans. London: Allen Lane, 1972); K. D. Bracher, *The German Dictator* (1969, trans. London: Weidenfeld and Nicolson, 1971).
6   Levi wrote a preface to the Italian edition of Höss's autobiography, R. Höss, *Comandante ad Auschwitz. Memoriale autobiografico* (Turin: Einaudi, 1958; published in English as *Commandant of Auschwitz*, London: Weidenfeld and Nicolson, 1959).

Return to Auschwitz (1982)

Daniel Toaff and Emanuele Ascarelli

[The interview begins in a train travelling through Poland towards Auschwitz.]

So, what effect does seeing these places again have on you?

It's all different. More than forty years have gone by. Poland then was emerging from five years of a frightful war, it was probably the country that had suffered most from the war in all of Europe, that had had the largest number of victims, and not only Jews. And then, in these past forty years, the world has changed everywhere. Also, I came through this landscape in winter, and the difference is total, because the Polish winter, then as now, is harsh, not like our Italian winters. There's snow for three or four months and we were inept, we had no idea how to survive it, during and after the time in the camp. I came through these towns as a sort of missing person, disorientated, in search of a centre of gravity, someone who could take me in. And the landscape was truly desolate.

And the wheels, the goods trains that run past us, what effect do they have?

From a transcript of a television interview carried out over the course of a journey to Auschwitz concentration camp in June 1982, broadcast by the RAI programme *Sorgente di vita* in April 1983 and again immediately following Levi's death in April 1987.

Yes, I'd say that it's the goods trains that trigger the strongest reflex, that upset me most. Even today, seeing one of these goods cars, let alone getting into one, affects me violently, reawakens strong memories, much more so than seeing these towns and places again, even, I'd say, seeing Auschwitz itself. A journey of five days shut up in a sealed cattle-car is an experience you never forget.

This morning you were telling me about the feelings you have when you hear Polish being spoken?

Yes, that's another conditioned reflex, at least for me. I am a talker and a listener: other people's language makes a great impact on me. I tend, I try to use my own Italian language as well as I can. Now, Polish was the incomprehensible language that greeted us at the end of our journey, and it wasn't the civil Polish we hear today, in the hotels, from our travel companions here. It was a rough Polish, full of swearing and imprecation that we couldn't understand; it was truly the language of hell. German was even more so, of course. German was the language of the oppressors, of our torturers, but many of us – myself included – could understand something of the German we heard, it wasn't unknown, the language of the void. Polish was the language of the void. And I was deeply struck, last night, by two drunken Poles in the hotel lift, who were speaking the language I remember, not like all the others around us: they were swearing, spitting out what seemed like a stream of consonants, a genuinely infernal language.

The same sensation, you were saying, that you get from the smell of coal.

Indeed. There's that too, perhaps because I'm a chemist. A chemist is trained to identify substances from their smell. Then, as now, as you enter Poland, Polish towns at least, there are two particular smells that you don't find in Italy; the smell of toasted malt and the acid smell of burning coal. This is a mining country, there's coal everywhere, even the heating in many homes is by coal, so in spring and autumn and all the more in winter, the smell spreads through the air. It's not even such a nasty smell, the acid smell of burning coal, but for us, for me at least, it is the smell of the *Lager*, of Poland and the *Lager*.

And the people?

No, the people aren't the same. Then we didn't get to see the people. We did see our torturers in the camp and their collaborators who were mostly Poles, both Jewish and Christian. But the ordinary people in the street, the Poles living in their own homes, we didn't see them or we saw them from afar, beyond the barbed wire. There was a country road that ran alongside the camp boundary, but hardly anyone used it. Later we found out that all the peasants had been moved out of the area. But coaches carrying Polish workers passed by and I remember that on one of these coaches there was an advertising board, just like nowadays, with the slogan 'Beste Suppe, Knorr Suppe' ('The Best Soup is Knorr Soup'). It was very strange for us to see an advert for soup, as if you could choose between one soup and another.

What effect did it have coming back and leaving for this journey this morning from a luxury hotel for foreigners?

An effect of displacement, I'm tempted to say of physical dislocation, of something impossible that is nevertheless happening. The contrast is too strong. We could never have even dreamed of such a thing then, of coming back to these places as tourists in luxury (or almost luxury) hotels. Although...

Yes, what does this contrast, what...

Like any contrast, this one is partly gratifying and partly alarming, because it could all return. The inverse would have been much worse: to have come first to the luxury hotel and then later been in total despair.

Did you know where you were going, what your destination was?

Basically we knew nothing. We had seen at the station in Fossoli[1] a sign hung on the cars with our destination, with Auschwitz scribbled on it, but we didn't know where it was, we thought it might be Austerlitz. We thought, who knows, it must be somewhere in Bohemia. At that time, in Italy, I don't think anyone, even the best informed people, knew what Auschwitz meant.

Forty years ago, what was the first impression of Auschwitz?

It was . . . oh, well, like another planet, at night, after five days of appalling travel, during which some in the wagon had died, arriving at a place whose language none of us understood, whose purpose none of us understood. There were meaningless signs: a shower, clean side, dirty side and clean side. No one explained anything, or they spoke at us in Yiddish or Polish and we couldn't understand. It was a profoundly alienating experience. We felt we had gone insane, that . . . that we had given up all possibility of reason, we could no longer think.

What had that journey been like, those five days? What do you remember most?

Oh, I remember it very well, I remember a great deal. There were forty-five of us in a very small wagon. There was just enough room for all of us to sit down, but not to lie down. There was a young mother breast-feeding her baby and they had told us to take food supplies with us, but stupidly we hadn't brought any water; we hadn't thought of it, we had a tiny amount, no one had warned us; we assumed we would find water en route. And although it was winter, the thirst was awful. Five days of thirst was really the first of many tortures. I remember that it was deep winter, that your breath froze on the wagon bolts, and we had a competition to scrape off the frozen dew – even though it was rusty, hanging off the bolts – to scrape it off to have at least a few drops of water to moisten our mouths. And the baby screamed from morning to night, because the mother had no more milk.

And what happened to the children and the mothers, when . . .

Oh, they were all killed at once. Of 650 in our train, four-fifths died the night we arrived or the night after; they were selected out immediately and taken to the gas chambers. In this grim scenario, at night, with reflector lights glaring and people screaming – screams like I had never heard before, screaming orders that we didn't understand – we left our wagons and lined up, they made us line up. Before us was an NCO or an officer – later I found out he was a doctor, but we knew none of that then – who asked each of us: are you able to work or not? I talked it over with the man nearest to me; he was a friend, from

Padua, older than me and not in perfect health. I said to him, I'm going to say I can work. And he said to me, do as you please, it's all the same to me. He had already given up all hope; and in fact, he said he could not work and he never went into the camp. I never saw him nor indeed any of the others again.

What was the work like there, in Auschwitz?

The first thing to say is that, as you know, there wasn't just one camp at Auschwitz. There were many and several of them had been built to plan, as annexes to factories and mines. The camp of Birkenau, for example, was divided into a certain number of squads which worked for various factories, including armaments factories. My camp, Monowitz, with its 10,000 prisoners, was part of an industrial plant belonging to IG-Farben, an enormous chemical trust company which was dismantled after the war. The task of the plant was to construct a new factory for chemical products over an area of something like six square kilometres. The work was at an advanced stage, and everyone took part in it: English prisoners of war, French prisoners, Russians, and Germans of course, as well as free or volunteer Poles and also some Italian volunteers. There were something in the region of 40,000 individuals, of whom we 10,000 were the lowest of the low. The camp of Monowitz, made up almost exclusively of Jews, was there to provide the unskilled workforce. Despite this, however, because skilled workers were scarce in Germany at that time since the men were all at the front, after a certain time they began to look amongst us too – in theory labourers and slaves – for specialists . . . From the very first day in the camp at Monowitz there was a sort of census research going on: they asked everyone their age, qualifications, profession. And this was one of my great strokes of luck, because I said I was a chemist, without knowing that we were labourers in a chemical factory. Much later, this was to work to my advantage, because I was assigned to work for the last two months inside a laboratory.

And the food?

Well, food was problem number one. I can't agree with those who describe the soup and bread in Auschwitz as disgusting. As far as I was concerned, I was so starved that they seemed good to me, I never found them disgusting, even on the first day. There was very little food, the rations were minimal, roughly equivalent to 1600–1700 calories per day, in theory at least, since there were thefts along the way, so by the time it reached us there was always less than this. Anyway, that was the official allocation. Now, you know that a small man can just about survive on 1600 calories a day, but only without working, lying all day in bed. We had to work, hard labour in the freezing cold. So our ration of 1600 calories a day meant slow death by malnutrition. Afterwards I read the calculation made by the Germans. They worked out that in these conditions a prisoner might, using up this ration and their personal reserves of energy, last from two to three months.

But in the concentration camps did people adapt to everything?

The question is a strange one. The prisoner who survived adapted to everything; but the great majority did not adapt to everything, and died. They died because they couldn't adapt, even to things which seems to us today the most banal; shoes, for example. They shoved a pair of shoes at us; no, not even a pair, just two different shoes, one with a heel, one without. You almost had to be an athlete to learn to walk in them. One was too tight, the other too loose, you had to negotiate complex deals, and if you were lucky, you managed to find two shoes that went together reasonably well. In any case, all the shoes hurt your feet; and anyone with delicate feet ended up with infections. I know from experience, I still have the scars. By some miracle, mine healed on their own, without my losing a single day's work. But if you were prone to infections you died 'from shoes', from infected foot-wounds which never healed. Your feet swelled up and the more they swelled the more they rubbed up against the shoes; you might end up in the hospital, but swollen feet were not sufficient an illness to get you admitted to the hospital. They were too common a complaint, so if you had swollen feet you were sent to the gas chambers.

Today, we're being taken to eat in a restaurant in Auschwitz.

Yes, it's almost laughable. That there should be a restaurant in Auschwitz. I don't know, I don't know if I will eat, it feels almost profane, absurd. On the other hand, you have to remember that Auschwitz, Oswiecim in Polish, was and is a town with restaurants, cinemas, probably even a night-club, perhaps, they have them in

Poland too. There are schools and children. In parallel to the Auschwitz which is today more like a concept – Auschwitz *is* the *Lager* – there is also this civilian Auschwitz, just as there was then too.

When you left Auschwitz, your first contact with the Polish population...

They were suspicious. The Poles had in essence gone from one occupation to another, from the ferocious force of the German occupation to the somewhat less ferocious, perhaps more primitive force of the Russians. They were suspicious of everyone, us included. We were foreigners after all. They didn't understand us, we had on a strange uniform, the uniform of forced labour, which terrified them. They didn't want to talk to us, only a handful took pity and with them we managed to explain a little. It was very important to make ourselves understood. An abyss divides the person who can make himself understood from the person who cannot: one is saved and the other is lost. The same was true in the *Lager*: understanding and being understood was of fundamental importance.

The language problem for Italians?

This was one of the reasons for Italians having the highest group mortality rate. Italians and Greeks. Most of the Italians who were with me died in the first few days from not understanding. They didn't understand the orders and no account was taken of not understanding: an order had to be understood, it was screamed, repeated once and then no more, then came the beatings. They didn't understand when it was announced that shoes could be changed, when we were called to be shaved once a week. They were always the last, they always arrived late. When they needed something, needed to say something, even something quite simple, they couldn't say it and they were ridiculed. Even at the level of morale, they collapsed immediately. As I see it, of the many causes of ruin in the camps, language was among the worst.

A few minutes ago we passed through one of the stations you refer to in The Truce.

Trzebinia. Yes, it was a station somewhere between Katowice and Cracow where the train had stopped. It was always stopping, that train, it took us three or four days to travel 150 kilometres. It stopped and I got off and there for the first time I met a middle-class Pole, a civilian, he was a lawyer, and I managed to communicate with him as he spoke German and also French. I didn't know any Polish, as I don't today. And so he asked me where I came from. I told him that I came from Auschwitz; I was in uniform, I still had my striped rags on. He asked me why and I replied: I'm an Italian Jew. He was translating my replies for a crowd of curious onlookers that had gathered, Polish peasants, workers on their way to work, early in the morning, if I remember rightly. As I said, I didn't know any Polish, but I could work out that in his translation he had changed my reply. I had said 'I'm an Italian Jew' and he had translated 'he's an Italian political prisoner'. So, in French, I protested. I said, I'm not... I am also a political prisoner, but I was brought to Auschwitz as a Jew not as a political prisoner. And he replied to me in hurried French, 'it's better for you this way. Poland is a sad country'.

We're now back in our hotel in Cracow. What do you now think the Holocaust represents for the Jewish people?

It was nothing new, there had been others. As an aside, I've never liked the term 'Holocaust'. It is inappropriate, rhetorical and above all wrong. What it represented was a turning point: in its scale, in its modes of operation primarily, because it was the first time in recent epochs that anti-Semitism has been planned, ordered and organized by the state, not simply tacitly accepted, as happened in the Russian of the Tsars, but actually willed. And there was no escape, the whole of Europe was turned into an immense trap. That was the novelty and that is what made it a profound watershed for the Jews, not only in Europe but in America, throughout the world.

Do you believe that another Auschwitz, another massacre like the one carried out forty years ago, could come about?

In Europe no, I don't think so, if only for reasons of what you could call immunity. There is a sort of immunization at work, so that I think it unlikely, at least for some time... maybe in a few decades, fifty years, a hundred years, you could conceivably find something like Nazism in Germany or Fascism in Italy. No, I don't think it could happen in Europe. But the world is much bigger than Europe alone.

There are countries where you might find a desire to build an Auschwitz, where only the tools are lacking for now.

So the idea is not dead?

The idea is most certainly not dead, because nothing ever dies. Everything returns renewed, nothing ever dies.

The forms change?

The forms change. The forms are important.

Is it possible, in your view, to destroy the humanity in man?

Yes, I'm afraid so. I would say that what characterizes the German camps – I cannot comment on others, because I did not see them, perhaps the same applies to Russian camps – is precisely their annihilation of man's personality, on the outside and on the inside. This goes not only for the prisoner but also for the prison guard who loses his humanity in these places, even if along a different path. The result is the same. Only very few had the luck to keep their awareness intact during their imprisonment. Some rediscovered that sense of awareness of what had happened afterwards, but whilst there they had lost it. Many forgot everything, they never recorded their experiences mentally, they didn't engrave them on their memories, so to speak. So it did happen, yes, to all of us; a profound alteration in personality, a numbing of sensibilities; memories of home, of families, became secondary to the battle of urgent needs, to hunger, the need to protect ourselves from cold, from blows, to resist exhaustion. All this led to conditions you could reasonably call bestial, like beasts of burden. It is curious that this animal condition was even reflected in the language. In German there are two verbs for 'to eat': one is '*essen*' and is used for people, the other is '*fressen*', used for animals. A horse '*frisst*', it does not '*isst*'. A horse or a cat devours, you could say. And in the camps, without anyone decreeing it, the verb for eating was '*fressen*' not '*essen*', as if the perception of our regression to an animal state had spread among us all.

At the end of this second return to Auschwitz, what comes to mind?

Many things come to mind. One is this: I am rather angered by the fact that the Poles, the Polish government, have taken over Auschwitz and turned it into a memorial to the martyrdom of the Polish nation. It was that too, it was that in its first years, in 1941–2. But afterwards, with the opening of the Birkenau camp, with the building of the gas chambers and the crematoria, it became above all else the instrument of the destruction of the Jewish people. It isn't that this is denied here – we saw that there is a Jewish Block museum, just as there are Italian, French, Dutch Blocks, and so on – but the resounding fact that the overwhelming majority of victims of Auschwitz were Jews, and only in part Polish Jews, although it's not denied, is at least glossed over.

Do you not fear that others, that people today want to forget Auschwitz as soon as they can?

There are signs that it is happening – forgetting, even denial. And that is significant: to deny Auschwitz is to be ready to rebuild it.

Note

1   After his arrest in Piedmont and before his deportation to Auschwitz, Levi was held in the prison camp at Fossoli, near Modena in central Italy, as described in the opening pages of *If This is a Man*.

The Duty of Memory (1983)

Anna Bravo and Federico Cereja

One of the important aspects you touched on in your lecture at the university[1] was the series of rituals, of modes of behaviour suggested, imposed, decided on collectively; we had loosely labelled it something like the camp 'rule-book' or 'etiquette manual'.

Yes... I should say straight away that I might well repeat things I've already written in my books, it's inevitable. Like anywhere else, there was an official code in the camp, a range of precepts and proscriptions imposed by the German authorities. But intermingled with that system, overlaying it, there was also a spontaneous code of behaviour that I called the 'rule-book': some of the precepts and some of the proscriptions could be worked around, if you knew how. You had to learn with experience, once you had managed to survive the initiation crisis which was always the most serious. Whoever got through the first few days began to learn the side-roads, the short-cuts, such as the best way to be marked down as sick. You also learned – and this came as a surprise to all of us, especially to us Italian Jews – that corruption reigned throughout the *Lager*. We had only come into contact with

From a series of 220 oral history interviews with survivors carried out in Turin, 1982–3, and published in an anthology entitled *La vita offesa*, edited by Anna Bravo and Daniele Jalla (Milan: Franco Angeli, 1986). The interview with Levi was first published separately as 'Ex deportato Primo Levi: un intervista (27 January 1983)', *Rassegna mensile di Israel*, n.2–3, May-December 1987. An elaborated and tidied up version was later published in French as *Le Devoir de mémoire* (Paris: Editions Mille et une nuits, 1995). Some of the same minor alterations made for the French version have been preserved here.

Germans very recently and we still had intact that official image of them as cruel but incorruptible. In reality they were extremely corruptible. It was something you learned more or less quickly, through experience. Not only the Germans, who were on the outside as a rule, like unreachable gods, but the entire camp hierarchy running down from them was corruptible. One of the first words we learned was the Polish *protekcja*.

Then there was a system of rules which was not directly to do with survival but rather with good or bad manners: an example was when someone asked to borrow your spoon. In general you would only agree to this with someone you absolutely trusted, because your spoon was part of your capital, it was worth a whole ration of bread, so you only gave it up to someone trustworthy or someone you could watch over carefully. We weren't given spoons on arrival, it was not yours by right, you had to earn it, that is, to buy it early on with bread. As an aside, it's significant that when the camp was liberated we found a whole storeroom full of spoons; there was no reason not to let us have them . . . So, the new arrival was forced to lap at his soup like a dog, because he had no spoon and no one would give him one. Then if you did lend your spoon to someone, it was good manners to lick it first; you would eat your soup, then lick the spoon clean and only then give it to the supplicant.

Another thing that comes to mind is what you might call the dress code. It sounds strange, since it was all but impossible to be properly dressed, but just like in normal life, it was important to have clothes, a hat and shoes that were 'decent' – in inverted commas of course, since they were never really decent, unless you'd had quite an exceptional career. Nevertheless, this concern for propriety had its place in camp mores. At the start, I tended to neglect my clothes, it seemed a pointless, useless worry to think about dusting off my grease-smeared jacket, with its rust stains; but older companions put me right: 'no, you mustn't do it, here *you must* keep your shoes and your jacket clean and the rest, you must clean your face, you must accept the shaving'. We were shaved only once a week, but it was something that had to be done, not just to abide by camp rules, but also to reinforce the defensive shell of our moral life. A sort of collective instinct drove us to it: if you let yourself go you were in danger, you would come last in everything.

On this need for dignity, even external dignity, did you notice any difference in reaction based on class origins, on differing cultural models of propriety and decency?

I don't think so. In any case, class differences disappeared very rapidly as other factors came to the fore. I remember the way some intellectuals fell away very quickly whilst dockers and others who were used to manual labour were able to put up more resistance. But even this was not an absolute criterion, there were several others. One was body-weight. Clearly someone like me who arrived at the camp weighing 49 kilos, because I was constitutionally thin, needed fewer calories to survive than a man of 80 or 90 kilos. So this was another factor which favoured my survival, it was an advantage. Many intellectuals went under because they were faced with work they had never done before, with hard physical labour and tasks a well-off man does not do: polishing shoes, brushing clothes without a brush, with hands, nails . . .

Looking after themselves.

Looking after themselves, rather than having others do it for them.

Quite. In families, there were women – the wife or the maid – to do these things.

Exactly. Tasks were delegated. Instead, in the camp, you had to fend for yourself. I myself was in great danger in the first few days and here I would go back to the friendship factor. I believe I owe my survival to a handful of friends, if only because of that crucial additional problem for us Italians, the failure of communication. I felt it like a burning brand, like a form of torture, being in a world whose words, whose language was incomprehensible, where we could not make ourselves understood. Finding another Italian to talk to was a stroke of luck. And there were so few of us, maybe one hundred out of 10,000 in my camp, 1 per cent. Very few of the others spoke any Italian and very few of us spoke any German or Polish, maybe some French. We were gravely isolated, linguistically. Finding a gap, a hole, a passageway out of this isolation was a crucial factor for survival; and finding one's way to the other end of the passage, finding a friendly face, meant salvation. Alberto, the boy I have talked of a lot in my books, was that figure for me; he had courage to spare for himself and others, he was able to transmit his courage and I found him by pure chance, without ever really understanding . . . he was a saviour for me. As for what he found in me, he used to say 'you are a lucky man', I'm not sure why, but in the end destiny proved him right. I was lucky.

I've tried many times to theorize what precisely led to survival, but I have never got very far, just that luck was the dominant force. For example, in my case, I was someone who had not been particularly robust in health, but somehow I went through an entire year without falling ill, not even minor ailments which could so easily turn very serious there.

And then at the end...

I fell ill at precisely the right moment, when it became a stroke of good luck, because the Germans suddenly decided to leave the sick to their fate.

To come back to the 'rule-book', you referred to a sort of implicit code which forbade the mention of certain things.

Yes. It's related to the subject of death, which we'll talk about later. In normal life, it's improper, at least in informal or family settings, to speak about cancer. In exactly the same way, it was considered maladroit, a sort of gaffe, to talk about the crematorium or the gas chambers, in my camp at least. Yes, it was a subject you could avoid because they weren't materially present where we were, at Monowitz not Birkenau. We should perhaps talk about the geography of the camps: Auschwitz was more than one camp. There were many different camps and mine was the third down, Auschwitz III, the largest of the secondary camps. The crematorium was at Birkenau. I never set foot there and I can't say whether this particular rule held good there also, but in my camp it was seen as incorrect, anyone who mentioned it was made to shut up, shoulders were shrugged and the subject was changed.

Besides this, were there other forbidden topics?

No. Our obsessive topic was food, which was so general, so universal among us all that it was tolerated even though it was harmful. Conjuring up in our minds elegant menus in those conditions was an overwhelming instinct and it led to feelings of irritation and nervousness, but we all did it. I only encountered a handful of people able to resist the temptation to talk about what they used to eat at home, or rather an ideal version of it, of course. It truly dominated our talk, there was no way around it, it was *the* topic of conversation.

I wanted to go back to the question of death. Our fear of death was no different, *in quality* at least, from the fear of death in everyday existence. Today, living our lives in freedom, we all know that we will die, and there too we knew death would come, not in ten, twenty, thirty years' time, but in a few weeks, in a month. Strangely, though, this difference didn't alter much. It was still a thought that was suppressed, just like in normal life. Neither the word nor the fear of it returned to us every day. We were so acutely deprived of food and warmth, desperate to avoid fatigue and violence that death, which did not seem imminent, was overtaken by other concerns.

Still on the question of death, I wanted to ask, was there a selection as soon as you arrived?

Yes. As we got off the train. In the very first few minutes. That was the rule for all arrivals, although we didn't understand that then. Or at least, I didn't and nor did the rest of us Italians. It was all carried out extremely quickly, with a quota for each side that I found out later was more or less constant: roughly four-fifths or three-quarters of every convoy was sent straight to the gas chambers, and the remaining fifth or quarter was sent to work.

When did you know for sure of the existence of the gas chambers and the crematoria?

In our camp, this aspect was kept under wraps, as I was saying earlier. It was spoken of through the veil of a thousand acts of censorship. On occasion, someone would arrive from Birkenau ... I remember a boy I met very early on, he was Turkish or Greek and he spoke Italian, and he came from Birkenau. He said 'Yes, you work much less at Birkenau than here, but there there is death'. I said, 'what do you mean?' and he shrugged his shoulders and let it go at that. No, in our camp, the idea of the gas chamber was suppressed in every way possible. But I think elsewhere too, even at Birkenau, where possible ... You have to imagine the different sensitivities, the different emotions of the deportee in those conditions: he would turn dumb and this witlessness was a source of salvation that allowed him to get through the day just worrying about immediate, daily concerns and repressing the rest. Our sensibility, above all our emotions, were cut down.

As an aside, let me say that after forty years, I remember most of these things through what I have written, my writings are like a form of artificial memory and the rest, what I have never written down, does not amount to much now, just a few details.

We wanted to ask you a question on just this matter, the relation of writing to deportation, because of course when one writes, one cannot relate everything one has experienced. One has to weigh up, select, take on the work of literature, of the writer. What gets lost in the writing, what do you remember having to leave aside?

I did not make a conscious choice of that kind. At the time, I tried to write down the most serious, the most weighty, heavy and significant aspects. I didn't write down – because it seemed pointless to include them in a book, although I did not forget them either – certain conversations, certain discussions with friends and colleagues. So, later I put together a dozen of these omissions in a book of stories, *Lilìt*,[2] perhaps you know it. Mostly they are stories of encounters, of characters who seemed vaguely out of place in *If This is a Man*. There I felt that the note of indignation should prevail: it was testimony, almost juridical in form, as I saw it, a case for the prosecution, not a call for revenge, vendetta, punishment, but an act of witness. So certain subjects felt marginal: for example, one of the first stories in *Lilìt* is about the 'disciple', the Hungarian who refused to steal and to lie, who insisted on sticking to the morality he had had as a free man. He had just arrived and he felt that to carry a load that looked like it was twenty bricks, but had been reduced to seventeen by leaving a hole in the middle of the pile, was wrong, was a lie. And I tried to convince him that his past morality did not apply in that place, that this was a bipartite world, split in two, into us and them, where standard morality failed, where the others are so hostile and the separation between us and them so bitter and fierce that all standards of morality failed. And in fact later on he stole a radish and gave it to me as if in payment for the lesson I had taught him. Episodes like that, which needed a certain subtlety in the telling, jarred somewhat in the context of *If This is a Man*. They were, you might say, an octave lower and I only wrote them much later. I can't give you a precise reason for all of them . . . For example, the story of Cesare's return,[3] that I wrote much later because I didn't have permission to write it any earlier. The same goes for many stories about characters I thought were still alive; I didn't write them because I know that it is never a good idea to write about living people, even if to praise them, to speak highly of them. It's always a risk, and you almost always hurt them, because the image people have of them is different from how they perceive themselves, for better or worse.

This is a problem that comes up throughout our research project, the problem of the image people build up in their minds of other people or events which they then find represented differently by others. It resurfaces in all the interviews we are carrying out and will certainly resurface again when we have to present the material to a wider public, when we will have to condense, to emphasise certain points above others. It is a very delicate issue, so I understand very well your fear of naming specific individuals...

That's why, in *If This is a Man*, I talked about a certain Elias – perhaps you remember, the Herculean dwarf – and I used his real name and surname, but later on my scruples intervened and when the German translation of the book came out, I begged the editor to change the name. If Elias had survived it was highly unlikely that the Italian edition of my book would have reached him, but a book in German was a different matter, because he spoke German. No matter how hard you try, a written portrait never reproduces the person. Complicated factors get in the way, like failing memory, unknowing idealization, for good or ill, or even knowing idealization, because sometimes we take a person and try our best to make a 'character' out of them, don't we? Sometimes it can happen. As far as I remember, I tried not to do this in *If This is a Man*, but I gave in to the temptation quite frequently in *Lilít*. By then I'd become a writer. The man who wrote *If This is a Man* wasn't a writer in the normal sense of the word, he wasn't looking for literary success, he had no illusions, no ambitions to create a beautiful end-product.

Had you never thought of writing before then?

Not seriously. I confess I had written a long story before I was taken prisoner. I still have it, but it's worthless, it doesn't make any sense. I could easily throw it away, without any qualms.

The impulse was the same as that which made you write some notes there, in the laboratory?

Yes, the notes that I wrote there were real. I really did have a notebook, but the notes never amounted to more than twenty lines. I was too afraid, it was extremely dangerous to write. The very fact of writing was suspect, so no, it wasn't so much the notes, it was the desire to write them, when I found I had what I needed, pencil and paper, the desire to get across to my mother, my sister, my family, this inhuman life I was living through. But they weren't real and anyway I knew there was no way I could keep them. It was materially impossible. Where could I hide them? In some container, but which? In my pockets? We had nothing, they changed our beds, the mattresses were continually being moved, even our clothes. There was no way of holding on to anything. Except in our memory.

I wanted to return to the question of the initiation. In If This is a Man, *you also spoke in passing of a series of rituals, of little jokes at the expense of new arrivals, which made me think of many other similar rituals in large concentrations of people. I was interested by this because it's an area not often touched on in our other interviews, that is, how the community greets the new arrivals, what tests it imposes or puts them through before accepting them, since it seems that even there, there was something of that* . . .

We need to distinguish between the initiation by the authorities and the initiation by fellow inmates. The former was brutal, as in not giving out spoons and and – although not in my camp, I've read about it in other accounts – beatings dealt out as the first welcome for the new arrival to convince him from the outset that all hope is lost. In our camp, this didn't happen, because it was a mixed camp, we were workers and German industry needed us to arrive in a state fit to work, so we were spared this form of official initiation. So I cannot tell you much about the SS initiation. But initiation by fellow inmates, yes. The new arrival, the 'high number' (because new numbers were always higher than those gone before), was a funny creature; funny because he was disoriented, because he was fat, inept, because he didn't understand anything. And with a cruelty reminiscent of the school or the barracks, they were despised, tricks were played on them, they were sometimes given absurd, outrageously false information to get them into trouble. I was told, for example, 'you don't like the work you're doing? Go and peel potatoes. Ask if you can peel potatoes', and I did, I went, with my few words of German (that, too, was seen as comic, our linguistic ineptitude, the man who cannot speak, who does not have the gift of the word). You may not have heard much about this, because I imagine most of your interviewees were political deportees. Am I right?

I wouldn't say most. Perhaps half. Then there were also soldiers picked up from disbanded units, but only those who ended up in KZ [concentration camps].

Only those in the camps. But there were very few soldiers there.

True. Those we've interveiwed were often picked up as soldiers, perhaps in Yugoslavia, and then ended up fighting with Tito's partisans, or they joined the Resistance for a few days and then they were captured. In any case, many were not political, in the narrow sense of the term.

My point was that the linguistic isolation was less marked at Mauthausen,[4] because the number of Italians was much higher.

Of course. Indeed, we have relatively few accounts of camps such as Auschwitz, or camps to the north in general, where there were few Italians, or few Piedmontese at least. In all of those we have, the linguistic problem stands out right from the start; whereas in the plant at Gusen, 90 per cent of inmates were Italian, and what is more they were all workers, all of the same background, from Sesto San Giovanni [in Milan] or from Fiat in Turin.
　　I wanted to ask whether initiation was only ever negative or whether, apart from the aspects you've talked about, there were not also positive aspects, information transmitted to you which helped you survive?

Yes, but only rarely. First, because of the linguistic friction, and also because of the simple lack of good will, because the newcomer was not a matter of much interest. He was an annoyance, another mouth to feed, more competition. He did not arouse interest, there was no sense of solidarity. At least that was my experience; as I saw it, solidarity was scarce.

You mention the same thing when you draw parallels, perhaps even in If This is a Man *itself, with other situations of extreme oppression when the oppressed clash, at times violently, among themselves.*

Yes, I've said it explicitly: when prison is governed by extreme oppression, solidarity fails. Other factors prevail, above all personal survival.

Loss of identity probably also works in favour of this atomization: that is, it seems, the more impoverished identity becomes the more the individual is closed off and unable to communicate or to concern himself with others. The process could work in that way.

I'm not sure. What do you mean by losing your identity?

Realizing that all the cultural and moral models on which you have structured your life, there – as you were saying before – no longer hold.

I see.

That is, the loss of your fundamental frame of reference for living, which was firmly in place even though you were all relatively young. You had lived long enough to have already worked out for yourselves lessons and models which suddenly, there, came to nothing.

Well, yes, that certainly happened. Perhaps I just put it in other terms, less technical than 'loss of identity'. The worst thing was to be so unsettled, transplanted to a world that was not ours.

I wanted to ask you something else in this regard: you went to the camp as a Jew and as a partisan...

As a Jew... No, I was also a partisan.[5]

Precisely. Subjectively you went both as a Jew and as a partisan. But what was the reaction of those who found themselves there somehow, rather by chance, those who were simply Jewish or...

My experience as a partisan counted very little. Very little. I was a partisan for a few months only, and in name only, since I wasn't even armed, so my case is more or less the same as those taken simply for being Jewish, punished for the crime of being born, in short, taken

under the weight of an immense injustice. I remember that neither I
nor my Jewish companions in the camp ever ceased to be amazed at
the sheer iniquity of this fact. To punish your political enemies, to put
them in prison or even in a camp is cruel but at least it's rational. It
has always been done, just as prisoners of war used to be sold off as
slaves. It was ever thus, however despicable it may be, even in the
animal kingdom I believe – creatures like ants use slaves, they raid
other groups and use them as slaves. But to punish another because
he is other, on the basis of abstract ideology only, seemed to us the
height of injustice, stupidity and irrationality. Why am I different
from another, in what way? You see, there's an important distinction
to be drawn here: the pious Jews, the believers, like all believers, had
no sense of, no feeling of injustice, they attributed everything that was
happening to divine chastisement, to the incomprehensible,
unknown God who has the power of life and death, whose reasons
are unknowable, who plays... Whatever God decrees must be
accepted. But for a non-believer as I was then and still am today,
this was the very greatest of iniquities, absolutely incomparable and
inexplicable.

*Did this experience change anything in your Jewishness, either in the camp
or later?*

No. I'd say that it further weakened my religious convictions which
were already very feeble. My impression then and now was that no
religious credo could possibly justify the killing of children and the
like. An adult can be consciously or unconsciously guilty – anyone
who has lived has also sinned in some way – but not a child.

*But you did come into contact with the world of Eastern Jewry which you
had hardly known beforehand and which, as your stories show, fascinated
you...*

You're right, but that only happened much later, as part of a retrospective elaboration. The contact I had there with Eastern Judaism
was traumatic and negative. We were rejected, as Sephardi or in any
case Italian Jews, because we didn't speak Yiddish, we were doubly
foreign, both for the Germans of course because we were Jews and for
the other Jews from the East because we were not part of their world,
they had not the slightest idea that there was any other Judaism... A
great many of the Polish Jews who were of humble origin were

angered by our presence: 'but what sort of a Jew are you? *Redest keyn jiddisch, bist nit keyn jid'* they would say. You understand the logic? *Jiddisch* is the adjective from *jid* which means Jew: it's a sort of syllogism, like a Frenchman who doesn't speak French. If you don't speak French you aren't French. A *jid* who doesn't speak *jiddisch* isn't a *jid*. That was the form our contact took, with a handful of exceptions of course, some figures who had retained a certain nobility or discernment, who realized how defenceless we were. As Italian Jews we felt especially defenceless. Along with the Greeks we were the lowest of the low, and in some ways we were worse off than the Greeks because they were at least used to discrimination, there was a long history of anti-Semitism in Salonika and many of them were old hands, had developed hardened shells through their contacts with other Greeks. But the Italians, so used to being treated as equals of all other Italians, had no shield, we were as naked as eggs without shells.

Was there any form of religious practice among the Poles?

With some of them, yes. Our camp was made up almost exclusively, 90 per cent, of Jews and there were some rabbis who carried out their religious ceremonies in hiding, even praying in public, which drew large numbers, even non-believers.

I wanted to ask you a question prompted by a French book on the children of deportees and the traces left behind, according to the author, for three generations.[6] Many others have also noted this influence on future generations of that feeling of having suffered the extreme iniquity, as you put it. What are your thoughts on this, what impact has it all had on your relationship with your children, on the values you have given them or the young in general?

This is a very difficult question. There's a great difference between the young in general and one's own children in particular. My children have always refused to talk about this subject. I have two children and I have always got on very well indeed with them, but they have never wanted to hear about this. As for the young in general, well, they are like fluid matter, every generation and every class is different from the next. I have often been to talk in schools and I've found interest, horror, pity, sometimes incredulity, amazement, incomprehension... I wouldn't know what general diagnosis to propose, at present I feel that too much time has passed, I don't willingly accept invitations to schools any more because I feel like a old survivor, like one of Garibaldi's men,[7] a 'greybeard' essentially.

Although there has been a recent flourishing of interest, it seems.

Well...when... I don't know... My feeling is that it hasn't come from the young. What's your impression?

I'd say it has. I went to Mauthausen last September for a peace rally and there were a large number of schoolchildren who seemed very alert in their interest and in their understanding of what the concentration camps were. It had marked them deeply. I believe that the handing on of testimonies is still very important. You and your peers have positively influenced a whole generation, given them a sense of civic engagement which they will never lose.

Here you are touching on a very delicate issue for me. It may be my own fault that I don't feel happy going to talk in schools any more. In part, I admit, I'm just tired, because the questions are always the same; in part, I fear that my language has become inadequate, that you need to speak a different language today. And then I have to say that I was upset by one of the last times I went to a school when two boys, two brothers, got up and asked to my face: 'Why are you telling us all this stuff, after forty years, after Vietnam, after Stalin's gulag, Korea and all the rest? What for?' I felt cornered, on the ropes, trapped in my role as a returnee. I said that I came to speak of these things because I had lived through them; if I had been in Vietnam I would have told them about Vietnam, if I had been in Stalin's gulag I would have recounted that, but I knew how weak my reply was. I'm afraid of lapsing into panegyric, as can easily happen – I mean, privileging one's own experience above that of others'. I'm aware that we're living in a world in a process of very rapid transformation, which is part progress and part regression, and today's primary school children who use calculators with great nonchalance, who know, learn from television things I never learned, they rather put me to shame. I feel almost inferior to them. So even though I know I have had important things to say and I have no hesitation or doubt over the value of my books, I nevertheless have the sense that they are old, that they've aged.

Another impression is one I've gleaned more recently from the many letters I receive. On average I get one or two letters a day and they are almost all couched in religious terms. They ask me, a firm non-believer, whether there is a God and if so, why he allowed these things and other terrible things to happen. They disturb me, these matters, and I reply in the only way a non-believer can; that the world is ruled by chance, that there is no ruler, no director, only the need for a god-cum-father figure which seems to be growing ever more fearfully strong even among schoolchildren. These questions arose even in schools the last few times I went on visits. I don't know what your view on this is, whether you're religious?

No. Probably, in many young people today there is a need for a benevolent figure of authority, whether or not in the sense of a God and father, someone to refer to. I can see something like that in the air.

It must be a need for security, of any and every kind.

Quite, for those securities that were so much easier to find in the past... It reminds me of something you wrote in La Stampa *a while ago about how lucky we are that nowadays politicians are not charismatic figures, and how dangerous charisma is in politics...*

Yes, that's right. It's the old story of the 'lame-duck leader'.

But perhaps when they cannot look for charisma in politics they look for it on a broader, more general human level? It would be understandable, after all... I don't think it's a lack of interest. There is a gap in language between us and schoolchildren but that doesn't mean the experiences themselves are now irrelevant... Perhaps, as you say, you are simply tired of repeating the same things, the same old questions – and they are necessarily always the same, and must be wearying after a while.

There is another point, too, which I must add: one of the questions that gets repeated and repeated is the question of why it happened, why there are wars, why the camps were built, why the Jews were exterminated, and it is a question to which I have no answer. No one does. Why there are wars, why there was the First World War and the Second World War and now we talk all the time of a Third World War... is a question that torments me because I have no answer. My standard reply is that it is part of our animal make-up... that a sense, an awareness of territory is something we share with dogs, nightingales, all animals: but even as I say it, I don't believe it. So now I'd like to ask you some questions: can you tell me why, why we go to war, why (because this is war too) we crucify our enemies, as the Romans did and the Nazis after them, why, although we've had a brief half-century of sanity, of respect for prisoners of war, it lasted so briefly and now we've returned to the cruelties of before?... Well, I have only vague, generic answers, that man is evil, man is not good. And there is another question I am constantly asked: is man good? How can anyone answer such a question? There are good people and less good people, each of us is a mixture of good and not so good.

In the end, I think we have to talk about the impossibility of providing a complete explanation of historical events, which is an important point to arrive at, a lesson for us . . .

The impossibility of total explanations or the total impossibility of explanation of any kind?

I'd like to go back to the question we touched on earlier. In what ways does someone who has been in a concentration camp, in a Lager, *bring their children up differently from the rest of us? For the reasons we've been discussing, because deportation has a lesson for all generations, not only for those who went through it.*

Yes. But as I was saying, I'm afraid that both my children, around the age of fifteen, rejected the topic. And I fear they rejected it precisely because they had already perceived its presence. This house is full of the *Lager,* they will have seen all the books around them, the images and photos, all the talk – children are very sensitive to these things, and I think they reached that age either consciously or unconsciously weighed down with fear and repulsion and so they refused to hear any more about it and still do now. They have read my books but they will not admit it. They don't like to talk about it.

But Lisa [his daughter] whom I know, has held onto a strong anti-Fascist consciousness, an engaged social conscience which strikes me as an important product of that experience.

Yes, of course . . . But I'm not at all sure that comes from me. It's her generation . . . I think her generation, and yours too, were all in all a brave generation and a protesting one, but I'm not sure that had any roots in my experience . . .

You see, education is made up of at least three factors: there's transmission from parents to children, which comes in two forms, a genetic element carried by chromosomes at the moment of conception and an element of conscious teaching, and then there's a third factor of unconscious education by example. To be frank, I don't recall ever having given my children lessons in democracy, although it's perfectly possible that they absorbed them from the air they breathed, just as they did with the *Lager*.

Yes, that's it. I think it is the tacit example more than the lengthy explanation that is formative.

It's true that examples are very important.

I wanted to move on to another area. I've noticed that with many survivors, whenever we mention the work of Bruno Bettelheim, especially his books Surviving *and* The Informed Heart,[8] *there is a reaction either of indifference or of outright rejection and hostility.*

My reaction exactly.

I would be very interested to hear more about that.

My view is that Bettelheim's attitude and ideas are violently distorted by his belief in psychologizing explanation at all costs. He talks about a form of regression, if I'm right?

That's right, regression back to infancy.

Camp behaviour as a form of regression to infancy. No, I wouldn't agree. I felt myself grow older in the *Lager*, not return to childhood. I remember very clearly how after a year in the camp I was more mature, I was no longer a child. I had acquired a way of confronting reality that was more solid, more concrete and also more courageous and I saw the same change in all my fellow survivors. So regression, I don't know what regression he means. I've really forgotten Bettelheim completely, I hardly remember what he has written. I think that you could only talk of regression in one way: you could say that whoever regressed, died.

He says that the total dependence on others for food, sleep, time and movement tended to induce in the prisoner a form of regression and that this policy was quite consciously adopted in the camps. He says that, indeed, many fell into such a regressive state. So even if you emerged enriched by the experience, you only speak for a very small minority.

But I didn't see it happening. The constraints you mention on food and the rest, well, anyway, even in families there are meal-times and no one feels constrained by that.

Perhaps children do. Children want to eat when they are hungry.

Children are creatures of habit, they fall into patterns without fuss. I don't see this as an example of regression. Or, if it is, it is contradictory: if you say children don't like fixed timetables, forcing a prisoner to follow one cannot be a forced regression into childhood.

It is rather to be forced to depend on the whim and will of another; to be unable to intervene in any way in one's own life.

All I can say is this: each of us lived through the *Lager* in their own way and it would be hard to find two identical versions of the experience and then to deduce general rules from them. In my experience and that of many who were close to me, the dominant impulse was not so much a product of regression or constraint as our almost cynical curiosity, our scientific or anthropological interest in such a radically different mode of living. These were the factors that enriched and matured us, and I repeat what I've said many times before, that the *Lager* was a sort of university for me. The idea is not mine, I stole it from Lidia Rolfi, I imagine you've interviewed her too. Of course, the maturing came afterwards, there was no time to mature there, but later, when there was time for reflection. As for *Surviving*, I only read it recently and to no avail, nothing has stayed with me. I thought it a bad book, very bad, papers and lectures stitched together, and poorly stitched together at that.

It includes the article on Anne Frank's family which has come in for a great deal of criticism and has often been rejected outright. He analyses the behaviour of the Frank family, criticising them or rather explaining that there was a strong repression of danger in their desire to stay together at all costs that in the end turned out to be disastrous for all of them. A more realistic, concrete or flexible attitude would perhaps have saved at least some of the family members, and Bettelheim extends this analysis to various strata of Jewish families who similarly repressed the real dangers so that they actually paid a higher price in the long run. The excellent book by Debenedetti on the ghetto round-up in Rome comes to mind . . .

16 October 1943.[9]

Exactly. He also shows how there was this refusal to believe, a pretence that it wasn't happening.

That's a very weighty problem, the 'pretence'.

I'd like to know your view on this central issue.

Well, it certainly existed, the denial at all costs, these things won't happen here. It was my father's attitude at heart. Luckily for him, he died before, a year before, but this highly dangerous denial was there, for me too, in 1942–3 when I was living the life of a normal student, going off climbing, to the theatre and concerts and so on, without even realizing that Germany was invading the whole of Europe. It was a failure to act: but what could I have done? Do something else, emigrate for example, try to emigrate. But emigrating meant over-coming an enormous potential barrier: to crawl out of our hole, where we had family, affection, our own country where we were born, friendships and all the rest. Very few in Italy had the strength and far-sightedness to take that step, and in any case, you needed money too, a very great deal of money. It wasn't easy and to criticize the Frank family for failing to act differently is superficial, I would say. It may be that sticking together was a dangerous choice, but it was also the only way to preserve some semblance of life as it was before.

But Bettelheim's point is precisely that it was impossible to preserve that semblance and that anyone who tried paid the highest price for it. On the other hand, those who accepted that there was no way of carrying on as normal or those who actively resisted in the end suffered less...

Perhaps, but how can we expect such lucidity? Do we live our lives even today with lucidity? We should pack our bags and head for the New Hebrides, get out of Europe. Are we far-sighted enough? Even with the nuclear threat hanging over us? If there is to be war, we are living on the battleground, but which of us – even those of us who could afford it – which of us has gone and fished out our savings, perhaps hidden away in Switzerland, and headed for New Zealand? Then things weren't so different. We're in denial now as much as we were then.

Also, within the Italian Jewish community there was a legalistic tradition, too, I think...

That wasn't so much part of the Italian Jewish tradition as part of the Italian bourgeois tradition.

The Italian bourgeoisie, of course, but especially the Jewish community ever since emancipation in Piedmont, by Carlo Alberto,[10] which has meant that the community sees its own values in the law, in their legitimacy.

Certainly, Italian Jews were deeply assimilated, the most assimilated in the world and they still are. No other Jews are as assimilated as we are. Even the simple fact that I speak Italian, standard Piedmontese Italian, that I am, that we're all indistinguishable from the rest. It's not so common to find that, I'd say, in the rest of the world. But the legalistic attitude didn't *only* belong to Italian Jews, it was shared by all Italians.

Quite. I know that this led several Jews to present themselves voluntarily when the notices went up calling for them.

Yes, for some it happened that way.

Perhaps they took the view your father shared, that nothing would happen, these things have never happened here. The parents of Sion Segre[11] went voluntarily, I think, and the 'carabiniere' officer tried to get them away, told them to 'get out!'.

But what I wanted to say was that any Italian citizen, not only Jewish, could have acted in the same way. Just think of the air raids: how many people stayed in the city, even just stayed on in their homes in bed, saying 'these things don't happen to us'.

Yes. There was also the risk of being killed in the shelters, as happened a few times, so it was risk for risk, I suppose.

I don't think the risks were equal, though.

But I think the hostility to Bettelheim is linked to the fact he seems to be denying any sense of sacrifice. His analysis is far more subtle than I can do justice to here.

His story is a strange one, though. He paid, he was able to pay and get out. And there is perhaps some, a little too much of this privileged fate, of this ultra-privileged good fortune. I have to confess that I share that feeling of hostility towards Bettelheim, and it's a crude hostility, I can't really justify it. I dislike him, I dislike his presumptuousness, his belief that he can explain it all, his psychoanalytical armour which is like a gospel that brings light to all, without ever a chink of doubt.

But listen, that isn't right at all.

In what way?

Reading Bettelheim as someone not directly involved didn't give me an impression of a dogmatic figure. That's why we were interested in the hostility of survivors towards him. His isn't a rough, brutal schematic critique of the victims, it's a series of notes on a number of psychological mechanisms and their consequences . . . Listening to our interviewees, it almost seems that they feel violated by his sort of analysis, as if he wanted to read their minds. Probably there are just two different readings, and for those who were there, his work provokes a strongly emotive reaction, in the negative sense, obviously.

Let me say that I have read many books on the camps, and I love many of them, but not this one. I don't know how to justify my position more than I have already, except to say that it seems to want to look you in the eye and say 'now I'll explain how things really worked', but then it also wants to mix in his own personal experience with everyone else's. Now, he was, if I'm right, at Buchenwald or Oranienberg, I don't remember exactly which. In a *Lager* of political prisoners. He was there as a Jew, for one year, after which he managed to get away. He seems to ignore the enormous changes that went on after his departure, the different fate that so many suffered. He only very rarely cites personal encounters with others beyond his own case. It is as though he turns himself into the paradigm, what happened to me and around me happened to everyone, around everyone.

Of course, his experience was of a German camp, that is a Lager for Germans.

He is German, after all.

Until 1939. He left in 1939, I think.

Yes. And so that experience of alienation which was fundamental to us, he never had. He suffered greatly, physically, he was beaten, went hungry, was in forced labour, but *deportation*, with all it implied, the uprooting, he didn't go through it ... Perhaps that is why his book felt so alien to my own experience ...

By contrast, I find Hermann Langbein's works fascinating, although unfortunately they are not well known in Italy. Above all, his most recent book, *Menschen in Auschwitz* ('Human Beings in Auschwitz').[12] Langbein is over seventy, half-Jewish, he was a communist and he fought in Spain as a communist, then he escaped to France like many others and was captured by Pétain's government and handed over to the Germans who sent him first to Buchenwald, then from Buchenwald to Auschwitz as one of the squad of 'founder inmates' of Auschwitz. He has written a book or several books – but especially that one superb book, *Menschen in Auschwitz* – where he recounts not only the conditions of those on the inside but also outside, people beyond the camp. They are human beings too, and the stories he tells, the clinical cases of the SS, high and low, are new and important, only rarely told, how almost all of them behaved odiously, but without ever being born monsters, with a handful of exceptions. Only very few indeed were real monsters, mentally sick torturers, others applied themselves to the task with a sort of weary indifference. They didn't kill with any enthusiasm but they accepted it, they were the products of their education. I've hardly ever seen explained so well the impact of Nazi schooling, the National Socialist education system, on the formation of this subaltern class. For a long period, Langbein was the secretary of one of the chief SS doctors and also a member of the internal resistance in the camp, so he was in a key position to find out a great many things. He tells of how this doctor, Wirtz, who he worked under, was at heart just like the rest of them; he had gone into the system, had joined the SS as a career move, and then there was no way back out. Later, Wirtz committed suicide; after he had been tried, he killed himself in prison.

You said earlier that you've read many testimonies, many different personal and historical books on the camps... And then you are also a writer yourself. I wanted to know how you judge this field of work in general and whether you think there is still much ground to be covered in this area?

I cannot say for sure. Langbein's book, for example, is fairly exhaustive, it tells us a lot of what we need to know.

Our impression is that immediately after your return, say between 1945 and 1948, you survivors wrote a lot, driven above all by that almost Kantian imperative to bear witness for those who did not return. Then, perhaps in part because of the change in the political situation,[13] *there was a gradual abandonment of the question. In Italy at least, perhaps partly because it was inhibited by having already found a writer as important as Primo Levi early on, the field of memoir-writing dried up. Only now some are going back to writing. Do you think there was a link to the situation you found on your return, to the fact that you were not listened to, even not believed, in some cases? And then, people had all had their own troubles to deal with during the war – minor compared to what you went through, but looming large for them nevertheless.*

Is there a return to the subject now? Which books do you have in mind?

There was a book I didn't manage to read because it's very hard to get hold of... the story of a Jewish girl... Natalia Ginzburg reviewed it in La Stampa *in the summer, but no one picked up on it, this story of a baby who is still young now as she writes about her experience. Then there's the book by a French psychoanalyst who interviewed children of deportees, called* I Didn't Say Goodbye. *That was what made us ask you about your relations with your children. Then also there's the book on Ravensbrück,* Il ponte dei corvi.[14]

Yes, I read the manuscript of that one.

Mursia, the publisher, now has a series of two or three texts which were old testimonies that had remained unpublished for all these years.

I'm not sure. The book by Arata, *Il ponte dei corvi*, is a rather modest work. I wouldn't set too much store by what gets published nowadays, so many years after the event. I am not at all sure that there are fundamentally important works appearing now, and it would be terrible if it were simply coming back in fashion.

They may not be of fundamental importance, you are right, and perhaps it isn't part of our remit here to talk about this, but in our interviews many are speaking out for the very first time.

Really? Why is that? Do they feel forced into it, somehow?

No.

Are you sure this is really the first time they have spoken?

That's what they tell us.

No one has ever asked them before?

Perhaps yes, but many also refused to talk about it, like Elena Recanati or Natalia Tedeschi [two of the interviewees]. They are speaking out now precisely because they are speaking to another generation.

I don't know what to say. From where I am standing, I haven't seen the reflowering of interest in the camps, the *Lager*, the KZ, except perhaps in the strange religious questions I mentioned earlier: that is, asking us, me, to explain evil in the world. I have no quantitative measure, but I receive these requests a lot and not only from Italy. This morning, I received a letter from a young American theologian who is in Switzerland: he tells me that he read my books out loud in church, and this causes me real embarrassment, I don't know what to say in reply. I was even invited to a congress of American theologians, and I answered *'Non sum dignus'* [I am not worthy], I'd feel like a lamb among wolves or a wolf among lambs, either way... But as to why Elena Recanati or Natalia Tedeschi haven't spoken until now, surely it's because they've only now been tracked down. Did they refuse to say anything before?

No, they say that after their return, they felt so deeply misunderstood, that they were not believed, that they lost the desire to say anything more.

For myself I didn't feel that incomprehension. As you know, *If This is a Man* had a difficult career. It only became well known ten years after it was written. But nevertheless, I found understanding, solidarity, I never had any difficulty in telling the stories I had to tell.

I don't know if perhaps for women in particular there was a sense of violence, difficulty in speaking, a reluctance because of the morbid curiosity of some that reached its peak in that awful film by Liliana Cavani.[15]

Perhaps, yes.

That is, what we have seen up to now in our interviews is that it isn't so much the hypothetical sexual encounters that induces people not to talk as the lack of solidarity, the loss of identity. What Cavani chose to emphasize was precisely this reduction to a bestial state of which accepting certain lewd acts was just a minimal part, although she concentrates so much on it that she offends. Several women tell of indiscreet questions thrown at them on their return, or worse still, assumptions − there are cases when they were brutally confronted with the accusation: you've come back so you must have... In any case, it may well be that this made it harder for the women.

I'd put it slightly differently. I'd say that women felt the loss of human dignity more strongly than the men and some felt ashamed to talk about this, but to go from that to accusations of that kind . . .

When you talk about the Lager, *you also talk about the links between the German war industry and the camps. I'd like to know, because it strikes me as an important and little studied question, what the relations were between the companies, the SS and the* Lager. *Perhaps you were able to see from within.*

Of course. In the camp where I was there was a dual power system: we were simultaneously ruled by the SS and German industry, and they had conflicting interests. The SS wanted to destroy us, to kill us, the *Lager* was there for that purpose. German industry wanted us as a workforce and a worker who lives for three months and then dies is a bad worker because he has to be constantly replaced by a new worker who doesn't know the job. So there was a sort of deaf hostility between the two forces. German industrialists had, notoriously, funded the Nazis, but they were afraid of the SS, who acted like a sort of superpower.

Wasn't there an organic link between the camp chief and the companies in question?

Of course there were contacts at high level. The Monowitz camp where I was imprisoned was – this is something I learned only recently – paid, financed and even constructed by IG-Farben. They wanted their own *Lager*. And paradoxical things happened, because although IG-Farben didn't care in the least whether we lived or were killed, they did care about their workforce not being hampered, so I probably owe my survival at least in part to being a chemist. I don't know and I'll never know whether the rumour was true that I was saved from the October selection because I was a chemist and because I was part of the factory workforce by then. In the factory section, there was a list with the names and numbers of some employees, mine included; Mr So-and-so and Mr Such-and-such, number etc., are employed in this section. So there was simultaneously an interpenetration of the two powers, political and industrial, and also a rivalry. To be precise, the functionaries, the scientists employed in this enormous factory, that in practice was never put to work, was never finished, were people like any others. Perhaps you remember the story I told in *The Periodic Table* of Dr Müller [in the chapter 'Vanadium'] with whom I had some contact years later, who wanted some sort of absolution from me. I didn't know quite how to deal with it, I was thrown into a very conflictual situation. I'll tell you the story again, if you like. I didn't mention it in *If This is a Man*, but in the laboratory where I ended up working at one point, a large man appeared, tall and fat, and looked at me with a certain curiosity. He spoke to me in German, asking 'why do you' – he used the formal 'you' which was itself strange – 'why do you look so scared?', and then why was I so ill-shaven. He gave me a voucher that allowed me to be shaved twice a week and he also saw my shoes, or rather my wooden clogs, and he procured a pair of leather shoes for me. To his question 'why do you look so scared?', I forget what I replied, perhaps nothing at all, I was so bewildered, embarrassed, frightened, I didn't understand who this man was. But I remembered his name (Müller is just a stock name, he wasn't called Müller, I changed his name for the same reasons I mentioned earlier). Twenty years later I came into contact with a woman whose husband had worked for IG-Farben and so I asked her if she knew what had happened to this and that employee that I remembered. They had all vanished, except for this Dr Müller. [. . .]

So I found myself in an extremely embarrassing situation, in contact with a colleague, a fellow chemist, who had helped me out then, who had behaved in his own way with a modicum of compassion and who now wanted me to pardon him. I wrote to him saying that, as a lay person, I wouldn't understanding the meaning of the term pardon, I didn't understand what it would mean to say 'I absolve you of the crimes you have committed' without your telling me what you did. And so he told me, I think truthfully, the story of his career, of how he enrolled in the SA – not the SS[16] – and even then only because he was part of a student league that was incorporated into the SA. Of how he disliked the SA as a peaceful man, and so got a transfer into the anti-aircraft section and was then sent to Auschwitz as a chemist only a few days before I encountered him. He maintains that he never quite understood the nature of the *Lager*-factory complex, with all those unkempt and ill-dressed prisoners who he'd been told were all political prisoners, enemies of the state to whom it was forbidden to talk. He was clearly a frightened man. He even wrote to me that it was his doing that led me to being taken on in the lab, something I have no way of checking. I wrote back that if he was telling the truth, he should be at peace with himself, but that I had no right to absolve, to bind or release, to absolve or condemn. But he phoned me, asked if we could meet, and I agreed. We set up a meeting at Finale Ligure and he died just a few days before the meeting. Suddenly. I understood that it was foolish to talk of evil Germans: the system was demonic, the Nazi system was capable of dragging everyone down the road of cruelty and injustice. The good and the not so good. It was extremely hard to break out of, you had to have heroic strength. What I don't understand is why the same thing did not happen in Italy: in short, is there such a thing as a home-grown demon, intrinsic to Germany, which makes the demonic at home in Germany? Recently I was interviewed by Ferdinando Camon on this subject, in a written interview,[17] and he brought up the question of the demonic side that is intrinsic to Lutheranism. I don't know about such things, it's something I don't understand.

It's the herd instinct that is frightening.

The herd instinct, yes. The consent, the always saying yes.

I remember reading about the experiment carried out using American students, many years ago, in which they administered electric shocks to people in the presence of the students. Only very few of them pushed the button to interrupt the shocks when they had the chance.

And yet they were American... And we might ask why today Germans are so different from what they were then?

Indeed. They have the strongest pacifist movement in Europe.

They have pacifism, the Greens, they have a democracy that works. Why? I have come to the stage of believing in the heroic version of history, in which an evil, potent, charismatic man, the incarnation of the devil that Hitler was, drags behind him an entire people like a flock. What other explanation is there? To see the encounters between Hitler and the public on the newsreels is terrifying. It is like a flash of lightning, a giving and receiving. That is why I fear charisma. I cannot bring myself to accept the Marxist explanation of Nazism as a product of the class struggle: the behaviour of the German people and the figure of Hitler were both too peculiar, too singular, to be reduced to that schema. I don't know, it's something I wonder about.

In my view, much of the ground was laid for Nazism in the peace treaty at the end of the First World War. Forcing Germany to take on sole responsibility for the massacres of that war, humiliating it in absurd ways, was a strong impulse to the spirit of revenge that followed.

You're right, of course, but Germany after the Second World War was humiliated even more completely. It was split in two, occupied, by the French worst of all, and yet nothing similar occurred.

Perhaps precisely because it had been split in two. It is very difficult to talk sensibly about questions of mass psychology.

I always get nervous when I'm asked for reasons for historical events.

But even this nervousness represents a step forward, compared to an idea that history can explain everything, provide comfort or reinforce some notion of progress, a gradual progress towards a hypothetical endpoint... Your understanding of history is linked to a specific, personal, concrete experience, and yet it is also one we can pass on. It's a product of having lived through in the flesh, in the first person, this destruction of all reason. I'm not being very clear...

The fact of having seen all this from within hasn't given me the tools to explain it. I can provide data but I can't answer the whys. I've thought about this for a long time, without ever coming up with a conclusion that is any different from what an historian or a philosopher of history might tells us. In short, to tell the truth, I did not encounter monsters, so much as officials who behaved like monsters. If we then touch on the most burning question of all, the *Sonderkommando*,[18] what can we say? I am horrified by their existence. Do you know the book by that Hungarian doctor, Nyiszli,[19] who was a specialist doctor and part of the *Sonderkommando*? My first reaction is to say that there is no possibility of resilience in the face of such violence. I ask myself what I would have done if it had happened to me, whether I would have had the courage to kill myself, to let myself be killed if I had been offered the task? Perhaps they didn't understand at first what they were being asked to do. There are some cases of people who preferred to let themselves be killed rather than join the *Sonderkommando*, but there are many who didn't.

Were there also many suicides?

No. This is a very important point. There were very few suicides in the *Lager*, and indeed there were fewer suicides in general in wartime than there are now. I've read several different explanations for this phenomenon and few of them are convincing. My interpretation is that suicide is a human act, since animals don't commit suicide, and the human tended towards the level of the animal in the camps, so that, as I said earlier, it was the business of the day that mattered – what you were going to eat, how cold it was going to be, how heavy the work was and of what kind, in short, how you were going to make it through to the evening. There was no time to think about killing yourself.

But it must have been one way of putting an end to the suffering.

I thought about it a number of times, but never seriously.

There were people who let themselves die.

That was different, it wasn't an act of will.

On another aspect of the **Lager***, what about resistance, sabotage? Maybe only small acts of sabotage. Leonardo De Benedetti, the doctor,[20] relates that he had to plant some cabbages in a large field, and that he deluded himself – as he puts it – into sabotaging them by cutting the roots of the cabbages and planting them so that they would wither away. So there were episodes like that, but as he says, 'I deluded myself . . .'*

Yes. I remember wrecking a carriage by pushing and pushing it, knowing that the point was in the wrong position and that it would end up smashing against another carriage. I pretended it was all a mistake, I was with others and we did it all together, more or less consciously. Also I tried to ruin some rollers that I knew were import-ant. I was lucky not to be put on trial for that. I pretended to fall over on to them. That was all I did, and I don't know of any other significant acts of sabotage in the factory. Fear ruled everyone. As for the resistance, there is something I'd like to say. Much later I learned that there was an organized resistance even in Monowitz. At the time, I only had suspicions on two occasions. Once we had a

Jewish *Kapo* who was neurotic, and who beat up prisoners. Now every *Kapo* beat us up but this one went about it with particular violence, he did it to cause pain and harm, he would hit you on the nose, on the neck. I told a companion who was a communist, but also a Jew, about him and we discussed this character, and he said, 'You'll see, he won't last long'. And I said, 'What do you mean?' and he replied, 'You'll see, he won't last long'. And in fact, a few days later he disappeared. My communist friend said to me, 'I told you so'. I never found out nor worked out anything else about it.

The second episode concerned a certain engineer from Milan, another Levi, who stopped me a few days before the arrival of the Russians and said, 'Listen, if anything happens come and find me'. Again, I didn't understand what he meant, I asked him to say it again and he did, 'If anything happens come and find me'. Many years later I met a French Jewish communist who had been at Monowitz and I recounted the two episodes to him. And he told me, yes, both were explainable, that there was indeed a network of Resistance and of preparation for Resistance which on occasion had a power of life and death. That is, they were able at times to get their hands on the personal files of the camp and to erase or add a name. So the *Kapo* could well have been inserted in place of a 'selected' prisoner, there was a way of manipulating to some extent the lists of those who were destined for the gas chambers.

I asked the man who explained all this to me whether that meant that I, as a non-communist, could have ended up in the gas chambers to save the life of a communist? And he replied, yes, of course. In Auschwitz as elsewhere, the communists were in control of the resistance. It's hard to comment on such things. I think that in many ways they were justified in that only they had the capacity to sustain it, only the PC, the German communist party as it was then, and indeed all the monolithic communist parties as they were then, had the strength to organize in this way. And so I think we have to accept this fact, that any old individual might have been condemned to death to save one of their own. I no longer think of it as so monstrous as all that.

But we have also heard from others who had been connected to the resistance here in Italy and who were protected on arrival in the camp, without necessarily being communists. Information somehow reached the offices of the camp and the internal resistance tried to direct resistance members towards less heavy work duties, less uncomfortable situations, at least, so our witnesses tell us.

In camps for political prisoners, maybe. In mine, having been in the resistance was useless. On the contrary, when I said I used to be a partisan, they told me to shut up, not to tell a soul. French prisoners who knew better than any of us what was going on would tell me, if you're a partisan, keep quiet. The place is full of spies.

Notes

1 The interview with Levi was preceded by a lecture by him to the researchers on the oral history interviewing team at the University of Turin.

2 *Lilít e altri racconti. Moments of Reprieve* is a translation of the part of *Lilít* that deals with Auschwitz, with the addition of some new, previously uncollected material.

3 'Il ritorno di Cesare' in *Lilít* ('Cesare's Last Adventure' in *Moments of Reprieve*) tells the picaresque story of the final return to Italy of Cesare, Levi's companion for part of the journey home, as recounted in *The Truce*.

4 The most common destination for Italian political prisoners, mostly rounded-up resistance partisans from the centre and north of Italy, was the labour camp at Mauthausen, and a number of other similar camps, such as Gusen mentioned by Levi below.

5 As described in the opening pages of *If This is a Man* (pages added for the second, 1958 edition), Levi was briefly a partisan in the Val d'Aosta in late 1943, but when captured, he declared himself a Jew and was treated as such by the Nazis from that point on.

6 See note 14 below.

7 Garibaldi's famous 1860 expedition with 'The Thousand' to claim Sicily for a new united Italy created a group of veteran heroes many of whom wrote and spoke of their experiences afterwards.

8 Bruno Bettelheim (1903–90), survivor for over a year in a concentration camp (although in the early years before they took on their most horrific form) and emigré to America in 1939, wrote influential and controversial books on child psychiatry, psychoanalysis and the Holocaust, including *The Informed Heart* (London: Thames and Hudson, 1961) and *Surviving* (London: Thames and Hudson, 1979). He committed suicide in 1990.

9 Giacomo Debenedetti, *16 ottobre 1943* (Rome: Edizioni del secolo, 1944) tells the story of the Nazi round-up of Rome's Jewish ghetto. There is an English translation by Judith Woolf, published by University Texts (Market Harborough, 1996).

10 Carlo Alberto was king of Savoy at the time of the 1848 constitution, the 'Statuto', which formally emancipated the Jews in his kingdom, hence the tradition of loyalty to Savoy and then to the united Italy that the House of Savoy ruled after 1861.

11 Sion Segre Amar (1910–), Piedmontese Jew and author of several books.

12 Hermann Langbein, *Menschen in Auschwitz* ('Human Beings in Auschwitz') (Vienna: Europaverlag, 1972).

13 In the Italian context, the interviewer is referring to the end of the postwar hiatus in 1948 when the first democratic elections for the republic under the new Constitution were held and were won by the centre-right Christian Democrat party.

14 Claudine Vegh, *Je ne lui ai pas dit au revoir* (Paris: Gallimard, 1979; in English as *I Didn't Say Goodbye*, London: Caliban, 1984); Maria Massaniello Arata, *Il ponte dei corvi. Diario di una deportata a Ravensbrück* ('The Bridge of Crows. Diary of a Deportee to Ravensbrück') (Milan: Mursia, 1979).

15 Liliana Cavani (1937–) directed the film *Night Porter* (1974), with Dirk Bogarde and Charlotte Rampling as former camp guard and inmate respectively, who enter into a tortured sexual relationship. Levi attacked Cavani and *Night Porter* in particular on several occasions as representative of a 1970s trend for psychosexual, semi-pornographic representations of Nazism.

16 The SA was the *Sturmabteilung* (Assault Division, or Stormtroopers or Brownshirts), a Nazi paramilitary organization whose mass membership and influence was much reduced after the power struggle culminating in the 1934 Night of the Long Knives. The SS (*Schutzstaffel*, or protective squad) was first Hitler's personal bodyguard, then the elite and independent force of the Third Reich, the force behind much of the Final Solution.

17 Ferdinando Camon, *Autoritratto di Primo Levi* ('Self-Portrait of Primo Levi') (Padua: Nord-Est, 1987).

18 The *Sonderkommando* was the squad given the task of manning the crematoria and gas chambers.

19 Miklos Nyiszli, *Auschwitz: A Doctor's Eyewitness Account* (Greenwich, Conn.: Fawcett Crest, 1960).

20 Leonardo De Benedetti (1898–1983) was deported to Auschwitz with Levi, and first in a holding camp in Russia and then on their return, they co-wrote a medical report on sanitary conditions in the camps which was published in a medical journal, *Minerva medica*, in 1946. It was Levi's first published writing on the subject.

Words, Memory, Hope
(1984)

Marco Vigevani

Hannah Arendt[1] has written of accounts of the Nazi camps: 'The more authentic they are the less they try to communicate things which are beyond human understanding and experience, that is, suffering that turns men into unprotesting animals. No testimony of that kind can inspire the passion of indignant sympathy that has mobilized people of every age to fight for justice.' Would you agree that this opinion could be applied very well to If This is a Man with its dry, restrained style, with its rejection of rhetorical or literary description?

It's true. It is also true that when I wrote the book, almost forty years ago now, I had one precise idea in mind, and it was certainly not to write a work of literature. It was rather to bear witness, and a witness is all the more credible the less he exaggerates or the less he risks being taken for someone who is exaggerating. As I say at the end of the Preface, I was afraid that the events related might be taken as inventions, although unfortunately they were all true. Furthermore, in my testimony there is an element of extreme importance missing: the quantitative element. It is missing because when I wrote the book, no one knew the exact scale of the extermination and so I did not give any figures. I couldn't have and perhaps I didn't really want to. I wanted to recount what I had seen. I would like to add further that there is a question of temperament here also, of style: I don't like to talk too loudly and I have noticed from the innumerable testimonies

From 'Le parole, il ricordo, la speranza', *Bollettino della comunità israelitica di Milano*, XL, 5, May 1984.

that I have received that this has gone down well. It is more effective to bear witness with restraint rather than with scorn: the scorn should be the reader's, not the author's, and it is by no means inevitable that an author's scorn will become the reader's. I wanted to provide the readers with the primary matter for *their* scorn.

In that first book there are two sentences which struck me particularly: 'Then for the first time, we became aware that our language lacks words to express this offence, the demolition of a man' and 'If the Lagers *had lasted longer, a new, harsh language would have been born: and only this language could express what it means to toil the whole day in the wind, with the temperature below freezing, wearing only a shirt, underpants, cloth jacket and trousers, and in one's body nothing but weakness, hunger and the knowledge of the end drawing nearer.' My question is: how did you manage to live through again psychologically and to express in words an experience that was so much at the limits of what is human and what is imaginable?*

I realize that it is very difficult to put that experience into words. I tried to do so, and perhaps in part I succeeded, although at times I had the sensation of attempting an impossible task. Now, after so many years, it is hard even for me to return to the state of mind of the prisoner of that time, of myself back then. In particular, writing the book has worked for me as a sort of 'prosthesis', an external memory set up like a barrier between my life today and my life then. Today, I relive those events through what I have written. Also we need to distinguish, in talking about memory, between episodes you might call 'in technicolor', which I described because they seemed essential and worthy of record, and the grey material, 'in black and white', the everyday routine, which was so destructive, perhaps even more than the selections. The hardest thing to capture was precisely the boredom, the total boredom, the monotony, the lack of events, every single day the same. That is what being in prison feels like, and it generates a curious effect by which the days as you live them seem eternal but as soon as they are over they collapse into instants because they have nothing in them. The past is compressed, thinned, it has no depth. I think this is hard to render, because memory works in precisely the opposite way: the single, clamorous terrifying episodes, or conversely the happy moments, prevail and invade the canvas, whereas as one lives them they are a part of totally disintegrated reality. And there is another gap in any testimony: the witnesses, by definition, are survivors and thus all of them, to some degree, benefited from some privilege. I say this also of myself: if I had not been a chemist, if I had not known a smattering of German, my fate would have been different. The fate of the common prisoner has not been told by anyone, because it was materially impossible for him to survive. The common prisoner of the camps has been described, by me and others, when we speak of the *Muselmann*: but the *Muselmänner* themselves have not spoken.[2]

Then there was another, linguistic difficulty, this time internal to the *Lager*. This is an area still to be developed, something I will write about one of these days. There was an enormous gulf separating those who spoke German or Polish and those who did not. For many Italians this was a matter of life and death, the experience of suddenly becoming deaf-mutes. Hurled into an alien world, even the most banal means of communication no longer worked, the ways of making oneself understood and of understanding where you were. It was my good fortune to know some German, very little, but enough to understand the orders, enough to make myself understood. But I remember very clearly having realized that it was essential to set up lines of communication and so I struggled to absorb from around me, to retrain myself as a speaker and a listener. I even asked some Alsatian friends to translate what was going on around me, to give me that bare minimum of language that would allow me to live, first of all materially (you could have orders screamed at you and not understand, or you could miss the doling out of soup and bread) and then also to get over the psychological block of only being able to communicate with Italians, who were a hundred in 100,000. This problem was specific to the Italians and the Greeks. The Jews from Trieste or Fiume who did speak German seemed like supermen to me, they were one notch above us from the outset, you could say.

You yourself have posed the question of the 'possible meaning in the Lager *of the words "good" and "evil", "just" and "unjust" . . . how much of our ordinary moral world could survive on this side of the barbed wire'. Taking to its extreme this sort of annulment of the distinction between good and evil that the* Lager *produced, some have gone so far as to speak of an identification between victim and executioner. Rousset,[3] for example, writes: 'victim and executioner are equally ignoble, the lesson of the camps is the fraternity of abjection'. I know this is a delicate question: what is your opinion?*

It is a frightening proposition and it is acceptable from Rousset who was there, but not from Cavani and other aesthetes who have worked on it later.[4] There is an element of truth, with due exception made at the level of moral judgement of course, since the executioner is the executioner and the victim the victim. For example, on my return to Italy, I myself noticed with a certain horror but also some amusement that my German was the German of the SS. Language unifies, interlocutors tend to come together. So that when, much later, I went to Germany for work, and they asked me, 'Where did you learn German?', I replied, 'I learned it in Auschwitz', and then some of them understood. Certainly the title of my book (*If This is a Man*) is eloquent in this regard: neither one nor the other is more of a man. There was dehumanization on both sides: on one side imposed, on the other more or less chosen. It is a delicate subject, which is spoken about too much and too crudely, whereas it should be treated with extreme care. There is much more one could say, but I have given you some indications. For example, for practical reasons, there was a long chain linking together prisoners and executioners made up of all those prisoners who progressed, who in some way collaborated, and they were many, at least 10 per cent. There was an extensive hierarchy that went from the cleaners all the way to the barrack *Kapos*, who in some instances went over to the other side. This was rare among the Jews, but quite common amongst the criminal prisoners. The dividing line between victim and executioner was thus 'blurred': there were executioner-victims and victim-executioners. We thought we were heading for a place of suffering, but one where there would be some solidarity, a united front against the Germans and this was almost never the case. National differences were exacerbated and Italians were treated by all Germans, whether Nazis or not, as *Badogliani*.[5] The levels of the hierarchy were infinite, there was none of the clear-cut separation you might imagine.

Many former internees have described carrying with them from the Lager *a 'sense of guilt'? What is this guilt? What guilt can there be in an innocent victim?*

Almost all of us came out of the *Lager* with a sense of unease and to this unease we applied the label 'sense of guilt'. Certainly there is no overlap between this and what we were discussing just now about the so-called identification between victim and executioner. It is not that we feel the guilt that should be felt by the executioner: but to some degree, I believe, all of us or most of us have felt a certain unease at the thought that so many died who were at least as worthy as us, if not more so. It is not necessarily the best people who survive; in some cases, in fact, it is the worst. It is the feeling of being alive in someone else's stead. I mentioned it in *If This is a Man*: after the selection, I thought I had survived by chance, mistaken for someone much more robust than me. There I wrote: 'I do not know what I will think tomorrow and later; today I feel no distinct emotion.'

Then there is also a sense of guilt for perhaps not having done everything one could have done, for instance, putting up more resistance. This is a rationalization, perhaps a sublimation, but it is undoubtedly a thought we had afterwards. We could have done something more, organized ourselves better, at least have made plans to escape... For a long time now, I have had feelings of guilt about one episode: it was summer, during a phase of bombings, it was very hot and I had found some water, a piece of piping. There were perhaps three or four litres there and I only told one friend, not others. I felt guilty about this: on the other hand, if I had told too many others there wouldn't have been enough water to go around. But the sense of failed or incomplete solidarity, of having omitted to do something I could have done, that I have certainly felt. And then, finally, we also felt a certain shared, human responsibility, for the fact that Auschwitz was the work of humankind and we are humans. It is a product of the civilization we live in, even if Nazism was a degenerate branch of that civilization; it is the fruit of a Western philosophy that we have all had a hand in, with which we have all collaborated in some way. But these thoughts are all very elaborate and in the end posthumous, a posteriori. In any case, the fact of being victims is not contradicted by these feelings of guilt I have talked about, because they were marginal feelings. Furthermore, it is not always the case that the victim is pure, entirely innocent. On the contrary, it was typical of the *Lager* system to force us to make ourselves guilty in some way; myself, for example, for accepting to work in an IG-Farben laboratory.

I'd like to move on to another point that strikes me as important: the issue of memory, of how to remember the concentration camps and the extermination camps. It seems to me, for example, that behind the use of words such as 'Holocaust' to designate the planned and scientifically executed murder of millions of people, or behind the disproportionate attention that has often been paid to an event, which was certainly heroic, but which was also quite exceptional and in the end not representative of the Jewish tragedy – the uprising in the Warsaw ghetto – behind these there might lie a refusal to accept the extermination in all its overwhelming crudity and senselessness. What do you think?

I agree. 'Holocaust' literally means 'all burnt' and it refers to animal sacrifices made to the gods. It is a term that annoyed me when it was first used: then I learned that it had been Elie Wiesel who coined it, and who later regretted it and wished to withdraw it. I am also irritated by attempts by some religious extremists to interpret the extermination in the manner of the prophets: as a punishment for our sins. No. I cannot accept this: the fact of its senselessness makes it all the more appalling. If you think that the convoys even picked up the dying, from all four corners of Europe, only for them to die en route, this truly goes beyond any explanation. I understand the children more; in the psychology of a Nazi, a Jewish child was a future enemy, but the dying and the mentally ill, no. This was part of the Germans' *Gründlichkeit*, their fundamentalism, the going the whole way at all costs, so that when you say 'all', it must be all. Even those who will die tomorrow anyway are picked up and loaded on to the trains just so they can die where they are all supposed to die. Nor do I like the idea of presenting the camps as a place of resistance. It was not or it was so only marginally: all credit to those who did resist, but it was by no means the rule. The rule was to give way, to be cut down. Survival in itself proves nothing; as someone who survived I do not feel in any way either a hero or a resister. I am at peace with myself because I have borne witness, because I kept my eyes and ears open so that I could tell the story of what I saw truthfully, with accuracy. In any case, as I said, resistance was the work of a few dozen only and not common prisoners; they were all political prisoners, perhaps Jewish political prisoners, Zionists, people who had fought in Spain, people with military experience, and native German speakers, a fundamental asset for setting up conspiracy networks. For us it was quite extraneous and something that surprised me *afterwards*. Only after liberation did I learn that there was a nucleus of resistance even in Auschwitz. As for those open eyes and ears, this is something I noticed with amazement later on. Even today, after so many years, I have preserved a visual and acoustic memory of my experiences there that I cannot explain: I happened to be in Israel once and I met a camp comrade whom I had not seen for twenty-five years, and I recognized him at once. Not only that: I also still remember, as if recorded on to tape, phrases in languages I do not know, Polish or Hungarian. I have recited these phrases to Poles and Hungarians and they tell me they make sense. For some reason that I cannot fathom, something anomalous happened to me, almost an unconscious preparation for the task of bearing witness.

Do you see today any possibility, not that the same things could happen again, but that there could be a move in that direction?

It cannot be ruled out. You only have to see what happened in Argentina some years ago.[6] Fortunately, being a poorly organized country, the victims there numbered in tens of thousands, not millions, but if there had been a ruler in Argentina, a 'shamanic' figure like Hitler, the victims would have been millions and not tens of thousands. If they had had everything *gründlich*, through and through . . .

To turn to Germany and to the attitude of Germans today, do you have the impression that at least young Germans have come to terms and are coming to terms with their own history or are they rather trying to consign it to oblivion?

In West Germany lots of different things are happening. Today I received a circular from a German lady inviting me to sign a petition to stop SS meetings there. On the other hand, there *are* SS meetings. Germany has many different heads. Without doubt, the older generation still feels a certain nostalgia: as for the young, these days they resemble more and more their French or Italian peers. The Neo-Nazi party has not reached the 5 per cent threshold to enter Parliament, so it is weaker than the MSI in Italy.[7] Even that German pride in Germany above all things seems to have been calmed; they have no desire to make war. My impression is that there is a clear divide between the Germany of then and the Germany of today, without hiding the fact that residues of Nazism remain. I've been sent many letters from German readers of my books, although I realize they are not a representative sample. They are all letters of solidarity, some of them very moving. Of course, anyone who writes to the author of *If This is Man* is already sensitized, many are children of anti-Nazi ex-deportees or of people killed in the war.

Just as there is a scale with infinite gradations for those who collaborated with the Germans, is there also a scale of different degrees of responsibility amongst the German civilian population?

There certainly is. There are families who were victims of Nazism there too. The first to be deported were the political enemies of the Nazism – communists, social democrats, liberals. They, too, suffered under Nazism, indeed the first to suffer were the German people. And here, too, what can you say about families with war dead or wounded? I do not feel able to generalize, saying 'they were fighting for Germany and thus they were Nazis, and thus my enemies, so that I couldn't care less about their widows and orphans'. I will not reach that point: I know suffering and suffering is the same for us all.

As an Auschwitz survivor, how do you choose between the alternatives of 'not forgetting' what happened and hoping for a more humane future?

The duty of hope and the duty of not forgetting are neither synonyms nor opposites. They can coexist. All the combinations are possible: remembering and hoping, remembering and despairing, as many do – there are many survivors who live equally on memory and despair – forgetting and hoping, forgetting and not hoping. It can all happen. My position would be to remember and to hope, but as I said, this is something congenital, hormonal even, not the result of a studied, reasoned choice.

Notes

1   Hannah Arendt (1906–75) was a German-born philosopher who studied with Jaspers and Heidegger before moving to America after the rise of Nazism. She was the author of a famous study of the Eichmann trial, *Eichmann in Jerusalem. A Report on the Banality of Evil* (London: Faber and Faber, 1963).

2   *Muselmann* (Muslim), as Levi explains in the chapter 'The Drowned and the Saved' in *If This is a Man*, was the camp-jargon term used to describe those who were so weak or who had so lost their will to live that death seemed the inevitable next step for them.

3   David Rousset, *L'univers concentrationnaire* (Paris: Editions du Pavois, 1946), translated as *A World Apart* (London: Secker and Warburg, 1951).

4   Liliana Cavani, see note 15 to previous interview.

5   The nickname comes from Marshal Pietro Badoglio (1871–1956), the soldier-politician who took over from Mussolini after the latter's fall in 1943 and negotiated the Armistice with the Allies. Thus, for the Germans, *Badogliano* means turncoat or traitor.

6   Levi is referring to the military dictatorship in Argentina installed in 1976, and the torture and 'disappearance' of opponents that followed.

7   The MSI or Movimento sociale italiano (Italian Social Movement) was a party founded in 1946 by former Fascists.

Part VI
Judaism and Israel

Jewish, Up to a Point (1976)

Edith Bruck[1]

I met Primo Levi many years ago, our first embrace was that of two old friends who have lived through the same tragedy. He arrived, holding a rose, at the Turin television studios where they were filming one of my stories, about the camps inevitably. We looked each other in the eye and then we glanced over at the set, smiling, as if to say 'it's a game, perhaps it's all a game, for us reality is always double-edged, caught between the past and the present'. From that day on we have shared a bond that has no name. I have come to interview him because I am also (or I play at being) a journalist, and Primo has agreed to be interviewed because he is (or he plays at being) a writer and for once, we are able to play together. I ask him with a smile:

Are you still playing at being a chemist?

I've been a chemical engineer and a factory manager in all seriousness for twenty-six years. I stopped only a few months ago and I felt a great sense of relief for all the free time I now have and for the end to all that responsibility.

What does it mean to you to be Jewish?

From 'Ebreo fino a un certo punto', *Il Messaggero*, 9 January 1976.

I was turned into a Jew by others. [*Primo Levi replies in his sweet, persuasive voice.*] Before Hitler I was a middle-class Italian boy. The experience of the Race Laws helped me to recognize, amongst the many threads that made up the Jewish tradition, a number that I could accept.

For example?

Spiritual independence, for one: the same that provoked and guided the rebellions of the Judaeans against the Romans. And the Talmudic tradition of impassioned but precise argument, and the tradition of the religion of the Book. Other aspects, the more strictly religious or mystic, interested me much less. That *rapprochement* with tradition was confirmed by my time in Auschwitz, by my first contact with a civilization I hadn't known before, that of the Ashkenazi Jewry of Eastern Europe.

Do you think there is anti-Semitism in Italy today?

I would say that it is negligible. Even during Fascism the anti-Semitism imposed by law on the Italian people was never more than superficial and inconsistent. Today it seems to me to be limited to certain particularly reactionary neo-Fascist groups.

And yet the only newspapers that admire Israel are right-wing and . . .

With friends like that who needs enemies. Their love for Israel is just an offshoot of their anti-communism, and from the way they portray it, the Israel they admire is precisely the Israel I like least.

What does Israel mean to you?

I feel deeply split on Israel.

So I'm not alone.
(*I laugh. He laughs too, and then he turns serious again and adds:*)

So much so that I cannot give an objective judgement on it. In the years from 1935 to 1940 I was fascinated by Zionist propaganda, I admired the country it described and the future it was planning, the return to the earth, the restoration of a society founded on equality and fraternity, regeneration through manual labour, the rejection of property as the basis of our existence. Later on, during the Second World War, I accepted the need for a homeland for the Jews of all the countries threatened by Nazi occupation. But I must admit that after 1950 this image of the Jewish homeland gradually faded in me.

The Arabs continue to reiterate that their enemies are not the Jews but the Zionists. I've tried many times to distinguish Zionists from Jews but it never quite works; can you explain it to me?

In its origins, Zionism had a particular programme and a particular aim, the rebuilding of a single homeland which all those who declare themselves Jews, no matter where they may be, could recognize as theirs. For non-Zionist Jews, the very notion of a homeland was debatable. As far as I'm concerned, despite my deep attraction towards Jewish culture, history and tradition, I have to say that the formation of my own cultural base is predominantly Italian.

And your children, how have you brought them up?

With the full agreement of my wife. We sent our children to Jewish elementary school to counterbalance the pressure of the dominant Catholic culture around them, but after that we preferred to move them into state schools.

At home, do you observe any of the Jewish traditions?

No, nothing.

And today, what is your children's attitude now?

My daughter, who is twenty-six now, has made a choice in line with her friends. She is a non-religious woman, but she is seriously engaged in politics and has a deep civic conscience.

And your son?

My son is eighteen years old and it looks as though he will follow essentially the same path as his sister. Of course, no one can predict the future, and no one can exclude the possibility that they might be drawn back to an interest in Judaism, as happened to me.

And how do they judge the manifestations of anti-Semitism in communist régimes?

Very severely. They consider them a dangerous sign of the collapse of socialist ideals.

How do they see you, as a father and as a writer?

I have always had a very straight relationship with them. But there is a tacit understanding in our family that I have to leave behind my writer's garb at home. I have good reason to think that they have read my books, even though they have never said a word about them to me.

Have you asked them?

On occasion I have tried to discover what they think, but I have always come up against their implicit or explicit refusal to reply.

Do this upset you?

Yes, it does a little.

What are you writing now?

Just now, nothing at all.

Do you think that the subject of Judaism has a following among readers?

The subject of a book isn't what attracts readers. You can write about rabbits or ants just as well. Nevertheless, I believe that the Nazi massacres constitute in more than one way the central problem of the history of Europe in this century. So it isn't surprising that readers, especially young readers, are far from uninterested, indeed, they are more drawn to the subject than older generations who compromised with Fascism in so many ways.

Let's talk some more about minorities, about feminism as well. Are you anti-feminist, like most Italians?

Anti-feminist, me? I don't know, I don't think so. Let me examine my conscience. No, I am not an anti-feminist.

I see. You don't want to say any more.

No, no. I am a narcissist. I like it when the talk is about me.

I look at his high, prominent forehead, his lively eyes and sweet smile, and I realize that I can't describe him physically, because his beauty is on the inside.

Note

1   Edith Bruck (1932–) is herself a Jewish Holocaust survivor and a writer. Born in Hungary, she moved to Israel after the war and then to Italy in the 1950s, and is the author of several autobiographical narratives, beginning with *Chi ti ama così* (Milan: Lerici, 1959).

Interview with Primo Levi (1979)

Giorgio Segrè

In your most recent book, The Wrench, *as well as recounting the adventures of the Piedmontese crane-rigger Faussone, who journeys from one end of the globe to another as a skilled worker, you intervene yourself in dialogue with Faussone to explain your own experiences of life and work. These two elements – travel and going back over one's own experiences – which recur in different shapes and forms in your other novels, are they not also elements which characterize the Jew? In this I don't mean even vaguely to hint at a racial difference of some kind, but rather to put the accent on an aspect of character that is more or less evident in different instances?*

I would say certainly not. It is true that a writer, or indeed all of us as we live, does not always consciously know exactly what is motivating him, so I can't possibly say for sure what brought me to write that book in that way. But, as far as I am aware, I would say no, since the character Faussone is very different from me. At the very least he is far removed from my identity as a Jew. In fact, I'd say that this is the first time I've taken on the task of writing a book cut off from Auschwitz, and I did so for several reasons. First – although, of course, I don't wish to deny a thing, nor to forget, I don't want to forget anything, and it is more than likely that I will write again of my experiences as a deportee – I nevertheless wanted to try this experiment, to move away from that time, to draw on completely different source material for the book, i.e. my professional work, my many

From 'Intervista a Primo Levi', *Ha-tikwa*, April 1979.

years' work as a chemist and all the encounters of those years. So I'd say that my past, my present life as a Jew, although never denied, only appears in this book obliquely, by chance.

So you do not see these elements of travel and self-analysis as at some level, perhaps only at the level of subconscious, decidedly Jewish?

Luckily Jews aren't the only ones who travel. It would be awful indeed if only Jews were wanderers. No. My creation has his roots, if anywhere, in Conrad. I say as much almost explicitly in the note at the end of the book. He also has his roots in my own journeys: not in those of *The Truce*, but rather in later journeys made in completely different circumstances. No longer journeys of fear, but work trips, work stories and so on. So my answer is no, 95 per cent no.

Do you believe there is such a thing today as a Jewish culture of the Diaspora? And if so, in the field of literature particularly, can its practitioners, for all their inevitable subjective differences, be said to share common denominators?

I would say yes, without a doubt. There is a Jewish culture of the Diaspora. Just look at any list of Nobel prize-winners. There is a Jewish presence in all branches of our culture.

In every country where there are still Jewish communities aware of their Jewishness, that presence is to be found in the human sciences, in literature, in visual arts, in exact sciences and in natural science. It is not missing anywhere. As to whether there really are shared common denominators between them all, I would also say yes, although with many reservations. The shared elements might well be minimal. It would be interesting to explore and see how much Judaism there is, say, in Saba or Moravia[1] to see what remains of Judaism in non-Jews. Very interesting indeed. As is well known, American literature today is packed full of Jewish culture, not only in the work of Jewish authors, but across the board. America is the centre of gravity of Jewish culture now. You could say that throughout the United States there is a full spectrum of Jewish presence, a series of segments going from Chassidism at one extreme all the way to the lay Jewishness of Saul Bellow, just to give one specific example. It is a curious and large-scale phenomenon, this transmigration not of Judaism, but of the centre of gravity of Jewish culture, which is no longer to be found in Poland, White Russia, the Ukraine or Lithuania, but in New York. And it has lost nothing along the way; on the contrary, it has grown richer. Even Yiddish, that extraordinary, wondrous language which is unknown in Italy, is turning another linguistic somersault: after drawing on German, Hebrew, Russian, Polish and Lithuanian, now it is becoming English, adapting itself to English. These are phenomena that are gold-dust for linguists, because they can watch a truly hybrid language, the most hybrid in the world, surviving precisely because it is hybrid. The very idea of pure language is a folly. Think of how hybrid English is: Yiddish is even more so, or at least more so recently since it continues to reinvent itself even now. It has a glorious literature, even if small in volume, and within strict parameters, so it is not so weighed down. It carries on evolving with remarkable neologisms.

What can you tell us about Jewish culture in Israel?

I know very little about Jewish culture in Israel. My impression is that it is not very lively, or at least that it is rather provincial. It's a bald statement that I couldn't justify, since I haven't heard anything about modern Israeli writing. I know that there are some writers: Dayan's daughter, for one.[2] But I haven't read her books, so I cannot comment. Israel seems to be moving in the direction of becoming a Middle Eastern country, as is right and proper, and so it is cutting its links with European culture and Western culture in general. I'm told that the younger generation in Israel is no longer polyglot, that it speaks Hebrew and at best perhaps learns English at school. My generation, on the other hand, those of my age in Israel, speak four or five languages because they have held on to their roots. In these conditions, a specifically Israeli culture can certainly exist, is perhaps being born now, with its own more Middle Eastern characteristics. Which is not at all to disparage it: it means new links, links with the Arab world, even with the world of Islam. Why not? As far as I know, it has already happened in music. Today, Israeli music is already in fertile and active dialogue with Arab music. I cannot add much more. I am a Jew of the Diaspora and I feel much closer to Western culture. I know little of this new culture, so all I have said should be taken with a pinch of salt.

What is your assessment of the two Nobel prize-winners, Saul Bellow (1976) and Isaac Bashevis Singer (1978)?

I am a great enthusiast for Saul Bellow, almost without reservations. I see in him true intelligence in all its forms, intelligence and versatility... Bellow could come up with any number of different types of new work. He's still highly active. Every single line of his books oozes vitality and intelligence. Singer's is a somewhat different case. I think of him more with respect than with admiration. He's very old, the Nobel prize was his by right and they did well to give it to him. The Nobel prize, as is well known, sets the seal on a great career. His voice is different from Bellow's. It's the voice of the Eastern European Jew, made welcome in America as a guest, but not integrated; of a Jew who is always slightly uneasy after landing in America. Like the Jew of Joseph Roth;[3] like Roth's Job when he arrives, disconcerted, in that foreign land. Bellow, on the other hand, is not in a foreign land. He is perfectly integrated and has to the full that typical Diaspora capacity to adapt and transform, taking on whatever new aspect is needed. The Diaspora Jew can be conservative or reactionary, subversive or submissive, enlightened, mystical or rationalistic. And Bellow is all of these things.

Going back to something you said in your interview with Ha Keillah,[4] *would you be able to be more specific about what you said there of your intention to tackle one of the most painful subjects of all: the relation between the oppressor and the oppressed in the extermination camps, and the other related question of the torturer, the question of how the torturer reaches the stage of carrying out certain acts that perhaps he would not have contemplated in different circumstances?*

If I was vague in that interview it's because I am still unsure on the subject. I have few clear ideas on what I shall do and what I want to do. Roughly speaking, the problem is as follows: the situation of the persecution of the Jews, the Holocaust (the word cannot be avoided now), tends to be simplified, in part because everything tends to get simplified. We human beings are animals who prefer things kept simple. But here nothing is simple. Things are complex at every stage. I would like to put together what I'd call a sociological analysis. Of course, I'm no sociologist or I'm an amateur at best. But I am a witness, I know and lived through the experience. I'd like to re-establish that experience as it was in its own terms. And in this context, the victim–torturer pair needs examining. We need to understand how the torturer becomes what he becomes. By what means. If he was really always a torturer or not. Perhaps he was simply someone who carried out all the tasks, gestures and acts of a torturer, but who in all other respects was just like us. In all probability that is how it was, and if so, it could not be more significant nor more sad. It is Hannah Arendt's thesis on the 'banality of evil'. Her idea is very close to what I'm saying, that the environment was much more important than intrinsic human nature. These were not monsters. I didn't see a single monster in my time in the camp. Instead I saw people like you and I who were acting in that way because there was Fascism, Nazism in Germany. Were some form of Fascism or Nazism to return, there would be people, like us, who would act in the same way, everywhere. And the same goes for the victims, for the particular behaviour of the victims about which so much has been said, most typically by young Israelis who object 'but we would never act that way'. They're right. They would not act that way. But if they had been born forty years earlier, they would have. They would have behaved exactly as the deported Jews – and, it's worth adding, the deported Russians and Italians and the rest.

What do you think of the various anti-Semitic incidents and pronouncements that are growing ever more frequent in Italy and Europe?

It's hard to say anything that isn't obvious in reply. Clearly, incidents like that at Varese[5] cause pain and shock. Although I'd like to add one point. I think there is a link between the interview in *L'Express* with Darquier de Pellepoix, the interview in *Le Monde* with Faurisson and this act in Varese.[6] I offer it as a hypothesis, which needs discussing and debating. First of all, you could say the three are linked by their extreme stupidity, which they do not share with Hitler's Germany. You can accuse the Nazis of many things, but not of stupidity. In this case, by contrast, the idiots seem to have taken charge. Darquier is an idiot because he is senile. Faurisson is an idiot, or mentally ill, although perhaps we should speak more politely of the mentally ill? And the boys of Varese were, it seems, relatively unaware of what they were doing. I can believe it . . . the idiots have taken over for sure. There may well be more serious minds behind it all, probably there are. But it is not insignificant that this is the highest calibre they can find for their work, here and in France, that they use people of this ilk.

Notes

1   Both Jewish-Italian writers: Umberto Saba (1883–1957) was a Triestine poet and Alberto Moravia (1907–90) a novelist and major intellectual presence in twentieth-century Italian literature.
2   Yael Dayan, daughter of the famous soldier and politician Moshe Dayan, had published several novels in the 1960s, such as *New Face in the Mirror* (1959), *Envy the Frightened* (1961), *Dust* (1963) and *Death Had Two Sons* (1967), all published in London by Weidenfeld and Nicolson.
3   Joseph Roth (1894–1939), Austrian novelist, author of *Job* (1930; London: Chatto & Windus, 1983).
4   Levi had given an interview to Giorgina Arian Levi for the Jewish journal *Ha Keillah* in February 1979.
5   At a basketball match in the Northern Italian town of Varese in 1979, the home team taunted a visiting Israeli team with chants about the concentration camps, provoking a minor scandal in the national media.
6   Levi is referring to two of the protagonists of Holocaust negationism in France who achieved notoriety in late 1978 for the interview and article referred to. Levi wrote an article on the episode for *La Stampa*, 19 January 1979.

God and I (1983)

Giuseppe Grieco

Our second conversation about God. Interlocutor: Primo Levi, sixty-four years old, chemistry graduate, writer. He tells me straight away, at the start of the interview:

I think I'm an extreme case: up till now I have never really worried about the problem of God. Mine is the life of a man who has lived and who lives without God, indifferent to God.

And this leaves you unperturbed?

It allows me to go on with no illusions.

Primo Levi, from Turin, is Jewish by origin. He is a survivor of the Nazi concentration camps. His first book, If This is a Man, *is a terrifying account of the extermination camps, one of the most raw and dramatic testimonies that has ever been written by someone who lived through the hell of the Holocaust in the flesh. As a writer, he started from that awful experience that marked him forever.*

This was the second in a series of interviews about God with public figures, by Giuseppe Grieco, 'Io e Dio. Non l'ho mai incontrato, neppure nel "Lager" ', *Gente*, 48, 9 December 1983.

Last summer I met my fellow survivor Elie Wiesel in Milan. He has made the Holocaust the very centre of his life and his work as a writer. We were both prisoners in Auschwitz and we both survived. But in a sense he has become 'obsessed' with God whereas I have stuck to my non-faith. I hope to meet him again. Our meeting, after forty years of separation, was fascinating precisely because we are so different.

Talking to Elie Wiesel, did you not feel any twinge of envy for his faith, that has led him to state: 'I can live with God or against God, but not without God'?

Of course I felt some envy. I envy believers, all believers. But I cannot do anything about it. Faith is something you either have or you don't. You cannot invent it. You cannot invent your own God for your own personal use. It would not be honest.

Twenty years ago, Levi won the first ever Campiello Prize with his book The Truce. *This year he won the same prize again with the novel* If Not Now, When? *which is a vast, epic tale about the Jews of Eastern Europe and the groups of partisans who fought in the Second World War for a new freedom, unknown to their fathers and grandfathers.*
Did you have a religious upbringing?

I certainly did. But it passed me by without leaving any deep marks. My mother observed Jewish traditions but she didn't pay much attention to doing it. The real believer in the house was my father. But he was an odd believer. He feared God, he struggled to keep to the laws, he fasted on the right days, but he did so cursing because he couldn't quite stomach some of the restrictions. To give one small example, my father liked ham. To have to go without it because of God's will drove him mad. A believer of sorts, my father would give in with a snarl to the temptations of sin.

Was that the extent of your religious education?

No, of course not. Like all the children in the Jewish community in Turin, I was taught the fundamentals of our religion. At the age of thirteen I had my 'initiation', after which I was officially accepted as a full member of that same community, in terms of age and status. The ceremony of initiation is called *barmitzvah*, which literally means 'child of the law'. It is preceded by an examination carried out by the rabbi on Hebrew and Jewish history and culture.

Didn't you find God through this initiation ceremony?

I underwent the process passively. I have no pride in being Jewish. I have never felt part of a chosen people bound to God by an iron pact. I am Jewish by accident of birth. I am neither ashamed nor boastful about it. Being Jewish, for me, is a matter of 'identity': an 'identity', I must also say, that I have no intention of discarding.

So you entered into a Jewish community whilst at the same time not accepting the God into whose 'mysteries' you had been initiated?

To tell the truth, for a few months I was quite worried, but I got over this. I did try to find contact with God, but nothing ever came of it. I had been presented with a Ruler God, a punitive God who left me quite unmoved. After that short period of confusion, I cut myself off from him entirely, holding him at a distance like a sort of infantile phenomenon that had little to do with me.

A polemical rejection, all in all?

There's no polemic. Since I had never interiorized God, I never felt the need to detach from him in my conscience, to cut off from his horizon. In any case, my move away from God was encouraged in those years by my friends, who were almost all Christians, but also, in the end, uninterested. They were young men and women who maybe went to Mass to please their parents, but absentmindedly, and certainly with no authentic religious drive. They were rather cynical about it, I remember them laughing as they told me, a Jew, funny stories about the Church and priests.

And then, for you, came the awful experience of the extermination camps. How did you react?

I lived my imprisonment as a harsh confirmation of my indifference. In a way, it was all much easier for me than for my fellow camp-prisoner and believer, Elie Wiesel. He was forced to confront brutally the immense trauma of the triumph of evil, and he later came to blame God for allowing it to happen, for not intervening to stop the massacres. For me, on the other hand, I simply concluded: 'So it really is true: there is no God.' And in the absence of God, you might say that I put myself in the position of Giacomo Leopardi, the poet who charged nature with deceiving her children with false promises of happiness which she knows she cannot keep.

So you did not look to God for comfort even once?

In Auschwitz I had only one moment of religious temptation. It happened during the great selection of October 1944, when the group that picked out prisoners to send to the gas chambers was already at work. In short, I tried to commend myself to God, and I recall, with shame, having said to myself: 'No, you can't do this, you don't have the right. First, because you don't believe in God; secondly, because asking for favours, without having a special case, is the act of a *mafioso*.' The moral of the story: I gave up the doubtful comfort of prayer and I left it to chance, or whoever else it might be, to decide my fate.

What happened?

I escaped death and I really do not know why. After my return to Italy I met a friend, who was a believer of sorts, who said to me: 'It's clear why you were saved: God protected you.' His words set me in a state of extreme indignation which I did nothing to hide from the man who had caused it. They seemed to me grotesquely out of proportion, as I had seen suffering and dying all around me thousands of men more worthy than me, even innocent babies, and conversely, I had seen deplorable, most certainly malicious men survive. Thus salvation and death did not depend on God but on chance. Now we could call that chance 'God'. But that would mean accepting a blind God, a deaf God, and I don't see the merit in even considering that.

And so?

That is how things stand for me: either God is all-powerful or he is not God. But if he exists, and is thus omnipotent, why does he allow evil? Evil exists. Suffering is evil. Thus if God, at his bidding, can change good into evil or simply allow evil to spread on Earth, then God is bad. And the hypothesis of a bad God repels me. So I hold on to the simpler hypothesis: I deny him.

Several years ago, the writer Riccardo Bacchelli[1] told me, still on the subject of God: 'I lived till the age of eighty without paying him a great deal of attention, because I was sure that death was the definitive end of the game of existence. Unfortunately, now this certainty is beginning to waver. I confess this with some anger, because it disquiets me, disturbs me. But I cannot do anything about it. The idea of a beyond, of a God waiting to weigh us up on his scales, has planted itself in my mind like a nail and I cannot remove it.' My question is, have you never felt a disturbance of this kind?

Up till now, no. My situation in relation to God is the same as it was when I was fifteen, twenty, forty years old. Rather, there is another order of ideas which, I must confess, provokes a certain curiosity, a certain dissatisfaction in me. When I think about the cosmos, the universe, I begin suspecting that behind the enormous machine of the universe, there might be a driver who controls its movements, maybe even built the machine itself. But rest assured, my suspicion does not effect my conviction that the driver, if he exists, is indifferent to the matters of mankind. In short, he isn't someone to pray to.

I detect a certain regret in your voice...

You're not wrong. I would like the driver to exist, and I would like him still more to be a driver God. To have a father, a judge, a teacher would be good, calming. But this desire of mine does not authorize me to create a God built to order, it is not strong enough to push me as far as to invent a God to talk to.

Earlier you confessed to a sense of envy of believers. Why? Are they perhaps more tranquil?

No. On tranquillity, the non-believer is in a better position perhaps, because for him whatever happens, even evil, has no supernatural cause, it is all the product of the great machine of the universe. The believer, on the other hand, is constantly interrogating himself, interrogating God, always looking, however blindly, for a way out to justify the unjustifiable. Believe me, I know very well the tortuous paths believers travel . . .

And yet, there is much evidence to suggest that our time is marked by a return to God, or at least a return to the search for God. How do you explain this turnaround after the declared 'death' of God, which seemed to be taken for granted in our secular culture?

We are living in a time of crisis in our values, and the return to God is typical of such moments of crisis. The more things collapse around people and the more we feel alone and unarmed in the face of the enigma of the universe, the more man looks for clarity, for an answer to his questions, for someone to reassure him. The search for God thus becomes a search for protection, for a way out of loneliness. In short, the risk God runs, in this instance, is the risk of being seen as a short-cut, leading us beyond the void of our existence.

Can't this void be filled by science?

No. Science studies the great machine of the cosmos, it reveals to us bit by bit its secrets, but it gives no answers to mankind's big questions. The grand illusion that science could, in some sense, take God's place faded some time ago. If you ask science about the 'aims' of life, it will reply: 'Nothing to do with me'. And leave it at that.

So what can we do if we want to get out of the blind alley we've ended up in? If we leave God to one side, unlike your colleague Wiesel, should we then put man on trial as responsible for the evils of the world?

To put mankind on trial makes no sense. Man is a terrible mixture in which you can find everything. Some are wise, others mad, bastards, saints. I have always refused to make global judgements on mankind. Even on Nazis. For me, the only trials to be held, and then with caution in each case, are trials of single individuals.

So?

The situation is as it is, and we can do nothing but accept it. We are a mere detail in the great machine of the universe. And we do not know what margin of autonomy we have within the machine. We can and we must invent a morality, to behave 'as if...', but never forgetting that we are Nature's guests, and, what is more, curious guests bringing disorder wherever we go.

The interview is over: Primo Levi adds a codicil, a poem he gives me entitled 'The Girl-Child of Pompeii'. It is a very beautiful poem. It is about a 'thin child' brought to light by the excavations of the ancient city, buried beneath the ashes of Vesuvius 'clutching her mother convulsively'. He compares her to other innocent victims like Anne Frank or the school-girl of Hiroshima. Levi reads:

> In this way you stay with us, a twisted plaster case,
> Agony without end, terrible witness
> to how much our proud seed matters to the gods.

And he ends with an appeal to the 'powerful of the earth' not to push the button to unleash an atomic apocalypse, since

> the torments heaven sends us are enough.[2]

Notes

1   Riccardo Bacchelli (1891–1985), prolific writer, author of large-scale historical novels.
2   The translation of the poem is by Ruth Feldman, contained in Primo Levi, *Collected Poems* (London: Faber and Faber, 1988).

Primo Levi: Begin should Go (1982)

Giampaolo Pansa

I knock at Primo Levi's door. I have a long list of questions in my notebook and many more in my mind and heart. Yet he is the one to break the silence. Staring at me with his limpid, cool gaze, he says, almost in a whisper: 'OK, let's talk. But I must confess I am very unsure about giving this interview.'

Why, Dr Levi?

For two reasons. One internal, mine: the civil war I carry within me. The other reason is that I've received lots of letters in the last few days, a frightening pile of letters, about what I've said and written recently on the latest war in Israel.[1]

What sort of letters?

Both for and against. Those against were of two different kinds: some thought me too . . .

Too Zionist?

From an interview on the subject of the 1982 Israeli invasion of Lebanon and the massacres of Palestinians in the camps of Sabra and Chatila, 'Io, Primo Levi, chiedo le dimissioni di Begin', *La Repubblica*, 24 September 1982.

Yes, too Zionist. Others accuse me of not being Zionist enough.

Have you received any threatening letters?

No, I haven't.

Are you afraid, at this moment?

In what sense? Personally or as part of the Jewish people?

In both senses?

Personally, no, I'm not afraid. Fear is a deep instinct, and personally I do not suffer from it. But I'm not afraid as a Jew either. No, for us Jews I do not see the signs of a second Holocaust nor an imminent massacre like Hitler's. If anything, I am pained. This war of Israel's, this massacre in Beirut, is polluting the image of Jews throughout the world.

Dr Levi, is there a risk of a new wave of anti-Semitism? I ask the question with a feeling of fear and horror . . .

Yes, to an extent there is this risk. But for now it is limited to isolated instances. It is not by chance that the danger is most evident in Paris and Brussels. Ever since the Dreyfus affair[2] anti-Semitism has been alive in France. It is part of their profound xenophobia.

But even in Milan, the Jewish community has received threats and shows signs of fear. Is it the same in Turin?

Here I'm not aware of any incidents. Maybe you'll find a couple of slogans on the walls of Turin too, but to write on walls you only need one idiot with a spray can. What is more, the community in Turin is small, compact and much more liberal in outlook than the one in Milan . . . Anyway, yes, anti-Semitism is a beast that is stirring. But this is not a reason that Diaspora Jews can put to Begin.[3] It would not make sense to say to Begin, don't do what you are doing because you are harming us. There are other, more important objections.

What are they?

There are two, one moral and the other political. The moral objection is the following: not even a war justifies the bloody arrogance shown by Begin and his men. The political objection is just as clearcut: Israel is rapidly heading towards total isolation. It is a terrible, previously unheard-of fact. And in light of this, there is only one possible conclusion: not even *raison d'état,* so often invoked by Begin and Sharon,[4] can justify the Israeli government's most recent decisions.

Dr Levi, you talk of Begin, Begin . . . but Begin is not an isolated leader. He is in government with the consent of a majority of Israelis.

I realize that. Yes, I know, I know . . .

And what does this make you think?

It makes me think something obvious. Begin is in power largely with the support of the young and recent immigrants, that is, not refugees from Eastern Europe but rather Jews born in Israel of the Middle East. These people are strongly hostile to neighbouring states, from which many of them come, and in a sense this explains the war and what has happened during the war. Nevertheless, my condemnation is total. I say it clearly. And I also harbour a hope, the same hope that drove me to give this interview: I am not interested in having an impact on Italian readers, I'm more interested in the effect in Israel, on its leaders, its electorate and journalists.

Do you have some influence in Israel?

I don't think so. Of all my books, only *The Truce* has been translated there. But that doesn't prove anything. In Israel many people read books in German and English, so they can read my other books as well.

And what message would you like to send to Israel's rulers, Dr Levi?

That they should resign. I can say nothing else, since there is no chance of changing their minds. Of course, I know that asking them to resign at a moment like this is unrealistic. But if he still has a glimmer of reason in his head, Sharon should quit.

What sort of a man is Sharon?

I know Begin's history, but of Sharon I know very little. The image I have of him is just his present image, without any of its roots.

Tell me about this present image . . .

Begin, Sharon, well, the whole group governing Israel today look a lot like the ruling classes of other Middle Eastern states. Paradoxically, Begin and his men are realizing an old Zionist dream: turning Israel into a Middle Eastern country. But they are doing it in the worst possible way. That is, they are adopting the demagogy, instability, unreliability in their promises and treatises that marks out so many rulers in that area.

Can Sharon be defined as a Fascist?

I can't talk about Sharon because, as I say, I don't know his background. But for Begin, 'Fascist' is a definition I can accept. I think even Begin would not deny it. He was a student of Jabotinsky,[5] who represented the right-wing of Zionism, who called himself a Fascist and was one of Mussolini's interlocutors. Yes, Begin was his pupil. That is Begin's history. All I know about Sharon is that he is a hard, unscrupulous soldier. But in my position here, from afar, I cannot read his mind.

Listen, Dr Levi, there is one question that is on many people's lips today. Fascism has reared its head again in many parts of the world. Could it take hold in Israel too?

Fascism as such, I would say not . . . but your question is not a precise one. Take the question back and ask it again in another way.

I'll put it to you again like this: could Israel become a totalitarian state?

It could happen, although only through civil war. Today, opposition to Begin is, certainly, in the minority, but in a large minority. No, I don't think what happened in Chile could happen in Israel. That's not one of the risks as I see it. Israel is extremely vital in terms of its politics, its democracy.

Do you mean that Israel has the antibodies to react against this dark evil within it?

I would say so. I see it in the demonstrations that have taken place in recent days. And in any case, friends of my age there, and indirectly their children and grandchildren, have direct experience of the horrors of Fascism in Europe.

And yet some are saying, even here in La Repubblica *some are writing that there is risk of the state of Israel becoming the worst enemy of Jews, of the people of Israel...*

That seems rather harsh to me, and also rather generic. It might stand at best as a comment on a brief moment, on this moment today.

And if we replaced the words 'the state of Israel' with 'the present government of Israel'?

In that case, yes. But a more correct position would be the following: the present behaviour of the present government of Israel risks become the Jewish people's worst enemy. But not even this would work as an argument to stand up against Begin. An Israeli could reply: 'What do we care of the risks you run? We have our own problems.' The best arguments are the two I gave earlier on. And it is precisely based on these that we have the right to say to Israel: as long as things remain as they are today, you have no right to claim help, whether economic or moral, from the Jews of the Diaspora. No, you cannot ask those of us who criticize Israel for its militarism for money and then spend that money on arms.

But isn't there a real problem of military security for Israel?

I'm not an expert in the matter, but I really don't think so. Begin is waging this war with all the states bordering Israel and across the region staying quite passive. Begin undertook the liquidation of the armed wing of the Palestinians with the support of everyone concerned.

Quite, Arafat. Let's talk about Arafat...

I do not like Begin, but nor do I like Arafat. I don't for a moment trust Arafat's olive branch. He keeps an open mind, he is intelligent, but he is also as unscrupulous as Begin. And it was Begin who offered him on a plate both political victory and the crown as leader of all Palestinians, a crown he previously did not hold.

What is your view of the welcome Arafat received in Italy?

I saw it, I saw it... and my reaction was one of diffidence and also irritation. But let me say again, it was Begin who gave Arafat the glory of defeat.

But after defeat came the massacres of Palestinians in the two camps in Beirut [Sabra and Chatila]. What was your instinctive reaction to the news of what had happened there?

I never have instinctive reactions. If I have them, I repress them. Initially I was not convinced that it had actually happened. Then I understood that it was all true. Then, the slaughter in those two camps brought vividly back to me the Russians in Warsaw in August 1944. They stopped and waited at the Vistula whilst the Nazis exterminated all the Polish partisans of the uprising. Of course, like all historical analogies, mine doesn't quite work. But Israel, just like the Russians in 1944, could have intervened and had the force to stop the gangs who were carrying out the massacre of those people, but they did not.

Why did Israel not intervene?

I don't know, I don't know...perhaps there is some truth even in Begin's hypocrisies. That slaughter is not Israel's style. The situation must have got out of hand. And then again, maybe someone deliberately held back, wasting time before intervening to defend those women and children...what more can I say? As you see, I still have a certain sense of loyalty towards Israel, a sentimental bond. I am not such a pessimist as to think that Israel will always be like this.

But what can you Jews and we non-Jews do to make sure that Israel will not always be like this?

You say 'you and we'...that's a mistake. There is no distinction. God willing, for once there is no difference here between Jew and non-Jew. There is one response valid for all. And it is not, as some suggest, breaking off diplomatic relations or cutting economic links. Those are senseless reactions which would only help reinforce Begin.

And so?

We must all do a number of things. Realize exactly what is going on. Suppress our own impulse towards an emotional solidarity with Israel, so that we can think through coldly the errors of the present Israeli ruling class. Remove this ruling class. Help Israel rediscover its European roots, the balance of its founding fathers, Ben Gurion, Golda Meir.[6] Not that they all had spotless records, but who does? Abba Eban,[7] for example, seems to me to be a safe pair of hands for the future, and he is not that old. But today, the situation is awful. I receive letters from friends there which are harrowing. These are men who have fought in all Israel's wars and have seen children die fighting. They write to me saying, are you blind, can't you see all the Israeli blood, Jewish blood spilled in all these years?

And how do you reply?

I reply that the blood spilled pains me just as much as the blood spilled by all other human beings. But there are still harrowing letters. And I am tormented by them, because I know that Israel was founded by people like me, only less fortunate than me. Men with a number from Auschwitz tattooed on their arms, with no home nor homeland, escaping from the horrors of the Second World War, who found in Israel a home and a homeland. I know all of this. But I also know that this is Begin's favourite defence. And I deny any validity to that defence.

Dr Levi, I see that you are genuinely able to think this through quite coolly...

I do as best as I can, even if this is a dramatic time for us. There is an old play, written in the last century by Shalom Aleichem. Do you know the title? *It's Hard Being Jewish*, and today this is true more than ever. Yes, today it's harder than ever.

Notes

1   Levi had signed a peace appeal soon after the outbreak of the war and had also attacked the war and the Israeli government on the front page of *La Stampa* on 24 June 1982.
2   Alfred Dreyfus (1859–1935), a Jewish French army official, was wrongly convicted of spying for Germany in 1894 and cleared in 1906. In the interim, his case became the centre of an extraordinary battle between democratic and reactionary forces in France and is a watershed in the history of modern anti-Semitism.
3   Menachem Begin (1913–92) was Prime Minister of Israel from 1977 to 1983 at the head of a Likud Party government.
4   Ariel Sharon (1928–   ) was Minister of Defence and the leading 'hawk' military figure in the Lebanon war.
5   Vladimir Jabotinsky (1880–1940) was a writer and leading militant activist in the Zionist movement.
6   David Ben Gurion (1886–1943) was the first Prime Minister of the new independent state of Israel after 1948; Golda Meir (1898–1976) was Prime Minister of Israel, 1969–74.
7   Abba Eban (1915–   ), Israeli diplomat, politician and writer.

If This is a State (1984)

Gad Lerner

Only once in the course of his tormented and passionate relationship with Israel did Primo Levi decide to speak out. It was exactly two years ago, during the invasion of Lebanon, after the massacres in the Palestinian camps of Sabra and Chatila. He spoke out, demanding the resignations of Menachem Begin and Ariel Sharon even before they had been condemned by the famous Kahan Commission as indirectly responsible for those events.

Then Primo Levi shut himself away again. This Turinese Jew and concentration-camp survivor, the chemist who turned into a writer because of the need to tell the story – in *If This is a Man* – of Auschwitz and of the most terrible persecution ever suffered by his people, today he feels tired. He prefers to live apart, to think in the silence of his own home in the centre of Turin, to think about the difficult bond between him, a Diaspora Jew, and what was once called the 'hearth' of Israel.

There, in the ranks of the government of that 'hearth', in the last few days, Ariel Sharon, the most popular leader on the right in Israeli, has come back. He is back in alliance with the Labour party, that is, with those who – like Levi – saw his removal two years ago as fundamental for the future of democracy in Israel.

The Jewish world is in ferment. Behind the scenes of the 'grand coalition' between Likud and Ma'arach,[1] much has changed. For good or ill? It is a very difficult question, but one which today Levi does not refuse to tackle nor to give an answer that is perhaps for him

From 'Se questo è uno Stato', *L'Espresso*, 30 September 1984.

the most difficult of all: 'I am sure that the role of Israel as the unifying centre for Judaism now – and I emphasize the word 'now' – is in eclipse. So the centre of gravity of the Jewish world must turn back, must move out of Israel and back into the Jewish Diaspora. Our task is to remind our Israeli friends of the Jewish tradition of tolerance.'

Why, Dr Levi? Perhaps you see the return of the hawk Sharon as a definitive break, as a threat?

I wouldn't speak of a definitive break, I don't believe that we are facing an irreversible regression. And in any case, the degradation of political life is far from being an exclusively Israeli phenomenon. The fading of ideals is something we see throughout the world. Certainly, there has been a qualitative decline in Israel, but let's not forget that this is a country blessed with an anomalous intellectual agility, where what might take ten years elsewhere can take as little as one.

What is your worry then? Perhaps the rise of Rabbi Meir Kahane,[2] the one who proposes the expulsion of the entire Arab population from the Promised Land, who has put out a television ad which shows blood flowing down across a marble stone?

Kahane is just a loose cannon, I am sure of it. Unless some new disaster occurs, his political force is sure to wane. Someone might object that Hitler in 1923 was just a loose cannon. I would reply that no one can foresee the future, but I cannot see Israel taking the road towards Kahane's fanaticism. Come on, it wouldn't be racist to say that the Jews are not the Germans! To become racist, a country must be compact, must have the potential to work as a massive, uniform and controllable block. Hitler's Germany managed it, but, for example, in Italy it failed, simply because the difference between Piedmont and Calabria was too great. There is no way it could happen in a community such as Israel, fragmented by a 3000–year history, characterized by a mosaic of different ethnic origins and traditions. Having said that, I realize that there is a thread of racism running through the Torah. It contains everything and the opposite of everything. When Kahane brings up the proscription against sexual relations between Jews and 'gentiles' in the Torah, he is telling the truth. But elsewhere in the Torah, there are stories, such as that of Ruth and Samson, which treat it as the norm, as accepted.

Isn't rather the spread of anti-Arab intolerance, then, at the source of your worries?

I could reply that in recent times Israel is also living through a phenomenon that unfortunately does not make the news: in the universities and hospitals there is a massive and deep process of integration between Israeli Arabs and Jews. Amongst the 700,000 Arabs who have lived in Israel since 1948, a large number have integrated. The situation is very different for the million and a half Palestinians living in the occupied West Bank.

Precisely. In his delirium, Rabbi Kahane poses a problem that worries many Israelis: according to recent birth rates, by the year 2000 there will be an Arab majority in Israel. The date is put back another twenty years if you only count Arabs who are Israeli citizens, but the fact remains that they will be able to elect democratically the majority in the parliament of the 'Jewish State'. So, says Kahane, before that day comes, Israel will have to stop being a democratic state, to safeguard its Jewish identity.

These demographic projections are debatable, to say the least. No one can make reasoned projections more than five years ahead. I think I am right in saying, for example, that the birth rate amongst Israeli Jews is rising and amongst Israeli Arabs it is falling. The situation on the West Bank is again very different, and this should lead the Israeli government towards a rapid withdrawal from the occupied territories. If it were not for the heavy burden of the West Bank and Gaza, I think the Palestinian problem in Israel would have already been resolved.

So what is it then that worries you, Dr Levi? What are you referring to when you speak of the degradation of political life in Israel?

Above all, the agreement between Likud and Ma'arach, as with any other grand coalition, strikes me as a temporary and paralysing patching up that cannot last long. I am thinking first and foremost of the way in which before the elections repulsive policies were taken on board simply to garner votes. This isn't exclusive to Israel either, but perhaps we aren't used to it happening there. We're more used to Israel as the land of miracles, to the Israel of 1948, to a Zionism that coincides with a certain idea of socialism. Today the degradation we are seeing is in fact a process of normalization. Unfortunately, Israel is becoming a normal country. Furthermore, since it is a Middle Eastern country, it is tending to become rather similar to the other nations of that region. For example, we might worry about the contagion of Islamic Khomeinism and its impact on religious fundamentalism in Israel, although looking ahead I don't see Israeli masses prostrate before a new Ayatollah, be it Kahane or Sharon himself.

Don't you think that since the majority of Israeli Jews of today were born in Israel, they have changed position, compared to the Diaspora Jews who had always been accustomed to feeling themselves 'in the minority' in their own country, moulded by their 'difference'? The Jews of Europe whom you write about in your books are dramatically attached to the fragile value of tolerance. In becoming a normal country, is it not also that Israel is changing its very identity?

What you describe is part of a foreseeable future. I believe it is up to us Jews of the Diaspora to fight against it. To remind our Israeli friends that being Jewish means something else. To guard jealously the Jewish tradition of tolerance. Of course I am aware that I am touching on a crucial point here, and that is the question: where is the centre of gravity of Judaism today?

From at least 1948 onwards, the central Zionist organizations have had no doubts on this: the centre of gravity is in Israel.

No, I have thought about this a great deal: the centre is in the Diaspora, it is coming back to the Diaspora. As a Diaspora Jew, who feels much more Italian than Jewish, I would prefer the centre of gravity of Judaism to stay outside Israel.

That could sound like a declaration of your rejection of the Israeli nation and the ways it has changed.

Not at all, it is another stage in a deep-felt and passionate rapport. I just believe that the main current of Judaism is better preserved elsewhere than in Israel. Jewish culture itself, in particular Ashkenazi Jewish culture, is more alive elsewhere, in America for example, where it is in a sense dominant.

From what you are saying, it might seem that staying in the Diaspora, that is, remaining in the minority, is almost a compulsory condition for the continuation of Jewish identity. Taking it to extremes, that Jews are Jewish only in so far as they are in the Diaspora?

I would say yes. I would say that the best of Jewish culture is bound to the fact of being dispersed, polycentric.

By suggesting that it is up to Diaspora Jews to educate Israelis in Jewish values, you are opening yourself up to a great deal of hostile reaction. Isn't the reverse closer to the truth? Wasn't it Israel that infused in Jews throughout the world a sense of strength and security?

Unfortunately this is a case of role reversal. From that same source of strength, today's Diaspora Jews draw instead a sense of preoccupation and anguish. That's why I speak of an eclipse, which I hope will be momentary, of the role of Israel as the unifying centre of Judaism. We must support Israel, as its diplomats ask us to, but we must also impress upon it the numerical, cultural, traditional and even economic weight of the Diaspora. We have the power and also the duty to bring our influence to bear in some way on Israeli politics.

In which direction?

First of all, I believe that we should argue for a withdrawal from Lebanon. Then it is just as urgent to stop further construction of settlements in the occupied territories. After that, as I was saying, I would cautiously but firmly move on a withdrawal from the West Bank and Gaza.

What about links with the PLO?

The PLO is another protean body, there is no way of understanding what face it will show today. In words it offers to shake hands . . . But no, I don't think that the time is yet ripe to make contact with the PLO. Arafat is in decline, we cannot be sure of what he is doing or thinking, where he is, even of whether he is still really president of the PLO. Perhaps the time will come when an Israeli government can negotiate with the PLO, but not today. Both parties are in a fluid phase.

If, as you wish, the centre of Judaism is to move back into the Diaspora, does that mean that within Jewish communities some sort of reawakening is needed, that Jews will need to search out their own roots, their own 'difference' within their respective countries?

Yes. Even if it is not yet happening, this should and could happen in a country like Italy, where the Jewish community is small numerically, but relatively unified. This is also our limit: we are few and integrated.

Two years ago, along with other Italian Jews, you created a public protest against the Israeli government. Could, then, indignation be the catalyst that might bring together the Jews of the Diaspora?

Let's use a less inflammatory term, like disapproval. Yes, it is a catalyst, even if I always imagine an Israeli coming and reprimanding me, 'it's easy for you, an Italian Jew sitting in your armchair, to decide what we should do!'. But I insist. The history of the Diaspora has been a history of persecution but also of interethnic exchange and relations, in other words a school for tolerance. Especially in Italy. If I were not so weary, if I had more strength, I would agitate in the Italian Jewish community for it to take on this role. Because I am in favour of the integration of Jews in Italy, but not of their assimilation, their disappearance, the dissolution of their culture. Right here in Turin, there is an example of a Jewish community that is fully integrated into the life and culture of the city, but not assimilated.

Is it difficult, given your views, for you to maintain relations with Jewish and Israeli institutions?

I have a sort of affectionate and polemical rapport; one that runs very deep. Because I am certain that Israel should be defended, I believe in the painful necessity of an efficient army. But I am equally sure that it would do the Israeli government good to deal with support from us which is never unconditional.

Notes

1   The Likud and Ma'arach groupings were respectively right and left wing political formations in the coalition.
2   Kahane was the most vocal figure on the extreme right-wing of Israeli politics in this period.

Bibliography of Primo Levi's Works in Italian and English

Se questo è un uomo (Turin: De Silva, 1947; 2nd edition, Turin: Einaudi, 1958); *If This is a Man*, trans. by Stuart Woolf (London: Orion Press, 1959)

La tregua (Turin: Einaudi, 1963); *The Truce*, trans. by Stuart Woolf (London: Bodley Head, 1965)

Storie naturali ('Natural Histories') (Turin: Einaudi, 1966); selections in *The Sixth Day*, trans. by Raymond Rosenthal (London: Michael Joseph, 1990)

Vizio di forma ('Formal Defect') (Turin: Einaudi, 1971); selections in *The Sixth Day*

L'osteria di Brema ('Brema Inn') (Milan: Scheiwiller, 1975); *Shema. Collected Poems*, trans. by Ruth Feldman and Brian Swann (London: Menard Press, 1976)

Il sistema periodico (Turin: Einaudi, 1975); *The Periodic Table*, trans. by Raymond Rosenthal (London: Michael Joseph, 1985)

La chiave a stella (Turin: Einaudi, 1978); *The Wrench*, trans. by William Weaver (London: Michael Joseph, 1987)

Lilìt e altri racconti (Turin: Einaudi, 1981); with variations as *Moments of Reprieve*, trans. by Ruth Feldman (London: Michael Joseph, 1986)

La ricerca delle radici ('The Search for Roots') (Turin: Einaudi, 1981); not in English

Se non ora, quando? (Turin: Einaudi, 1982); *If Not Now, When?*, trans. by William Weaver (London: Michael Joseph, 1986)

Ad ora incerta ('At an Uncertain Hour') (Milan: Garzanti, 1984); *Collected Poems*, trans. by Ruth Feldman and Brian Swann (London: Faber and Faber, 1988)

L'altrui mestiere (Turin: Einaudi, 1985); *Other People's Trades*, trans. by Raymond Rosenthal (London: Michael Joseph, 1989)

I sommersi e i salvati (Turin: Einaudi, 1986); *The Drowned and the Saved*, trans. by Raymond Rosenthal (London: Michael Joseph, 1988)

Racconti e saggi ('Stories and Essays') (Turin: Edizioni La Stampa, 1986); selections as *The Mirror Maker*, trans. by Raymond Rosenthal (London: Methuen, 1990)

Note that for several of Levi's books the American edition (of the same translation) appeared earlier than the English edition.

Index